# MEDIEVAL HUMANISM
## and Other Studies

*For*
## V. H. GALBRAITH
*on his eightieth birthday*

# MEDIEVAL HUMANISM

and Other Studies

by

R. W. SOUTHERN

Basil Blackwell

© R. W. Southern 1970

First published 1970
Reprinted and first published in paperback 1984

Basil Blackwell Publisher Limited
108 Cowley Road, Oxford OX4 1JF, England

ISBN 0 631 12440 3

Library of Congress Number 70-120932

(32316)

Printed in Great Britain by Billing & Sons Ltd, Worcester

# PREFACE

In their present form the essays which follow have all been written during the last eight or nine years, but the origins of several of them go back to a much earlier time. The essay on Ranulf Flambard is an extensive revision of a paper published in the *Transactions of the Royal Historical Society* for 1933, but written in 1930–31 at the suggestion of the friend and master to whom this volume is dedicated. The rewriting of so ancient a piece would scarcely have been undertaken if it had not seemed an appropriate present for his eightieth birthday, and I offer it to him in grateful recollection of his help and friendship over forty years. The essay on Peter of Blois preserves the substance of the David Murray Lecture in the University of Glasgow in 1963; it is based on work on Peter of Blois's letters that I did over thirty years ago when I intended to make an edition of these letters. This work must now be left to others, but digging into the old notes has brought to the surface a few small studies that may still see the light. The essay on Abelard and Heloise began with some work on the manuscripts of their letters nearly twenty years ago, and it took its first shape in a paper read to the Dean Kitchen Society of St. Catherine's College in about 1953. The essay on the School of Chartres contains the substance of a paper read at the Ecclesiastical History Society Conference in 1965. The essay on King Henry I is a slightly modified version of the Raleigh Lecture in 1962, without the appendix on the royal demesne which would have needed extensive revision and will soon be superseded by work on which Mr. J. O. Prestwich and Miss J. A. Aveyard are now engaged. 'England's First Entry into Europe' preserves the substance of the Creighton Lecture delivered in the University of London in 1966, and 'Medieval Humanism' is a development of the Samuel Dill Lecture in Belfast University in 1964. Parts of these lectures and of the first three essays in the volume have been given as talks on the Third Programme and printed in *The Listener*. 'The Place of England in the Twelfth Century Renaissance' is based on a paper given to the Anglo-American Historical Conference in 1953 and printed in *History* in 1960; and the last essay in the volume started its life as a commemorative essay in *The*

*Times* for 1 September 1959 on the seven-hundredth anniversary of the death of Adrian IV.

Although the contents of this book have such a long and confusing history, I hope they will nevertheless be found to have a unity of theme and treatment which justifies their collection in a single volume. They bring together two sides of medieval history which should never be separated: the practical, business-like and earthy, and the intellectual, spiritual and aspiring. The combination of these elements in a single environment and often in the same persons has given western European civilization its peculiar strength and movement, and I have tried in writing or rewriting these essays to catch some reflections of this native amalgam.

Even so slight a volume, the result of work pursued over many years, owes more to the help of others than can be briefly acknowledged. It must suffice here to mention the publishers and editors who have allowed me to use work that has appeared in their publications, the librarians who have given permission for the reproduction of manuscripts in their collections, and Dr. Richard Hunt and my wife for their help with the proofs. To these and all who have helped me I offer my warmest thanks.

# CONTENTS

# CHARTS AND PLATES

(following on p. 252)

Chart I  Tree of Knowledge (School of Hugh of St. Victor)

Chart II  Tree of Knowledge (School of Abelard)

## Plates

I  The beginning of St. John's Gospel in a Jarrow-Wearmouth Gospel Book.

This Gospel book of c. 700 is preserved in a fragmentary state. It was written by the scribe of the Gospel which was placed in the tomb of St. Cuthbert in 687 or 698, and it is closely connected with the greatest of all the MSS. of Bede's monastery—the *Codex Amiatinus* which was written between 689 and 716 and taken to Rome as a present for St. Peter. For the group of MSS. to which it belongs, see E. A. Lowe, *Codices Latini Antiquiores*, ii, nos. 150, 177, 260. The pages from which our illustration is taken were reproduced in a facsimile edition of the Utrecht Psalter in 1873; they are described in *C.L.A.*, x, no. 1587. The art of book-making at Jarrow in Bede's day has recently been brilliantly investigated by R. L. S. Bruce-Mitford, 'The art of the Codex Amiatinus', *Journal of the Archaeological Association*, 1969, xxxii, 1–25.

II  The beginning of St. John's Gospel in the Lindisfarne Gospel Book.

The Lindisfarne Gospels were written between 687 and 698 (and 'probably near the latter date') by Eadfrith, a monk and later bishop of Lindisfarne. For a full discussion and reproduction of the manuscript see *Codex Lindisfarnensis*, ed. T. D. Kendrick, T. J. Brown and others, 1960.

III  *Mappa Mundi*, 1109–1110. St. John's College, Oxford, MS. 17, f. 6, from Thorney Abbey.

This map shows schematically the position of the British Isles as an *alter orbis* on, or beyond, the edge of the populated globe.

IV  The organisation of Nature, c. 1100. British Museum, Harleian MS. 3667, from Peterborough Abbey.

This chart is a copy of a picture ascribed to Bryhtferth in the St. John's College MS. 17, f.7 ᵛ (reproduced in *Bodleian Quarterly Record*, 1917, ii, 47–51, and in S. J. Crawford, *Byrhtferth's Manual*, Early English Text Society, 1929). The learning which it represents comes from Bede.

V   The Divisions of Philosophy, 1109–1110. St. John's College
    MS. 17, f. 7.

This tree of knowledge from Thorney Abbey may be compared
with the charts on pp. 254–5 which show the influence of the
schools of Paris a generation later. There is a less accurate copy of
this *Divisio Philosophiae* in British Museum MS. Harley 3667,
f. 6ᵛ, from Peterborough: probably they are both copies of draw-
ings made about a century earlier. The picture shows two different
ways of dividing Philosophy: the literary source of the first is
Cassiodorus, *Institutiones*, ii, 4–7; and of the second, Isidore,
*Etymologiae*, ii, 24.

VI  The music and movements of the planets, 1109–1110. St.
    John's College, MS. 17, f. 38.

This is an exceptionally fine example of a diagram, current in
MSS. from the ninth to twelfth centuries, designed to illustrate
Bede's *De Natura Rerum* and (as here) derivative works such as
Abbo of Fleury's *De cursu vii planetarum per zodiacum circulum*.
For the distribution of these MSS. in England before the Norman
Conquest, see A. van der Vyver, 'Les oeuvres inédites d'Abbon de
Fleury', *Rev. Bénédictine*, 1935, xlvii, 140–5.

VII Sun-spots observed at Worcester, Saturday, 8 December,
    1128. Corpus Christi College, Oxford, MS. 157, p. 380.

On a misty winter's day it would be quite possible for the observation here described to be made with the naked eye, but such
observations are of extreme rarity in the Middle Ages. See G.
Sarton, 'Early observations of the sunspots?', *Isis*, xxxvii, 1947,
69–71, where only one other example before 1450 is quoted, and
this in error: the phenomenon there mentioned was a transit of
Mercury across the Sun (*Ann. Regni Francorum*, 807; Einhard, *Vita
Karoli Magni*, c. 32).

VIII A scientific drawing from Worcester, c. 1130. Bodleian
    MS. Auct. F.1.9, f. 88.

This is a scientific drawing of an astrolabe, adapted, as Dr. J. D.
North tells me, for a latitude of about 53½° N. Since the MS. was
written at Worcester, which lies about 52.10° N., it seems quite
likely that the drawing was designed for this latitude.

# LIST OF ABBREVIATIONS

*A.H.D.L.*   *Archives d'histoire doctrinale et litteraire du Moyen Age.*

*B.E.C.*   *Bibliothèque de l'Ecole des Chartes.*

*E.H.R.*   *English Historical Review.*

*Historiens de France.*   M. Bouquet, *Recueil des historiens des Gaules et de la France,* 1738–1904 (new ed. L. Delisle, 1869–1880).

*M.A.R.S.*   *Mediaeval and Renaissance Studies.*

*M.G.H.*   *Monumenta Germaniae Historica.*

*P.L.*   J. P. Migne, *Patrologia Latina.*

*Regesta.*   *Regesta Regum Anglo-Normannorum,*
> i 1913 (1066–1100) ed. H. W. C. Davis and R. J. Whitwell;
> ii 1946 (1100–1135) ed. C. Johnson and H. A. Cronne;
> iii 1968 (1135–1154) ed. H. A. Cronne and R. H. C. Davis.

*R.S.*   *Chronicles and Memorials of Great Britain and Ireland, publ. under the direction of the Master of the Rolls (Rolls Series),* 1858–96.

*R.T.A.M.*   *Recherches de Théologie ancienne et médiévale.*

*V.C.H.*   *Victoria History of the Counties of England.*

# I

## THREE STAGES OF EUROPEAN EXPERIENCE

# 1

## BEDE

Few men can have spent more years or worked more hours on the same spot than Bede did; and to me at least the site of the monastery at Jarrow, where he lived and died, is one of the most moving things in England. It is a small and undistinguished spit of land about ten or fifteen feet above the waters of the Tyne; across the river are the cranes of the modern docks; at one's feet lie the mud-flats of Bede's day, now partly reclaimed to form timber-yards; on the site itself the blackened ruins of monastic buildings surround a small, somewhat dingy, church with a thin Anglo-Saxon tower. The dedication stone in the church gives a date which can be referred to the year 685. But the stone marks more than a ceremony of dedication—it marks nothing less than a new beginning in English civilization. It may seem an odd place for such a beginning, and to many visitors it will suggest the grave of civilization rather than the cradle. It has no grace, and whatever beauty there may be is distinctly austere. But in fact the setting is not an inappropriate one for the work that was done in Bede's day. Even in the seventh century there were more interesting places than Jarrow, probably more interesting men than Bede, and certainly more immediately exciting works than his: but no one did work which lasted better, and into the foundations of his work he put an energy and originality of mind which are hidden behind the modest exterior.

It would be wrong to think of him as a lonely worker in a barbarous age. During his lifetime England was going through one of the great creative periods in her history. The ideas and energy which emanated from England were soon to become the dominant force in Europe. The manifestations of that energy which survive are mere fragments, but the variety of excellence they display is astonishing: the stone crosses of Bewcastle and Ruthwell which stand for all to see; the Lindisfarne Gospels; the books written at Jarrow; the laws, biographies, poems, in Latin and Anglo-Saxon; the varied expressions of pagan and Christian, of Celtic and Anglo-Saxon sentiment which these works contain; the careeers of men who transformed not only the face of England but of Europe—all tell the same story of intense activity. It was a time when the traditional stock of pagan Germanic ideas was making its last appearance, and new influences were flooding in from all sides—from Ireland, Gaul, Italy and the eastern Mediterranean. As sometimes happens in such circumstances, both the old and the new seem to have inspired enough faith and confidence to produce works that are the best of their kind, though they point in contradictory directions. There was a struggle for the mind of a people not yet committed to any settled frame of thought or imagination. There are works of conscious propagandists for one or other set of ideas; and there are works of artists or ascetics who simply expressed in the most forcible way at their command the ideas and images which had captured their imagination. Whatever the degree of conscious campaigning, the result was a variety of activity which in quality of achievement has never been surpassed.

In all this activity the work of Bede and of the community at Jarrow has a severe and sombre appearance. If you compare the manuscripts from Jarrow with the famous Gospel book from Lindisfarne you will at once see the difference.[1] The Jarrow books are sober and unadorned, written without frills by craftsmen who have rediscovered the finest proportions of ancient script. The Lindisfarne book, on the other hand, is an extravagant artistic masterpiece in which the forms of Irish imagination are adapted to a somewhat more restrained, but still luxuriant pattern of visual images. And there is a similar contrast in the religious life. Bede's life seems to have been one of steady discipline without extravagance. There is nothing in it to catch the eye. We must look elsewhere for the qualities that made Christianity seem a religion of convincing power to contemporaries—for instance to Crowland in the Fens, where the hermit Guthlac was living one of those lives of heroic warfare against evil spirits dear to a people who loved war. Guthlac's visions, his struggles against the demonic forces

---

[1] See Plates I and II. The characteristics of the Jarrow-Wearmouth manuscripts are described by E. A. Lowe, *English Uncial*, 1960, 8–13. This slender but deeply learned book has been the subject of two important reviews, by B. Bischoff (repr. in his *Mittelalterliche Studien*, 1967, ii, esp. 329–34) and D. L. Wright (*Traditio*, 1961, xvii, 441–56). I am greatly indebted to Professor T. J. Brown for his help on this subject.

arrayed against him, and the sufferings of his distracted mind and fever-racked body give us a more vivid insight into the springs of Anglo-Saxon religion than anything in Bede's experience.[1]

In this exciting and tumultuous scene Bede is essentially calm. His gifts and habits were those of a scholar. His capacious mind was seldom swayed by prejudice, firm in its judgments, well fitted to deal with a large mass of disorderly material and to present it systematically and succinctly. Like many men of this stamp, he never obtrudes his own personality, seldom mentions his own experience, keeps his eye steadily on the material before him, and expresses his condemnation more often by silence than by strictures. His piety was exact and unwavering, and his diligence unremitting. His last hours, spent in translating the Bible and abbreviating a learned work, dividing his few belongings among his friends, breaking out unexpectedly at one moment into the poetic idiom of his ancestors, perfectly reflect the range of his activity and the unruffled temper of his life and death.

Throughout the whole range of our history this combination of temperament and talent is not so very uncommon. The University of Oxford produces perhaps one such scholar in a hundred years. But Oxford University has long existed to produce this sort of man, and it would be surprising if it did not sometimes supremely succeed. But Bede was alone in his generation, the first Englishman of his type, the first scientific intellect produced by the Germanic peoples of Europe. Some of his English contemporaries were gifted men, but none had gifts like his. Among the artists, statesmen, missionaries, athletes of the spiritual life, who proliferated in England in the late seventh and eighth centuries, he was the most unexpected of all products of a primitive age: a really great scholar. The circumstances of the time gave him a great opportunity.

To understand the nature of his opportunity we must turn our eyes once more to Jarrow. Physically, it lay on the very edge of the old Roman world. The Wall's end which marked the boundary between Mediterranean civilization and the barbarians was within an afternoon's excursion from the monastery, and Bede had certainly inspected it. In his lifetime the foresight of one man had made Jarrow the chief centre of Roman civilization in Europe.

[1] For Guthlac see his *Life* by Felix, monk of Crowland, ed. B. Colgrave, 1956.

Rome itself was falling into ruins. The economy of Italy was being stifled by the collapse of Mediterranean trade. The West everywhere had fallen into a deep disorder. Into this scene there came Benedict Biscop. He was a wealthy Northumbrian nobleman who had turned to the monastic life at the time of life when most men of his class began to think of raising a family. Like a wealthy warlord, he descended on libraries of the decaying society in southern Italy and carried off (no doubt at a price) their neglected treasures. By modern standards they were not many—perhaps 200 or 300 volumes—but they brought together in his Northumbrian outpost most of the best works of Christian scholarship in the later Roman empire. From these books it was possible to get a fairly complete and coherent view of the work of the Latin Fathers of the Church, together with a good deal of ancient history, grammar, chronology, and miscellaneous biblical scholarship. Benedict Biscop must be reckoned the first collector to use the wealth of a new aristocracy to appropriate the fruits of civilization from a people who could no longer afford to preserve them; he is the prototype of the great American collectors of our century.[1]

What England lacked in the seventh century was a tradition. No one could say for certain which of the traditions of Anglo-Saxon, Roman and Celtic origin that were struggling for mastery in England would have the power to survive. What Benedict Biscop brought to Jarrow was the learning of the Christian Roman Empire, and in doing this he picked the future winner. That is to say, he extracted from the welter of conflicting materials the most important element for the growth of a new European civilization.

Benedict Biscop, however, could do no more than provide the tools; it was still necessary to find someone to use them. A library is an act of faith, and no one can tell what will come of it. There were no doubt other libraries in Europe as well stocked with books as that at Jarrow, but on most of them the dust was gathering ever more thickly, and the damp penetrating ever more deeply. This might easily have happened at Jarrow where dust and damp are in plentiful supply. To utilize a collection of materials which

---

[1] For Benedict Biscop's life and travels, see Bede, *Gesta Abbatum* (ed. C. Plummer, *Venerabilis Baedae Opera Historica*, 1896, i. 364–77, ii. 355–65). The books available to Bede have been studied by M. L. W. Laistner, 'The Library of the Venerable Bede' in A. H. Thompson, *Bede: His Life, Times and Writings*, 1935, 237–66 (reprinted in Laistner, *The intellectual Heritage of the early Middle Ages*, 1957, 117–149).

no English mind had yet mastered required a genius and determination of the highest order. How great a genius was required we can easily see if we consider the great social, political and intellectual gulf which separated the Anglo-Saxon heroic age of the seventh century from the sophisticated society of the later Roman Empire. The two societies were bound together by nothing more than the thin thread of a common Christianity. In every external condition of life and habit of thought the gap was immense.

The greatness of Bede lay in this, that apparently without an effort he bridged the gap between the ancient world and his own day. Perhaps it is wrong to say 'without an effort', for among the few things he tells us about himself is an avowal of ceaseless labour. He was obsessed by the fear that inertia might lead to the loss of that which could, as he says, be ours; and this was the mainspring of his energy. Never did a man work with a more distinct idea of what he was aiming at. His aim was simple, and grand: to make the raw new nation, not yet a nation till he pronounced it one, at home in the past—not the past of pagan genealogies, folktales and heroic legend that he could see all round him, but the past of the Latin learning of the Christian Church.

Bede wrote many works with this general aim. His most famous, the *Ecclesiastical History of the English People*, is in one way the least typical of all, for it told a story which for the most part was to be found not in books but in the memories of living men. Bede's chief labours lay in transmitting the contents of ancient books in an intelligible way to his contemporaries and successors. The great *History* did not do this, but it grew out of the task of restoring ancient learning. It linked the earliest history of the Romans in Britain with the present, and applied the rules of ancient historical writing to a new age—the age of Bede's own day and people. No doubt it was the greatest, as it was also the last, of his works. But if we want to understand its place in his worldview, to appreciate the extent of his labours, and to see where his main influence lay, we shall look not to his *History* but to his biblical commentaries.[1]

---

[1] It must here suffice to say that, out of about thirty-five works, twenty are biblical commentaries, six are works of chronology, and there are two each on language, history and hagiography. The only modern editions of Bede's biblical commentaries are those by M. L. W. Laistner on the Acts of the Apostles (1939, with a valuable introduction), and by D. Hurst O.S.B. on Samuel and Kings (1962, *Corpus Christianorum, series latina*, cxix). The most widely read of the commentaries would appear to have been those on Exodus (69 MSS), Proverbs

Bede's commentaries have not had many readers for the last four hundred years, and they are not likely to whet many appetites today. Yet they are books which we should be glad to read if we had nothing else. They provide plenty of subjects for reflection, a stream of good sense, and (through their quotations) a daily contact with some of the greatest minds of the past. Anyone who has other books to read will probably read those other books. But it was precisely for men who had few other books that Bede wrote, and no author of the early Middle Ages had a greater success. His books were the handbooks of the English missionaries who converted Germany in the eighth century; they were among the foundation works of the Carolingian renaissance; and they continued as a main source of monastic learning until the twelfth century.

It is often said that Bede lacked originality, and he would doubtless have agreed. It was his task to make the past accessible to the barbarian present, and this required not primarily originality but judgment and patience. No one would deny that he possessed these qualities in a high degree, but we may also think that to conceive such a plan, to see how it could be carried out, and to carry it out just in the way he did, required a powerful imagination and independence of mind. The Christian learning of the past lay scattered in many volumes by many hands. Even to those who had access to these volumes, they were not easily usable or even intelligible. Bede reduced a great mass of materials to the single, simple and usable form of continuous biblical exposition. Even today a preacher might do worse than take his material from Bede's rational and lucid summary.

Though his main aim was to digest for others what they could not digest for themselves, he also aimed at adding to the learning of the past. He chose to explain those books of the Bible which had not been expounded before, or which offered scope for his own special interests in history and allegory. At first we are surprised by his omissions. For instance, among the Gospels, Bede chose to comment only on Mark and Luke, not on Matthew and John,

---

(86 MSS.), Song of Songs (65 MSS.), Tobias (74 MSS.), Mark (95 MSS.), Luke (90 MSS.), Acts (128 MSS.), Catholic Epistles (112 MSS.), Apocalypse (73 MSS.). In assessing Bede's influence in the early Middle Ages it should be remembered that the great majority of these copies were made before the end of the twelfth century, and a high proportion before the end of the tenth century. See M. L. W. Laistner and H. H. King, *A Handlist of Bede MSS.*, 1943.

which have (at least till recent times) been universally acclaimed as the richest treasuries of Christian doctrine. Similarly, he wrote two commentaries on the relatively neglected *Acts of the Apostles*, but on the Pauline Epistle he was content to put together a long series of extracts from St. Augustine.[1] He wrote at great length on Genesis, Samuel and Kings, but not on the Psalms; he devoted much time and labour to the minor, but very little to the major, prophets. Beneath the surface appearance of plodding compilation there was in fact a highly sensitive and selective scholar who aimed not only at copying the thoughts of greater men, but at completing them. It was a startling ambition for an obscure writer in an obscure monastery in a far corner of Europe, to think that he could make an original contribution to the body of ancient learning.

It is astonishing when we think of it that a man of the newest of the new nations of Europe could move with such confidence among ancient learning. As a master of technical chronology and as a historical writer he is among the greatest; as a theologian and exegete he had, if not the highest qualities—he is no Augustine or Jerome—at least the qualities most necessary for his plan. He had no known master. He was the first Englishman who understood the past and could view it as a whole. In the exciting England of his day, which was neither fully pagan nor fully Christian, neither Roman nor Celtic nor Teutonic but something of all of them, a country of dead-ends and new beginnings, Bede stood for sobriety and order in thought, common sense in politics, and moderation in the religious life. He was the first Englishman who could look back over the chasm which the collapse of the Roman empire had opened in the history of thought, and see clearly the landscape on the other side; the first, therefore, whose religion was wholly articulate and whose thoughts are entirely intelligible to us today.

In the main square of Jarrow there is a recent monument on which two large figures are prominently displayed. They are not the figures of the two greatest men of Jarrow, Benedict Biscop and Bede, preservers of the old and chief builders of a new civilization, but of two Vikings, the destroyers who in 796 erased Jarrow from

[1] Although Bede did not contribute a single word of his own on St. Paul's Epistles, his choice of relevant extracts from the works of St. Augustine shows an astonishingly wide, and in its day probably unique, mastery of Augustine's works. The extracts are analysed by I. Fransen, 'Description de la collection de Bède le Vénérable sur l'Apôtre', *Revue Bénédictine*, 1961, lxxi, 22–70.

the map of Europe for a thousand years. It is a strange perspective which gives these destroyers the chief monument in modern Jarrow; but perhaps like everything else in this strange story it has a certain appropriateness. Whatever happened to Jarrow after Bede's death was irrelevant to the spread of his influence throughout Europe. Like the ships from the yards across the river, Bede's works were not made to stay in harbour, but for a long future in distant parts. Even during his lifetime, even before he was well-known at home, his works were in demand on the Continent. At first they were mainly sought for by Englishmen abroad, by monks and missionaries far from their native land, who needed these works for the practical purposes of the religious life and for the instruction of the newly converted. Once established, Bede's works spread by the mere force of their immense usefulness. When England became cut off in the ninth century from the main centres of vigorous learning, most of Bede's works fell into disuse at home while they flourished abroad, and they had to be reimported after the Norman Conquest. Jarrow, which the Vikings destroyed, did not become great again until the nineteenth century. By then Bede's works were largely forgotten, but for four centuries after his death they played a conspicuous part in bringing order into the intellectual life of Europe.

# 2

## ST. ANSELM

Anselm was born almost exactly three hundred years after the death of Bede and at the other end of Europe. In mind and spirit the two men are quite different, and their differences are an index of the changing intellectual climate of Europe. Anselm's thought is rapid and penetrating, a bundle of nervous sensibility. Bede is conspicuously solid, and we must look twice to see his originality. Anselm is conspicuously original, and we must often look several times to see how solid is the learning on which his originality is based. Bede is a man of calm in the midst of crisis; Anselm is a man of crisis at a time when the storms which had shaken Europe seemed to be over. The storms and stresses of Bede's lifetime were all without. Those of Anselm were all within; and if they reflected—as they certainly did—a widespread unease, it was an uneasiness of mind and spirit at a time of unexpected safety and prosperity.[1]

Anselm was born in 1033 in the town of Aosta, at the foot of the St. Bernard Pass. Although it was on an important route over the Alps, Aosta was itself a shut-in little town where the Roman past was, and still is, extraordinarily pervasive. In the eleventh century the forum and amphitheatre, the walls, the streets, and the colonnaded square must have been oppressive reminders of the past. Unlike Bede, the young Anselm did not suffer from too little contact with the ancient world, but from too much. We do not known all the causes of his discontents, but when he was a young man he quarrelled with his father, turned his back for ever on his native town and came north. After some years of wandering he arrived in Normandy, and at the age of twenty-six he became a monk at Bec. Here he stayed until he was sixty. Then from 1093 to 1109 he was archbishop of Canterbury, and died at the age of seventy-six.

Why do I commemorate him? Not assuredly because he was

---

[1] In what follows I draw largely on my book, *St. Anselm and his Biographer*, 1963, where further references to the literature will be found.

archbishop of Canterbury, for there have been many better ones, but because his flight from Aosta is a symbol of his escape from the heavy hand of the past. He felt the need to break out and to seek something new. In the mid-eleventh century the time for rejuvenation had come. There were many who felt this—men who in different ways were helping to bring about one of the great revolutions in European life and thought. The need for rejuvenation came to some as a call to a new sort of religious life, to others as a desire for the renewal of ecclesiastical discipline, to others as a new enthusiasm for papal authority, to others as a call to intellectual adventure. Anselm felt all these impulses in varying degrees, but what distinguished him from all his contemporaries was the power and originality of his theological insight.

In the middle of the eleventh century there had not been a really constructive religious philosopher in western Christendom for six hundred years—not since the death of St. Augustine in 430. That is to say, there had been no one who had systematically asked fundamental questions about the Christian religion, such as: How do we know that the attributes of God are those affirmed by the Christian religion? How do we know that God exists? Did God become man in Jesus Christ? Was this necessary? What exactly did it achieve and how? Is the Trinity a demonstrable fact about the nature of God? What are sin, omnipotence, and freedom, and how are they related? What is the relation between our reasoning on these subjects and faith?

I do not mean that questions of this kind had never arisen at all for six hundred years. Of course they had; but they were thought of as questions which had long ago been effectively answered. They did not inspire any systematic enquiry into the credentials of the Christian religion. The pressing problems of the intervening centuries were not theoretical but practical: the organization and discipline of the Church; the preservation of a basic literary culture; the development of the liturgy for the purpose of organized religious life; the foundation of monasteries, and the long struggle for stability. The intellectual foundations were already laid, and there seemed no need to dig them up again. When anyone showed a tendency to do this he aroused immediate suspicion and fear. It was generally thought that such men were up to no good, especially if their efforts were directed towards extending the area of reason in matters of faith. We can understand the reluctance to appeal to reason. After all, the truth of the Christian religion was guaranteed not by reason but by events— by the events of the Bible, by the miracles of the saints, by the miracle of the Church. The problem of the Church in barbarian Europe was not unbelief, but unlimited credulity and lack of organization. What was needed was order and discipline, not new and doubtful enquiries.

In saying therefore that western Christianity had lacked a constructive religious philosopher for six hundred years I do not mean to suggest that there had been any lack of activity, or that this activity had not been what the circumstances of the time required. Nevertheless, the absence of fundamental enquiry into the credibility and coherence of the Christian religion as a whole was a weakness. In course of time it made the basic doctrines of the Church increasingly formal, and it was then easy to allege that these doctrines were formal because they were irrational. There are a good many signs that this weakness was beginning to be felt in the eleventh century. An interest in theological debate, in logical conundrums, and in the objections of unbelievers to the Christian faith suddenly appeared in surprising places, not only in monasteries and schools but in the market-place. The critical faculty awoke from a long sleep, and men asked whether, after all, the Christian religion was true.

Scattered throughout Europe in considerable numbers, and enjoying a level of prosperity and intellectual culture far above the average, were communities of Jews, testifying that it was not true. The Jews had lived fairly peacefully in Europe for several centuries protected by rulers, including the Popes, who needed their services. But towards the end of the eleventh century, riots and violence began to be increasingly common. The causes of these riots are difficult to determine but they are all associated with the fears and uncertainties of western Christian society. The recognition of the existence of the Jewish community as a distinct and alien society which positively rejected the Christian faith gave the West a shock of alarm. Their point of view seemed to require an answer, and the eleventh century saw the beginning of attempts to provide one.[1]

[1] For the part played by the Jews in stimulating discussion of fundamental problems of Christian theology, see St. Anselm and his Biographer, 88–91, and 'St. Anselm and Gilbert Crispin, Abbot of Westminster,' Medieval and Renaissance Studies, 1954, iii, 78–99.

An even more alarming symptom of unease was to be found within the Christian body itself. Spreading from Italy into France and Germany were missionaries of a new anti-hierarchical, anti-sacramental, anti-sacerdotal, and (in its extreme form) anti-Christian creed. With such men there was not much debate. They were hurried to the fire; but they added to the insecurity of the time.[1]

Then, quite apart from these external incentives to fundamental enquiry, there were many reasons within the Christian community why ordinary intelligent men should begin to ask new and disturbing questions. A society of growing affluence produced a growing number of students; masters competed with each other for their attention, and for the fame and fees that went with reputation, and those who had something new to say succeeded best. Once the process had started, there was no stopping it, and by the end of the eleventh century the practice of scholastic debate was emerging as a central feature of the educational system. Naturally the process did not stop at the walls of the monasteries. Monks asked questions like other men, and though the monasteries soon fell out of the scholastic race they had at first some great advantages over the secular schools in the pursuit of theological enquiry. The greatest of these advantages was the close and continuous contact between the teacher and the taught which stimulated enquiry. In favourable circumstances—with a teacher of genius, a tradition of learning, and the unhurried peace of a disciplined community—the results could not fail to be impressive. Nowhere were these conditions more fully met than at Bec from 1063 to 1093 while Anselm was prior, then abbot.

Anselm wrote most of his important works in the form of dialogues with monastic pupils; and we shall not understand them fully unless we see that the dialogue was more than a literary artifice. It was an expression of the fact that his thought grew out of the questions of young men who belonged to a worried generation. Whether Anselm himself experienced the crisis of faith which some of his pupils experienced we cannot tell. He never allows it to appear. The crises of his life which we can trace were crises of personal affection. He loved his mother and lost her in

[1] For the beginnings of the burning of heretics in the eleventh century, see J. Havet, 'L'hérésie et le bras séculier au moyen âge jusqu' au XIIIe siècle', *B.E.C.*, 1880, xli, 498–507.

early adolescence. He hated his father and left him. He found at Bec a teacher, Lanfranc, to whom he committed his affections and his whole future. Through his influence he became a monk. He loved a young monk who died; and then his affections were lavished on all who sought his friendship, on some whom he never met, and on others with whom he disagreed. Love and friendship are the dominant feature of his early and middle years. He had a gift for friendship which is only found in those who enter into the minds and anxieties of others, no matter how remote from their own.

His friendships were famous in his own day, and we can still read the record of them in his letters. From these friendships, and the discussions which cemented them, came the theological treatises. His biographer says that many came to him to ask questions, and stayed because he gave them answers which seemed to be convincing. Anselm spoke a language that they wished to hear: it was the language of rational argument, leaving no question unattempted however trivial or however fundamental, and never failing in the end to give some kind of answer.

Was Anselm, then, a rationalist? Certainly not a rationalist in our modern sense; quite the opposite, as we shall see. But if he had been asked, I think he would have allowed himself to be called a rationalist—on his own terms. He might have justified himself somewhat as follows: 'God is reason in its highest power, and every created thing has been created in accordance with the immutable reason of God. Man, created in the divine image, has the power of apprehending the divine reason, hence of understanding why things are as they are and not otherwise, why God is as He is and not otherwise, and why the whole course of creation and redemption has taken the course it has taken and no other.'

Anselm expressed his confidence in the power of reason in a most uncompromising way at the beginning of his earliest theological work. His pupils, he said, had asked him to prove that God's nature is as the Christian religion declares, and to do this simply by rational argument without any support from authority. He protested his insufficiency but I am not sure that he was quite sincere in this, for he approached his task with immense confidence. In the first sentence of this his first work, he claimed that he could prove to anyone of moderate ability that God's nature is as the Christian religion affirms. What he meant by 'prove' in this and other contexts has been the subject of almost endless debate. Probably he changed his ground as time went on, but here at least he seems to mean what anyone means, namely that his argument could compel the assent of anyone who aspired to the most humble forms of reasoning.

Later his idea of a 'proof' came to be more subtle and circumspect. He would say no more than that his arguments were proof against all known objections, and that they showed the Christian faith to be rational in the sense that it has no internal contradictions and is consistent with everything that is knowable about the nature of God and the universe. This is perhaps weaker than the earlier claim, but it is still a very great claim.

Even if we are right—and it is always difficult to be sure that we are interpreting aright the shifting emphasis that comes with growing experience—in thinking that Anselm lost some of his early rational confidence in the course of time, his method of rational enquiry, his rigid exclusion of any appeal to authority and his form of philosophical dialogue with his monastic pupils, did not vary over forty years of intellectual effort. During this long period he ranged over all the most difficult problems of Christian doctrine. At first he alleged that there was nothing original in what he had to say, that it had all been said by St. Augustine, and that he was only finding new and shorter ways of saying it. But from the first he had no interest in the simple restatement of old answers, and in his proof of the existence of God and of the *necessity* of God's incarnation he developed arguments that are as new and lasting as any in the history of western thought.

New thoughts in any much traversed field of study are never easy to come by. They are reserved for the very few, and Anselm is one of the few. He belongs to the company of Augustine, Pascal, Newman; and of these I think he is nearest to Pascal. Even new thoughts have affinities and lines of descent, and this is true of Anselm's new proofs of the existence of God and the necessity of the Incarnation. They owed most to Augustine, and yet they have a mathematical conciseness and finality quite unlike anything in Augustine. This is a quality all the more surprising since mathematics was the form of thought for which the medieval West showed least aptitude. It is this mathematical quality that links Anselm most closely with Pascal. Indeed I feel fairly confident that if Anselm had lived in the seventeenth century he would, like Pascal, have made fundamental discoveries in mathematics.

What is more important in an idea than its intellectual affinities is the quality of appealing to everyone, however inexpert in the subject, and of exciting a response even when imperfectly understood, even when rejected. Anselm's ideas have these qualities in a high degree. His two greatest arguments are very easy to state, though not so easy to state correctly except in his own words. Both of them can give an amateur like myself intense pleasure, the same kind of pleasure that a layman gets from the proof that there is an infinity of prime numbers. No doubt the amateur misses much, but he also gains by not seeing further than Anselm did, and by enjoying the freshness of his ideas with all the force of inexperience.

Anselm did not willingly tackle easy problems, and especially not practical problems, and when he did he was not conspicuously successful in solving them. He sought the heights, and breathed comfortably only in the pure and rarefied air of the most abstract speculation. After Pascal he reminds me of another seventeenth century philosopher, Thomas Hobbes, whose habit was to brood with intense concentration on a single theme for many days, and who said that if he had read as much as other men he would have known as little as other men. They were both men who at a crisis of human thought saw that the way forward was, so to speak, inwards, through meditation, simplification, and intensity of vision.

This parallel between St. Anselm and Hobbes, surprising though it may seem, could be developed in various ways, and not least in this, that despite their confidence in reason they both believed in the still greater importance of authority. Hobbes wrote to persuade men to obey: so did Anselm. They both believed that the strong tendencies to disobedience which their age displayed came not from ignorance, still less from knowledge, but from half-truths. They wrote to enlighten the ignorant and to confound those who thought they saw further than other men.

Naturally the parallel breaks down if it is pressed too far. Anselm and Hobbes were philosophers of diametrically opposed camps, and the ultimate authorities to which they appealed were consequently quite different. For Hobbes reason begins at the bottom, with counting and comparing; and the authority he sought to recommend was the *de facto* secular ruler. For Anselm reason comes from above. To reason well a man must purify his heart and seek in prayer a restoration of the divine image in his soul. Above all, he must first believe the doctrines of the Christian Church, because only in this way can the outline of the divine image be restored in his soul: 'Not only,' he wrote, 'is the mind unable to ascend without faith and obedience to the commands of God, but sometimes, even when understanding has been given, it is taken away, and faith itself collapses by neglect of a good conscience'.[1] The necessity for faith as a foundation and support for philosophical speculation at every stage is the subject of Anselm's most characteristic utterances. He called his first work 'An example of meditating on the rationality of what we believe', and his second 'Faith seeking understanding'. Fifteen years later he wrote, 'I do not seek to understand that I may believe, but I believe that I may understand: for this I also believe, that unless I believe I shall not understand'. He compared those who try to understand before they believe to bats, who 'having only seen the sky at night, presume to argue with eagles about the midday sun'.[2]

These phrases bring us back to our starting point, and they raise a fundamental question about Anselm's rational programme. In its simplest form the question is this. If we are to take seriously the objections of unbelievers and the questions of believers, what possible help can it be to say to the first, 'Unless you believe you cannot understand' and to the second 'Only those reasons which agree with the data of faith can be right—and even they are only provisional'? Anselm's answers to this question are scattered throughout his works. They are found only in *obiter dicta*, and they are never developed in a systematic way, but the gist of them is something like this:

Nothing can be finally and completely proved in this world. This is not because of the limitations of reason but because of the conditions under which reason operates in sinful man. If man

---

[1] *Epistola de Incarnatione Verbi*, c.i (F. S. Schmitt, *S. Anselmi Opera Omnia*, ii 9).

[2] For these phrases, see Schmitt, *op. cit.*, i, 13n, 94 ('Exemplum meditandi de ratione fidei'); i, 94, 97n. ('Fides quaerens intellectum'); i, 100 ('Neque enim quaero intelligere ut credam, sed credo ut intelligam. Nam et hoc credo, quia nisi credidero non intelligam.'); ii, 8 ('Velut si vespertiliones et noctuae non nisi in nocte caelum videntes de meridianis solis radiis disceptent contra aquilas ipsum solem inverberato visu intuentes.')

were in that state of union with God in which he was created, and for which he was created, reason would at once apprehend those truths which now appear only dimly even after intense effort. As things are, we can see only one thing at a time, and we cannot equally see all the possible objections to what we think we have proved. All proofs therefore have in them an element of the conjectural and provisional. They are not, however, useless on this account. They fill out the bare scheme of faith, and they make it part of our own experience: even if the proof is not valid, it is a means whereby we appropriate the substance of faith. Besides, although the proof may not be valid *in toto*, the fact that it stands up to all known objections is an indication that we are on the right lines. And even if we are not, it would be folly to reject provisional conclusions because of objections which we cannot see. Even if a man were determined to accept only what reason can demonstrate he would still be right to accept provisional proofs as the best that can be found, and it would be irrational and stultifying to the intellect to reject them.

Unbelievers therefore, should accept an argument which they cannot answer, even if they have no complete conviction of its truth. They should recognize too, that the 'proof' which they cannot answer, could never have been discovered in the uncharted maze of intellectual possibilities without the guidance of faith. Since mankind has lost the direct vision, God has provided him with the only possible substitute—faith. Faith provides an outline of reality, a map to guide our steps. The intuitive certainty, which would have been ours in a state of innocence, cannot be recalled. Faith takes its place. It is an essential starting-point for thought. Without the starting point of faith, reason would be simply bewildered by the maze of inconclusive intellectual possibilities. It is true that rational proofs based on faith must be provisional in the sense that they cannot foresee all possible future objections, but all the objections at present advanced can be shown to be either self-contradictory or inadequate, and that is enough to satisfy the enquiries of believers and the objections of unbelievers who here and now exist.

This, then, or something like it, is what Anselm would have replied to those who claimed that his arguments left them exactly where they were at the beginning. He would have claimed to have enlarged the worship of the believer, to have silenced the unbeliever, and to have refuted a variety of beliefs which are contrary to the Christian faith.

Whether or not these arguments will now appear to have any force I do not know. But the important point is this. It is possible to explain and discuss however inadequately, Anselm's arguments in a modern way—not as a piece of fossilized intellectual history, but as possible arguments that anyone might put forward today. The questions which they attempt to answer are questions to which we still seek an answer; and the answers he gives are answers which we can at once recognize as relevant, even if they are wrong. And even if we think they are wrong, it is not at all easy to determine the point at which they go wrong. Highly critical and sceptical minds in our own day have been convinced by some of the arguments which Anselm first thought out. To say the least, therefore, they have retained their power to puzzle and to stimulate longer than most arguments can hope to do. I do not think that this can be said of any other western writer in the six hundred years before the death of Anselm. The modern preacher can find plenty of valuable material in Bede's sermons and commentaries; but the modern enquirer will find no help till he comes to Anselm. That is one reason why the eleventh century is in an important sense the beginning of the modern world.

In the two centuries after Anselm's death, from Abelard to Duns Scotus, there is a line of speculative theologians whose works must still be reckoned with in any attempt to give a rational account of the Christian faith. But even in comparison with these successors, Anselm appears more modern than they. His resolute attacking of problems de novo, his refusal to support his arguments by the quotation of authorities, his general lack of philosophical baggage, the lucidity, firmness, and brevity of his arguments, and his recognition of the provisional nature of his proofs, all these characteristics stir a more immediate response in our minds than the wonderful mosaic of authorities and the carefully articulated pros and cons of St. Thomas Aquinas. St. Thomas may be the better theologian, but St. Anselm's problems are nearer to ours. In reading his works we can still experience some of the thrill of discovery of the first enquirers who came to him at Bec and stayed with him because he had an answer to their questions.

# 3

## MEISTER ECKHART

St. Anselm was the first great writer of the Middle Ages to tackle fundamental theological problems. For the next two hundred years the impulse of theological enquiry continued to produce some very impressive monuments of intellectual construction. But an intellectual interest remains powerful only so long as there is a goal to work towards, and the promise of success in reaching it. When the goal appears either to have been attained or to be unattainable, then the interest of the subject dies away. In the early years of the fourteenth century it appeared to some people that all the main positions had been occupied and that there was little to do except to defend them, while to others it appeared that the basis of the whole advance was so insecure that almost everything still remained to be done. In other words, instead of the relative order and optimism of the previous two centuries, there was a situation of bewildering confusion and intellectual despair.

There is a wide choice of writers who could be used to illustrate the confusion of the early fourteenth century, but the choice I have made is of a man who illustrates less the wreckage of the past than a new promise of the future: the German friar Eckhart. I am aware that the choice is more difficult to justify than that of Bede and Anselm. I can imagine somebody complaining that, whereas Bede and Anselm each stand high above all other candidates in their own time, Eckhart is a minority candidate if ever there was one. Everything is against him. A comprehensive list of his doctrines was condemned by Pope John XXII in 1329; also, he was a mystic, and this is not a word which inspires much confidence; then to crown his misfortunes, six hundred years after his death he became one of the idols of Nazi propagandists, who saw him as founder of their absurd Aryan ethos. These are severe handicaps for any man; yet I hope to show that my choice can be justified, and that it opens a new world of thought and experience, and a new social background of the highest significance.

Before we plunge into the novelties of the subject, it is important to emphasize how very ordinary much of the picture is.

Eckhart's life conformed to a pattern which was already well established by the end of the thirteenth century. He was born about 1260 in central Germany near Gotha. At the age of about fifteen he became a novice in the Dominican Order in Erfurt, and from that time until his death in 1327 or 1328, the main part of his career was that of a learned and successful member of his Order. He lived a life of teaching and administering, preaching, guiding and directing, which has been the common lot of distinguished churchmen throughout the centuries. Externally there is nothing to invite special attention.

When we turn from his career to his writings, once more all the familiar landmarks are there. At the university of Paris he performed the usual scholastic exercises, and on the great philosophical questions of the day he adopted the views we should expect of a member of his Order. His strictly academic writings attracted no great attention in his own time and were forgotten after his death. They would certainly not occupy us now if he had left nothing else behind him: they contain clear evidence of a powerful mind, but one that was not at ease or not fully extended in academic work.

The place where Eckhart exerted his full strength was not in the lecture room but in the pulpit; and there, not in his Latin sermons to the learned, but in his vernacular sermons to the unlearned. It was by his preaching that he drew attention to himself, and although many of the sermons traditionally ascribed to him have been found to be of doubtful authenticity, nevertheless it is to the sermons that we must go if we wish to judge the significance of Eckhart. Even the fact that he had imitators who exaggerated and distorted his teaching is of importance. It shows that there was an eager audience, even if it was not an intelligent one, and that his thoughts, however orthodox they might be, were curiously provocative as soon as he stood in the pulpit. This is the irresistible conclusion to be drawn from a single fact about the surviving evidence: there are two hundred manuscripts with German sermons ascribed to Eckhart and only three which contain his scholarly Latin works.

Since it is the audience which determines success or failure, we may look first at the people to whom Eckhart spoke before we look at the man himself. The audience which provoked the writings of Anselm was an audience of monks, young men eager for new light on old problems. During the two hundred years that separate Anselm from Eckhart the answers to intelligent and searching questions had become highly specialised, and most of them were extremely complicated and difficult to understand. They were intelligible only to a highly trained and professional section of the clergy. It was almost impossible for anyone to participate in the intellectual discussion of religious, theological, or even broad political questions without a university education, which was confined to relatively few clergy. Two classes of people were inevitably excluded: the laity in general, and women, whether members of religious orders or not, in particular.

It was to these classes of people, and especially to women in religious communities, that Eckhart's sermons brought something new. The first element in his greatness was this: his was the first academic voice which delivered arresting and original truths to an audience far beyond the lecture room, beyond the religious orders, beyond the ecclesiastical hierarchy. He spoke in the language of the people. This in itself was not new, but nearly all previous examples of vernacular sermons are colourless affairs, a distillation of academic recollections, seasoned with lurid stories. Eckhart's sermons were different from anything before his time. He said new things, and said them in a language which still gives the reader a curious physical sensation of power. His language has the stamp of all later German eloquence. We may not like it; it lacks lucidity and grace, and it is filled with that groping, guttural earnestness which Carlyle admired and we have learnt to distrust. But we can have no doubt as we read that a new vernacular eloquence has been born.

The orderly and systematic thought of the century before Eckhart had been made possible by an orderly hierarchial society. But there was one element in this society which the thought of the period found difficult to accommodate: the towns. Great towns were coming into existence and creating a new way of life in various parts of Europe, especially in northern Italy, western Germany, and the Netherlands. They brought with them new problems and new attitudes of mind. They had grown up in struggle, and they continued as an unruly intrusion into a mainly agrarian society. There is something about towns which makes their inhabitants restive, rebellious, and above all, articulate. Long before the thirteenth century Aristotle had noticed these characteristics and disliked them: they were the result, he said, of the too great ease with which mechanics, traders, and labourers— men who lacked moral excellence in their employments and were easily corrupted by foreigners—could come together in assemblies. The best thinkers of the twelfth and thirteenth centuries echoed this dislike and were glad to find that their instinctive fears were supported by Aristotle's arguments. But the towns grew never- theless, and as they grew they exhibited all those characteristics which Aristotle and Aquinas agreed in deploring. It is tempting to think that there is a critical size of population in towns which suddenly tips the balance and creates a new climate of opinion. This point had been reached in Western Europe by the early years of the fourteenth century. For the first time for nearly a thousand years in Western Europe towns were the source of new thoughts and new modes of expression of general and lasting importance.

It is in this context that Eckhart's sermons mark a new beginning. His was the first powerful voice of the northern towns. He founded no religious order, drew up no rule. His name became almost forgotten and he had no biographer, but the things he said and the way he said them reverberated far and wide; they became part of the general stock of religious ideas in the heterogeneous populations of the great towns throughout northern Europe.[1]

Eckhart's sermons have a single dominant theme, and this theme is the immediate presence of God in the individual soul: how to prepare the soul for this presence, how to recognise it, how to express it—these are some of the developments of the theme pursued throughout a hundred sermons. Nearly everything he said can be given a perfectly orthodox interpretation; but his words contained a challenge to established ecclesiastical society, however unintentional it might be. His contemporaries seized on his words, felt their inflammatory power, and reacted to them,

---

[1] The modern study of Eckhart's life and works began with two articles by H. Denifle in *Archiv für Literatur– und Kirchengeschichte des Mittelalters*, ii, 1886, and v, 1889. Since then, and especially since 1920 there has been a vast development of these studies, and a new edition of Eckhart's Latin and German works has been appearing spasmodically since 1936 under the patronage of the Deutsche Forschungsgemeinschaft (Stuttgart: W. Kohlhammer). There is a good survey of the literature down to 1958 in the *Dictionnaire d'histoire et de géographie ecclésiastiques*, xiv, 1960, 1385–1403, by Dom F. Vandenbroncke O.S.B.

for or against, without too much enquiry about their context. We can still feel the inflammation in his words, as a few examples will suffice to show:

I have often said that there is a power in the soul which neither time nor the world can touch. This power proceeds from the soul and belongs to the soul for ever.

I have sometimes called this power in the soul a fortress, sometimes a light, sometimes a spark in the soul; but now I can say that it is more than any of these things.

I wish to give it a nobler name than I have ever given it, but it disowns all names.

It is pure and free from all forms and all names; as pure and free as God is. (*Sermon* no. 2).

God's foundation is my foundation, and my foundation is God's foundation: here I am on my own ground, just as God is on his own ground. Actions spring up from this ground without asking *Why?*

Base your whole life on this inner foundation; seek no other ground of action, neither heaven, nor God, nor your eternal salvation.

If anyone thinks he will obtain God in meditation and sweet thoughts and special devotions rather than by the fireside or in the byre, he is seeking to take God and wrap his head in a blanket and thrust him under the table.

He who seeks God in some external routine will find the routine and lose God.

But he who seeks Him without external routine will obtain him as He is. (*Sermon* no. 5b).

The just man is so devoted to justice that if God were not just he would not care a bean for God or for the pains of hell or the joys of heaven.

People who do good deeds to the glory of God such as fasting, watching, praying and the like—and yet do these things so that the Lord will give them something they want in exchange—these people are the money-changers whom Jesus cast out of the temple.

When God made woman, He made her from man's side so that she should be equal with man, neither below nor above.

In the same way the just soul is equal with God, neither above nor below. (*Sermon* no. 6).[1]

Surely these are difficult, obscure, and dangerous doctrines to scatter abroad. They brought the deepest problems of personal religion to minds in varying degrees untrained and undisciplined. They attacked, at least implicitly, some of the main foundations of medieval religious life: large gifts to religious foundations as a payment for sin; the adoption of a religious habit at the end of life as a means of escaping Purgatory; the purchase of vast quantities of Masses for the release of souls from Purgatory; the conviction that the chief safety for the soul was to be found in membership of a religious Order; the centuries-long proliferation and extension of church services, and the accumulating costliness and splendour of the apparatus of worship; the immense enlargement of the legal and administrative functions of the Church since the eleventh century. All these features of medieval religion were in some degree called in question and threatened by the sentences I have quoted.

One can understand the anxiety of those responsible for the orthodoxy of the church, especially when these doctrines were passed round in popular form. But Eckhart's words had the quality of all great oratory: a certain indefinite power which created vague images, and released unexpected energies in those who listened. 'The spark in the soul', 'the fortress of the soul,' 'God in the soul', 'the equality of man with God': these thoughts and phrases came like a liberation to men and women who lived in the crowded cities on the fringe of the orderly society of the Church. We can only recapture their power if we remember the towering impersonal structure of the thirteenth century Church, its power over men's lives, and the inarticulate discontent which —though often misguided—expressed the desire for greater liberty. The fully developed intellectual and disciplinary system of the thirteenth century Church, regarded simply as a human achievement, is the greatest creation of the Middle Ages. It is one of the greatest practical and intellectual achievements of all

---

[1] These quotations are taken from three of Eckhart's sermons in the edition of the German works of Eckhart mentioned in the previous note: Josef Quint, *Meister Eckharts Predigten*, i, 32, 39–40 (Predigt 2); 90–91 (Predigt 5b); 103, 106–7 (Predigt 6). There is an English translation of these sermons by R. B. Blakney, *Meister Eckhart: a modern translation* (Harper Torchbooks, 1957), which I have found helpful.

time. But to live under it must, for the underprivileged, have been like living under a harrow. And it was to the underprivileged that Eckhart spoke.

His sermons are remarkable as much for what they leave out as for what they contain. They break away from the themes long associated with the biblical passages which he chose as his texts. The stories, legends, and allegories of Christ and the Virgin Mary, of saints and relics, even the sacraments and discipline of the Church—in fact all the most common landmarks of medieval religion—disappear. And in their place is the stark confrontation of God and the individual soul. I do not suggest that what Eckhart left out of his sermons he left out of his thought and life. But the emphasis is unmistakeable. Eckhart's depreciation of external practices, rules, disciplines and vows, his incipient nihilism, his insistence that the soul's joys could be fulfilled in the world and in the market-place no less than in church or in the cloister, cut across the carefully articulated system of the medieval church like a deep wound.

Eckhart's orthodoxy has found vigorous defenders in our own day, and it seems likely that his worst enemies and his warmest friends have been equally wrong in their interpretation of his thought. He was probably not a heretic and he was certainly not an embryonic Nazi. He was a prophet of the individual in religion. Anyone who cares to read him today will find that, even in translation, the force of his words has hardly diminished with the passage of time. He will never lack friends and enemies. His enemies will say that he tended to obliterate the distinctive character of Christian religious experience and to submerge it in a generalized experience of the divine. His friends will reply that he looked through the thick accumulation of rules and disciplines to truths which they were designed to safeguard and too often only obscured. Certainly, however, into the intellectual confusion and deepening despair of the fourteenth century Eckhart and his followers infused an optimism about the destiny of man and the extent to which even the least privileged could realize that destiny. The doctrine of man's closeness to God, of the existence of an impregnable fortress in the soul where God and man meet and are united, had a long and stormy history ahead of it. It proved capable of overthrowing systems and states, and even perhaps of overthrowing religion itself.

It may seem a long journey from the religious women and pious laity who heard his words in Cologne to the Puritan rebels of the seventeenth century, but the road is sign-posted with words like those I have quoted from Eckhart. At a further remove, Eckhart's deification of man has a distant echo in the over-ripe romanticism exemplified by Swinburne. These developments were very far from Eckhart's intention, but he opened a door which led to many different destinations. The people whom he roused could never again be kept in order, the thoughts he suggested could never be suppressed, and Europe, could never be the same again. He brings us into the tumult of the modern world.

# II

## ASPECTS OF HUMANISM

# 4

## MEDIEVAL HUMANISM

### I

As a general rule medieval historians do well to avoid words which end in 'ism'. They are words which belong to a recent period of history, and their use injects into the past the ideas of a later age. But some of these words like feudalism, romanticism, and humanism have become so closely bound up with our conception of various periods of history that it is almost impossible to write of these periods without some reference to the words which have been so often used to describe their main characteristics. They distort, but they also summarise a large assortment of facts and impressions; and we are obliged sometimes to ask what they mean and whether they correctly describe the main traits of the ages to which they have been applied.

One of the main difficulties with the word 'humanism' is that it has two distinct, though related, meanings, and historians have used the word sometimes in one sense and sometimes in the other, and sometimes in a mixture of the two. This has caused a good deal of confusion. The most general meaning of the word according to the Oxford English Dictionary is 'any system of thought or action which is concerned with merely human interests or with those of the human race in general'. It is in this sense that this word is now in popular use, especially among those who call themselves humanists. This meaning of the word associates humanism with the extension of the area of human knowledge and activity, and consequently with the activity of limiting (or abolishing) the supernatural in human affairs. Its main instrument is scientific knowledge leading ultimately to a single coherent rational view of the whole of nature, including the nature of men. I shall call this the 'scientific' view of humanism. I suppose that most people who support this type of humanism look on the medieval period—with its emphasis on the supernatural end of man, with its insistence on the primacy of theology among the sciences, with its predominantly clerical culture and hierarchical organization under a universal papal authority—as the embodiment of all that they most bitterly oppose.

Alongside this popular view of humanism, there is also an academic view which goes back to the Renaissance. In this view, the essential feature of humanism is the study of ancient Latin and Greek literature: hence the use of phrases like 'Professor of Humanity' and 'literae humaniores' in our academic jargon. These studies were regarded as pre-eminently *humane* in contrast to the formal and systematic studies of the Middle Ages in scholastic theology, canon law and logic, which were thought to have excluded humanity, destroyed style, and to have dissociated scholarship from the affairs of the world and men. I shall call this the 'literary' view of humanism. On this view of the matter the Middle Ages, in the eyes of the early literary humanists, represented the enemy, not only in their comparative neglect of the literary qualities of the ancient masterpieces, but also in their supposed neglect of the human qualities which the study of these masterpieces inculcated.

The protagonists of both these types of humanism, therefore, have generally looked on the Middle Ages as hostile country. Historians indeed have protested, and on many grounds. They have pointed out that the Middle Ages cannot be lumped together in a single undifferentiated period of a thousand years, and they have singled out the Carolingian age and the twelfth century as periods of 'Renaissance' and 'humanism' in one sense or another; they have brought to light medieval lovers of classical literature and writers of elegant Latin prose and poetry; they have spoken of medieval science, and medieval Platonism, and medieval influences on Renaissance scholarship and so on. But there is a confusion of voices. Those who have spoken most forcibly about the humanism of the twelfth century have been inclined to admit that it was short-lived, and that there was a falling-away long before the beginning of the thirteenth century. Those who have extolled the medieval stylists and lovers of the classics have found them disconcertingly indifferent to the authors whose words they quoted so lavishly. As we watch so notable a humanist as John of Salisbury striding through the classics, heaping up each page with quotations from half a dozen authors, with sovereign indifference to the source, we are forced to ask what kind of sensitivity to ancient literature this great man possessed. Certainly it was not the sensitivity of a Petrarch.

The confusions of the subject could be discussed without end —confusions in the use of words, confusions in the views of historians, confusions in the subject itself. Instead of pursuing these shadows let me attempt to state quite simply why, and in what sense, I believe the period from about 1100 to about 1320 to have been one of the great ages of humanism in the history of Europe: perhaps the greatest of all. As a corollary of this I shall argue that, far from the humanism of the twelfth century running into the sand after about 1150 to re-emerge two centuries later, it had its fufilment in the thirteenth and early fourteenth centuries— in the period which the humanists of the Renaissance most despised. Lastly I shall ask why the humanism of this period appeared so repellent to the humanists of a later age.

In order to discuss these questions, we must first be clear what we are looking for. What are the symptoms which will establish the existence of a deep-seated humanism in the period we are to study? I take them to be these:

In the first place there can be no humanism without a strong sense of the dignity of human nature. That man is a fallen creature, that he has lost his immediate knowledge of God, that his instincts and reason are often in conflict, and that he is radically disorganized and disorientated—all this is common ground to all Christian thinkers. We must not expect a denial of these facts in the Middle Ages, or even for that matter in the Renaissance; but we may expect a humanist to assert not only that man is the noblest of God's creatures, but also that his nobility continues even in his fallen state, that it is capable of development in this world, that the instruments exist by which it can be developed, and that it should be the chief aim of human endeavour to perfect these instruments.

Along with this large view of man's natural dignity there must go a recognition of the dignity of nature itself. This second feature of humanism is a consequence of the first, for if man is by nature noble, the natural order itself, of which he forms part, must be noble. The two are linked together by indissoluble ties, and the power to recognize the grandeur and splendour of the universe is itself one of the greatest expressions of the grandeur and splendour of man. Thus man takes his place in nature; and human society is seen as part of the grand complex of the natural order bound together by laws similar to those which tie all things into one.

Finally the whole universe appears intelligible and accessible to human reason: nature is seen as an orderly system, and man— in understanding the laws of nature—understands himself as the main part, the key-stone, of nature. Without this understanding it is hard to see how men can experience that confidence in human powers which humanism implies.

When those elements of dignity, order, reason and intelligibility are prominent in human experience, we may reasonably describe as humanistic the outlook which ensues. This humanism will be much nearer to the type I have described as 'scientific' than to 'literary' humanism, but I believe that this must be our starting point in any study of the central period of the Middle Ages.

The starting point is important because the subject has been confused by the tendency to start with the humanism of the Renaissance. This has given the love of ancient literature and the ability to imitate the style of ancient authors an exaggerated importance in judging medieval humanism. If we start with the concepts of natural nobility and of reason and intelligible order in the universe, the whole subject takes on a different appearance.

We may at once say that there is little evidence that these concepts played an important part in medieval experience before about 1050. In the main tradition of the early Middle Ages nearly all the order and dignity in the world was closely associated with supernatural power. There was order in symbolism and ritual, and order in worship and sacrament, and both of them were very elaborate and impressive. Man's links with the supernatural gave his life a framework of order and dignity; but in the natural order the chaos was almost complete. Almost nothing was known about secondary causes in natural events. Rational procedures in law, in government, in medicine, in argument, were scarcely understood or practised even in the most elementary way. Man chiefly knew himself as a vehicle for divine activity. There was a profound sense of the littleness and sinfulness of man. Both physically and mentally human life had narrow limits: only in prayer and penance, in clinging to the saints, was there any enlargement. Man was an abject being, except when he was clad in symbolic garments, performing symbolic and sacramental acts, and holding in his hands the earthly remains of those who already belonged to the spiritual world.

That at least is how I interpret the main evidence for the period before the late eleventh century. Perhaps this awe-struck, sacramental view of man's place and powerlessness in the world gives a more satisfactory account of man's situation in the universe than the optimism of the succeeding centuries; and optimism never overcame the final impotence of man and his need for supernatural aid. But there is a sharp change of emphasis after about 1050. It is this change of emphasis that we are to examine.

## II

We shall look first into the monasteries, for they were the great centres of supernatural influence in the early Middle Ages, and it is in them that we see the first signs of a change that had a profound effect on the religious life of Europe. Briefly, the change took the form of a greater concentration on man and on human experience as a means of knowing God. This was a significant step towards the restoration of the dignity of man, for it made the study of man an integral part of religious life. The search for God within the soul became one of the chief preoccupations of the monastic leaders of the late eleventh and twelfth centuries and this search expanded into a general demand for self-knowledge. The search took many forms and can be found in many places. For my part I find one of its most significant moments in Normandy in 1079. In this year Anselm at Bec entered into the chamber of his mind, excluded everything but the word 'God', and found that suddenly the word articulated itself into a demonstration of God's existence, which he believed to be both new and true.[1] It was new, and whether or not it was true, it was a triumph of an analytical introspective method. It seemed to show that men could find new truths of the greatest general importance simply by looking within themselves. The idea of finding something new was itself new to a generation which had believed itself to be at the end of the road; and to find the new things so close at hand, and so entirely central, was a revelation of the powers that lay within man's mind.

It was St. Bernard, a generation later, who popularized the

[1] For Anselm's experience of discovering the proof of the existence of God, see Eadmer, *Vita S. Anselmi*, I, xix (ed. R. W. Southern, 1962, pp. 28–31).

method of introspection and made it the property of a school of monastic writers. He gave the whole exercise a new direction. He was not interested, like Anselm, in logic or analysis, but only in spiritual growth. According to Bernard, man's love of God begins with man's love of himself for himself alone. This love can be refined by reason and virtue until it gives birth to the love of one's neighbour, and this in turn to the love of God.[1] So here too we find a programme of spiritual growth starting with man, and with a most unpromising aspect of man, his self-love. The programme is rooted in nature, and it uses the instruments of natural virtue to reach a supernatural end. From nature itself arises the necessity for turning to God.

To begin with man and nature and to find in them the road to God is very characteristic of the new age. As St. Bernard's younger contemporary, Richard of St. Victor, said:

> A man raises his eyes in vain to see God who has not yet succeeded in seeing himself. Let a man first learn to under-stand the invisible things of himself before he presumes to stretch out to the invisible things of God . . . for unless you can understand yourself, how can you try to understand those things which are above yourself?[2]

This search for man was at first a monastic programme, and it was in the monasteries also that another aspect of human experi-ence began to be appreciated—the experience of friendship. Without the cultivation of friendship there can be no true human-ism. If self-knowledge is the first step in the rehabilitation of man, friendship—which is the sharing of this knowledge with someone else—is an important auxiliary. This was understood by the humanists of the Renaissance; but the discovery was made in the monasteries of the late eleventh century.

Here again, it was St. Anselm who first in his generation groped for words to express the intensity of his feelings for his friends.[3]

---

[1] For the four stages of love, from the *amor carnalis quo ante omnia homo diligit seipsum propter seipsum* to the spiritual love *quo nec seipsum diligit homo nisi propter Deum*, see Bernard, *Tractatus de diligendo deo*, cc. viii–x (*P.L.* 182, 987–990).

[2] *Benjamin minor*, c. lxxi, *P.L.* 196, 51.

[3] The following letters of Anselm are especially relevant here: nos. 5, 11, 22, 34, 41, 59, 68, 69, 120, 140 (Schmitt, vol.iii). For a discussion of the sense of some of the phrases used in these letters, see *St. Anselm and his Biographer*, pp. 67–76.

But very soon in many places friendship came to appear an essential part of a full religious life. By 1160 Aelred of Rievaulx was able to sum up the results of the monastic experience of the past century in the words 'Friendship is wisdom', *amicitia nihil aliud est quam sapientia*, or even 'God is friendship', *'Deus est amicitia'*.[1] He was careful to say that these phrases had to be accepted with some reserve, but they expressed the close relationship between human friendship and the nature of God. The experience of friendship lay along the road to God. Nature, said Aelred, makes man desire friendship, experience fortifies it, reason regulates it, and the religious life perfects it.[2] So here again we start with nature and end with God. The treatise that Aelred wrote on friendship is the most beautiful example of the casting of an ancient humanistic theme into a Christian mould, and the sequence which it elaborates—nature prompting, reason regulating, experience strengthening, religion perfecting—is the basis of all religious humanism.

Of all the forms of friendship rediscovered in the twelfth century, there was none more eagerly sought than the friendship between God and man. This may seem a commonplace theme, and one which has been debased by countless sentimentalities and trivialities. But it was once fresh, and it lifted a great weight from men's lives. In the early Middle Ages God had not appeared as a friend. By great labour and exertion, by crippling penances and gifts to the Church, by turning from the world to the monastic life, men might avert God's anger: but of God as a friend they knew little or nothing. It was terribly difficult to approach Him. Then quite suddenly the terror faded and the sun shone.

There were many forces working in this direction. One of them was just a new way of thinking about God. Prayers, poems, devotions of all kinds, poured forth from the twelfth century onwards, which had one predominant theme—the humanity of God. I do not forget that one of these poems—the greatest of them, of about 1250—begins with the tremendous words:

> Dies irae, dies illa,
> solvet saeclum in favilla . . .

But it is wrong to think that this superb poem simply describes a

[1] Aelred *De Spirituali Amicitia*, i (*P.L.* 195, 669–70).
[2] *Ibid.* 666 C–D, 671D, 672 B–D.

scene of terror. Its second half mitigates the terror by an appeal
to the sufferings and humanity of Christ:

> Recordare, Jesu pie
> quod sum causa tuae viae,
> ne me perdas illa die.
> Quaerens me sedisti lassus;
> redemisti, crucem passus:
> tantus labor non sit cassus.[1]

This is just one of the many signs that since the days of St.
Anselm the God of human sufferings and emotions had become
an object of tender contemplation. The whole creation had become
filled with humanity. The theme is capable of an infinite amount of
illustration, but I shall quote only a few sentences from an anonymous thirteenth century treatise on the uses of adversity. It shows
how even this theme so redolent of sin, misery and impotence has
been sweetened by the common humanity of God and man:

> Tribulations illuminate the heart of man with self-
> knowledge, and this is the perfection of the human condition.
> Just as lovers send letters to each other to refresh their
> memories one of another, so Christ sends tribulations to
> refresh our memories of him and his sufferings.
> By denying us earthly satisfactions God forces us to seek
> those which are heavenly, just as an earthly lord who wants
> to sell his own wine orders the public houses to close until he
> has sold it.[2]

We may object that these gentle similes cover the harsh
realities of the world with sentimentality, and this may be an
inevitable result of humanism in religion. But it is a form of
humanism that has survived all the religious divisions of Europe,
and it has made a lasting contribution to the way in which ordinary
people have looked at the universe. Popular piety has never lost
this sentimental familiarity.

Some may think that these religious themes, however

---

[1] There is a good text of this famous poem, which was probably written by
the Fransiscan Thomas of Celano, in *The Oxford Book of Medieval Latin Verse*,
ed. F. J. E. Raby, 1959, pp. 342–4.

[2] These sentences come from the *Tractatus de duodecim utilitatibus tribu-
lationum*, *P.L.*, ccvii, 989–1006. There is a recent edition by A. Auer, *Leidens-
theologie im Spätmittelalter*, 1952.

expressed, are far from the themes of humanism. But if we are looking for a growing sense of human dignity, and for an enlargement of man's powers and place in the universe, the hymns and meditations of the twelfth and thirteenth centuries supply us with abundant evidence. Indeed these religious developments are perhaps the greatest triumph that humanism has ever achieved, for they conquered the universe for humanity, and made God so much man's friend that his actions became almost indistinguishable from our own.

## III

The greatest triumph of medieval humanism was to make God seem human. The Ruler of the Universe, who had seemed so terrifying and remote, took on the appearance of a familiar friend. The next triumph was to make the universe itself friendly, familiar, and intelligible. This is an essential part of the heritage of western Europe which we owe to the scholars of the twelfth and thirteenth centuries. The experience of earlier centuries had suggested that so far as man could see, the universe was a scene of chaos and mystery, and that renunciation, submission to the supernatural, and a grateful acceptance of miraculous aid were the best that men could aim at. But in the late eleventh century, secular schools began to multiply which were dedicated to the task of extending the area of intelligibility and order in the world in a systematic way.

The importance of these schools for the intellectual development of Europe is very great. They provided permanent centres of learning which faced the world instead of facing away from it. The studies of the monasteries were necessarily dominated by the needs of the monastic life, but the secular schools belonged to the world. They were normally found in centres of urban life. They drew their scholars from a class of men who expected to live in the world and to make their careers in the government of church and state. The greatest of these schools became the prototypes of all modern universities. Oxford, Paris and Bologna have had a continuous history since the twelfth century: likewise our academic faculties and disciplines have had an unbroken development since that time. These schools and universities and disciplines have many achievements to their credit, but their first achievement was the foundation of all others: they brought the idea of an indefinitely expanding order and rationality into every area of human experience.

The emancipating role of the medieval schools has been obscured partly by the prejudices and misconceptions of a later age, and partly by the hardening of the arteries that afflicts all institutions in the course of time. Later scholars, who saw that the medieval secular schools existed to train tonsured clerks in sciences necessary for running ecclesiastical courts and institutions, could not understand that they had once been the great liberating force in European thought. They could not see how small was the gap that separated the clerks of these schools from the secular world. The masters and scholars wore the ecclesiastical tonsure and were subject to ecclesiastical courts, but many of them looked forward to employment in secular business. They were willing to use their skills as much to oppose ecclesiastical claims as to promote them. They had no sense of separation from secular affairs. Contemporaries criticised them for wasting the resources of the Church on studies irrelevant or hostile to the purposes of the Church, and though this was a narrow-minded criticism it was nearer the truth than the later charge of subservience to ecclesiastical interests. Certainly it would be difficult to imagine a less clerical body, in any modern sense of the word, than the unruly and undisciplined communities of the medieval universities. This was an aspect of the medieval schools hidden from the view of later critics who could only see them engaged in a long struggle to preserve a clerical monopoly in academic effort.

As for the curriculum and methods of study of the schools, they came to seem very arid to almost all thinking men. In the early days of the revival of medieval studies, no more than a century ago, the best that a deeply learned and serious observer could find to say about medieval scholastic writers was that:

> those men handed down to us much precious knowledge, with much verbiage and false logic. . . . They ticketed every portion of man's moral anatomy, found a rule for every possible case of choice, a reason and a reward for every virtue, and a punishment for every conceivable crime; they turned generalizations into law, and deduced from them as laws the very facts from which they had generalized. They

benefited mankind by exercising and training subtle wits, and they reduced dialectics, almost, we might say, logic itself, to absurdity. . . . In reading Thomas Aquinas one is constantly provoked to say, What could not such a mind have done if it had not been fettered by such a method?[1]

These are in their way very judicious remarks: this is what it all came to in the end. But in the beginning, the medieval scholastic curriculum met an urgent need for order in the intellectual outlook of a Europe first rising to independent thought. At that time the only available instrument of intellectual order was a thorough command of the sciences and techniques of the Greco-Roman world so far as they had been preserved in the West. This command was achieved, and it brought intellectual order into human life in a wonderfully short space of time. No doubt it is possible to imagine better starting-points. But none other was available, and we must judge the achievement in the light of the problems and the tools that lay to hand.

I have said that there can be no humanism without a strong sense of the dignity and intelligibility of man and nature; and if God exists, the same qualities must characterize the relations of God with his creation. These phrases could almost be taken as a description of the programme of the medieval secular schools. One of the first things they did was to renew a sense of the dignity and nobility of man. These terms are rare in the eleventh century, but very common in the twelfth. They meant that man's powers of reason and will, cultivated as they can be by study, give him a splendour which survives all the effects of sin and degeneration. As a twelfth century schoolmaster, Bernard Silvestris, wrote:

> The animals express their brute creation
> By head hung low and downward looking eyes;
> But man holds high his head in contemplation
> To show his natural kinship with the skies.
> He sees the stars obey God's legislation:
> *They* teach the laws by which mankind can rise.[2]

[1] W. Stubbs, *Seventeen Lectures on the Study of Medieval and Modern History*, 1886, pp. 103–4. The words quoted come from a lecture delivered in 1877.

[2] These lines are a rough translation of Bernard Silvestris, *De Mundi Universitate Libri duo*, ii, X, ll. 27–32, ed. C. S. Barach and J. Wrobel, 1876, p. 55.

These images were largely borrowed from Ovid, but whereas in Ovid they were a poetic fiction, for the twelfth century scholar they were a scientific fact. They provided a basis for intellectual ambition and optimism. For scholars of an earlier generation the dignity of man and nature had been lost through sin, and could only be restored by supernatural means. But the leading scholars of the secular schools, from the beginning of the twelfth century onwards, stressed the natural remedies to the ravages of sin, and saw the seven liberal arts as instruments for the mitigation of human frailties.

This view of the nature of man and his hopes for the future was based on man's apparently unlimited capacity for knowledge. It may seem strange that scholars who had so recently emerged from an extremely pessimistic view of human capacities, and who believed that man's faculties had been grievously impaired by sin, should rush to the other extreme and proclaim that everything, or almost everything, could be known. But in intellectual affairs almost all revolutions are violent, and this was no exception. Scholars discovered that there existed a scientific basis for optimism. They learnt from their sources that man's affinity with every part of nature gives him the power to understand everything in nature; that his elements and humours, and the influences playing upon his birth and development, are the raw materials for the whole universe. Hence man, being the epitome of the universe, is built to understand the universe. Despite the ravages of sin, he can still intellectually trace the primitive perfection of the creation, and collaborate with God in its restoration.

The instrument of this collaboration with God in the regeneration of nature is reason. With comprehensive enthusiasm, the secular masters of the early twelfth century began to let fall such *dicta* as these: 'The dignity of our mind is its capacity to know all things'; 'We who have been endowed by nature with genius must seek through philosophy the stature of our primeval nature'; 'In the solitude of this life the chief solace of our minds is the study of wisdom'; 'We have joined together science and letters, that from this marriage there may come forth a free nation of philosophers'.[1]

---

[1] These phrases are taken from the revised version of William of Conches's *Philosophia Mundi*, ed. C. Ottaviano, pp. 19–20 (see below), and from Thierry of Chartres, *Prologus in Eptatheucon*, ed. E. Jeauneau in *Mediaeval Studies*, 1954, xvi, 171–5. For the way in which the four elements are combined in the cells of the brain to make every kind of knowledge possible, see William of

These were ancient thoughts, but for the first time for many centuries we find men confident that all those things could be done and that nature could be known. Hence the future seemed bright. Men knew little as yet, but they could know everything, and already, as it seemed to those optimistic masters, they knew more than had ever been known before. At last, in a famous phrase of Bernard of Chartres, they 'stood on the shoulders of the giants, and could see further than their great predecessors'. They had mastered the past:

> His eagle eye could clearly see
> through each perplexed obscurity
> of all the seven liberal arts.
> He knew them well in all their parts,
> and made quite clear to everyone
> truths that for Plato dimly shone.[1]

This was the epitaph of Thierry, one of the great masters who died about 1150. The idea that he could see further than Plato, not through revelation but through superior science, was surely very bold. Thierry was only one of a large number of masters responsible for the intellectual revival I have been describing. A surprisingly high proportion of them died or retired in the decade before 1150; Abelard, Hugh of St. Victor, William of Conches, Thierry, Bernard Silvestris. It has seemed to many scholars that humanism died with them. Certainly some freshness and charm died with them. But if we look at the principles of enquiry for which they stood, the main current of their work suffered no setback. These men represented the intellectual adolescence of Europe, and it is natural to mourn the passing of youth. But we must not exaggerate their youthful achievement. What they made was partly a ground-plan and partly a castle in the air. It still remained to build on the foundation and to give reality to the vision.

Conches, *Phil. Mundi*, iv, 24, (*P.L.* 172, 95), and for the powers of *sensus, imaginatio, ratio* and *intellectus*, by which man knows, see his glosses on the *Timaeus*, (ed. E. Jeauneau, 1965, pp. 100–2). Similar doctrines are expounded by Thierry of Chartres in his glosses on Boethius *De Trinitate* (see below, p.81 n.2).

[1] A. Vernet, 'Une épitaphe inédite de Thierry de Chartres,' *Recueil de travaux offert à C. Brunel*, 1948, ii, 660–70: this brief extract can give only a dim impression of the fine eulogy (possibly the finest on any medieval scholar) contained in the long epitaph.

## IV

The extent of the problems which faced scholars at the end of the first phase of intense activity in the secular schools may be judged from two plans of knowledge drawn up in the middle years of the twelfth century. Plans such as these are a very common feature of the schools about this time, and they testify to the prevailing conceptions of a universal system. They also show us how little had been achieved and how much remained to be done.

Of the two plans which I have chosen, the first sums up what had so far been achieved, but it offers very little hope for the future; the second is very imperfect, but it opens up a rich prospect of progress.[1]

The first plan is drawn from a revised version of William of Conches's *Philosophia Mundi*.[2] It presents a conflation of several currents of thought of the second quarter of the twelfth century. We see in the plan the familiar idea of universal knowledge as a remedy for the frailties of man's nature caused by sin. We see also the characteristic attempt of this period to weave into the pattern of knowledge every part of ancient learning so far as it was known at the time. The various limbs of Philosophy and Eloquence (the remedies for ignorance) are mostly drawn from Boethius; the plan of ethics (the remedy for concupiscence) is borrowed from Cicero; the remedies for physical infirmity are drawn, for the magical arts, from Isidore of Seville, and for the mechanical arts— the only modern feature of the whole plan—from Hugh of St. Victor who died in 1141. In all this the central position of Man is very evident. All the arts and sciences have the single aim of restoring human nature to its original state of excellence. Placed in this light, the search for systematic universal knowledge, which later observers could easily decry as a vain attempt to ticket 'every portion of man's moral anatomy' is far from being the drab and lifeless process they imagined. It was a search which opened up a dazzling prospect of human improvement. At the end of the plan

---

[1] See following p. 252

[2] The treatise was edited by C. Ottaviano (*Un brano inedito della 'Philosophia' di Guglielmo di Conches*, 1935) as a genuine work of William of Conches. This attribution is mistaken, but the work is nevertheless an interesting attempt to enlarge the basis of William's system, mainly by conflating it with Hugh of St. Victor's *Didascalicon* of about the same date.

of knowledge which is outlined in our first chart there are four
lines of verse which express the aim of the whole enterprise:

Nobilitas hominis—naturae iura tenere;
Nobilitas hominis—nisi turpia nulla timere;
Nobilitas hominis—virtutum clara propago;
Nobilitas hominis—mens et deitatis imago.[1]

That is to say, man's nobility consists in keeping the laws of
nature, in fearing nothing but disgrace, in putting forth a clear
stream of virtuous acts, and in the possession of reason which is
the image of God. Reason, freedom, moral courage, and law:
these are the excellences of man, and they can all be improved by
the study of philosophy. These lines in one form or another
became very popular in medieval collections of verse, but here we
have them in their scholastic setting as a product and programme
of the schools.

It was a dazzling prospect, but was there any hope of arrival?
If man could understand the music of the elements and humours,
not to mention the music of the spheres, he might indeed be like
God. But information on these subjects is hard to come by, and
there is no way of learning. As for the human sciences in our
chart, the science of economics scarcely went beyond the knowledge of its possible existence; politics was a mixture of unfathom-
able custom and unresolvable dispute; the branches of ethics
were a farrago of ancient sayings without a plan; the mechanical
arts had no literature outside medicine and war; and only the
urge for completeness can have prompted the inclusion of magic.

The author of this outline must have known that, at the time
when he was writing, there was nothing more (or nothing at all) to
be said about most of the subjects which make such a fair show in
the general plan. His plan expresses some of the noblest aspirations of his generation without offering any hope of fulfilment.
This is the great weakness of many of the secular masters of the
first half of the twelfth century. They had mastered the learning
of the past, and they could do no more. They could point to no
way forward.

William of Conches's *Philosophia Mundi*, to which the plan

---

[1] Ottaviano, *op. cit.* p. 30. For some notes on the collections in which the
verses appear, see *Carmina Burana*, ed. A. Hilke and O. Schumann, 1930, i,
pp. 9–10.

was attached, is a striking example of this limitation. It is a powerful synthesis of earlier learning, and it is original in its aim and conception. For the first time in the Middle Ages it presents a systematic account of the whole natural world, not in the form of an encyclopaedia or a theological treatise, but in a scientific survey of the structure of the universe. It deals with the creation and organization of the universe, its elements and their combinations, the heavens and the earth, the animals and men; and in dealing with men it outlines the systems of generation, digestion, perception and thinking, of growing up and growing old. The conception of the work is original, but the ideas all come from old books. The cosmology comes principally from Plato's *Timaeus* with elaborations from Macrobius and Martianus Capella; the physiology comes from Galen, who had recently been translated into Latin by Constantine the African. Beyond this, William of Conches could not go. His grasp of the simple principles of order behind the complexities of the world, and the eagerness with which he used new translations of ancient works, are symptoms of his intellectual vigour. But here he stuck. At the end of the work he says that there are many problems in the field of grammar which still need to be cleared up, and he proposed to turn his attention to them. He was still a young man, but he had no more to say about the system of the world. His revisions of the work added nothing to its scientific content.[1] It was only in the humble field of grammar that he would make new discoveries, and it was as a grammarian that we hear of him ten or fifteen years after writing the *Philosophia Mundi*. It was a steep descent from surveying the universe to the problems of grammar; but in grammar there were problems which could be solved, in science there were no problems, or at least no way of solving them.

The exhaustion of available material was the main problem of scientific humanism in the mid-twelfth century. But there was another problem, at once less obvious and more insidious. This was the problem of criticising and evaluating the material which was available. Every age has its characteristic points of strength

---

[1] The second recension, in the form of a dialogue with the Duke of Normandy under the title *Dragmaticon Philosophiae*, was made about 1145 (Ed. by Guil. Gratarolus, *Dialogus de substantiis physicis a Willelmo aneponymo philosopho*, 1567). For an analysis of the manuscript tradition of the two recensions, see A. Vernet, 'Un remaniement de la Philosophia de Guillaume de Conches', *Scriptorium*, i, 1947, 252–9.

and weakness. The strength of this period lay in its power to deal with discordant texts, to seize on distinctions of meaning, and to clarify confusions of thought. Contradictions of authorities were the food of thought; where there were no contradictions there was a strong inclination to think that nothing more could be said. 'Who would strive to expound again felicity, which Aristotle has already expounded, or who would undertake again the apology of old age, which Cicero has already accomplished? Such superfluity can only provoke disgust.' Dante summed up in these words the sentiments of the Middle Ages.[1] Without contradictions within the source, there might still be room for eloquence or organization, but there was no incentive to think afresh. This is very clear in the *Philosophia Mundi*. It enters into the thoughts of the past with great success; it shows great powers of combination; but it initiates no new discoveries because the sources created no frictions and suggested no controversies.

Friction was necessary for intellectual progress, and our second chart illustrates the main source of friction in medieval thought. The work from which it is drawn is roughly contemporaneous with our first chart, but the picture of knowledge which it presents is entirely different.[2] Our first impression is that man and the natural world have been deprived of their central position. Man's needs and the correction of his frailties no longer dominate the scene. Theology, which in the first chart had been merely one of three branches of theoretical philosophy alongside mathematics and physics, is here at the centre. Man's nature and frailties are simply the starting point of an enquiry that leads through nature and the supernatural to the knowledge of God.

This is the first impression. But a closer inspection shows that man and the natural world play a greater part than is at first evident. Nearly the whole of the first plan is preserved in outline in the second, but the scope of the enquiry is now vastly greater. Moreover, it is much more actively pursued. The treatise from

---

[1] Dante, *Monarchia*, i, i, 4.

[2] Chart II summarises and simplifies the plan of study of an anonymous *Ysagoge in Theologiam*, ed. A. Landgraf, *Ecrits théologiques de l'école d'Abelard* (*Spicilegium Sacrum Lovaniense*, 1934, xiv). I retain the attribution to the school of Abelard, but D. E. Luscombe, *The School of Peter Abelard*, 1969, p. 237, has rightly pointed out that it 'could with good reason be claimed for the school of Hugh (of St. Victor) as well as for that of Abelard'. The truth is that the great activity and variety of Parisian masters make it impossible to draw simple lines of intellectual descent in the history of ideas at this time. For the date see below, p. 159, n. 1.

which I have extracted it bristles, as the *Philosophia Mundi* did not, with the record of fierce controversy. At hundreds of points within the framework of established theology it offers the possibility of choice. In this profusion of choice lay the hope of intellectual progress. Like the first chart, this second one is not without its confusions and some elements of wishful thinking; but it represents a new start in the organization of knowledge. Although some features of the plan fell out of date quite quickly, in one important respect it forecast the future with great accuracy. The necessity for a thorough study of the secular sciences as an introduction to theology became one of the basic principles of medieval theological teaching. Whether this was good for theology I do not know, but it was certainly good for the advancement of the secular sciences and for the progress of an orderly view of the universe.

This union of secular and sacred sciences in a single systematic exploration of the universe was not inevitable. It did not happen for instance in contemporary Islam, where the materials of secular science were far more abundant: there, after a time of prodigious activity, the two branches of secular and sacred science finally divided with the result that both stagnated. The secular schools of the West made such a division virtually impossible. Yet even in 1150 the union was not secure. Peter Lombard's *Sentences*, the chief theological work of the mid-century, gives no promise of the later union of science and theology. Among its thousands of quotations from the Church Fathers, there are only three from secular philosophy, and all these were borrowed from St. Ambrose or St. Augustine. By contrast, just a hundred years later, the *Summa Theologica* of Thomas Aquinas contains about 3,500 quotations from Aristotle, of which 1,500 come from the *Nichomachean Ethics* and 800 from the *Meteorology* or *Metaphysics*, works wholly unknown a century earlier.

These are crude statistics, but they tell the story of the penetration of natural reason into the domain of revelation more clearly and quickly than many words. The transformation of the subject-matter of theology which they reflect is one of the most astonishing facts in medieval history, and we may see in our second chart a forecast of what later happened. If an all-embracing intelligibility is a mark of humanism, it is here that the future of medieval humanism is to be found. Theology provided the friction necessary for the development of independent thought.

Put in its very simplest terms medieval thought became a dialogue between Aristotle and the Bible. Of course it was much more than this, but here lay the main tension which transformed the thought of Europe in the two centuries after 1150. Paradoxical though it may seem, it was the Bible that did most for humanism in its medieval form simply because it provided the most difficult problems. On the surface it seems to exclude the use of human reason; natural virtues and rational argument are not much in evidence, nor are they much praised when they appear. Abraham, Noah, Jacob, David are mystic figures of Christian truth, but scarcely edifying examples of the natural virtues; and a text accepted as the infallible word of God is not a likely vehicle to forward the *studia humanitatis*. But the power of the Bible to provoke thought about human values and human society arose precisely from its lack of interest in these values. The conflict between biblical precepts and the ordinary needs of man in society provided a greater stimulus to independent thought than Aristotle could ever have given: 'Take no thought for the morrow,' 'Turn the other cheek,' 'Thou shalt not kill,' 'Touch not the Lord's anointed,' 'The powers that be are ordained of God,' 'Blessed are the poor', 'Give all your goods to the poor,' 'Having food and raiment let us be therewith content'—these and many other precepts forced men to ask the simple question: What in an organized society, and in a rational world, can they mean? These were the precepts and doctrines which first provoked discussion about the ordering of human society and the connection between natural and supernatural virtues. They had the great merit that they presented a challenge. They had to be accepted as inspired words; but they had also somehow to be lived with.

Men learn after all by being puzzled and excited, not by being told. The placid teaching of Cicero on human virtue had no power to excite thought: it was all too obviously true. But the puzzling and impossible doctrine, drawn from the mystical meaning of the sons and daughters of Job, that he who has one virtue has all, and he who has lost one has lost all, started a long series of discussions which led to the original and realistic account of natural virtues that we find in Thomas Aquinas. Aristotle standing alone had no power to excite thought: at best, like alcohol, he first stimulated and then stupefied. What he said was so complete, so incontrovertible, so far beyond the range of conflicting authorities, that he hammered reason into submission. Curiously enough, therefore, the paradoxes of the Bible did more for rational argument by stimulating discussion than all the reasons of Aristotle which were swallowed whole.

## V

No reality is ever as beautiful as the vision. When people see the elaborate structures of thirteenth century thought and compare them with the visions of the age of William of Conches they find them less interesting in detail, less liberating in their effects, and less beautiful in their expression. Consequently they are apt to think that the intention of the later thinkers was quite different and much less humane. But the main difference is that the later writers knew vastly more than their predecessors and they had to work harder to integrate their material. The lack of new material, which had threatened to bring the humanism of the early twelfth century to a halt, was abundantly made good by the flow of new translations in the century after 1150. By 1250 virtually the whole corpus of Greek science was accessible to the western world, and scholars groaned under its weight as they strove to master it all. The days had gone when two large volumes could hold all that was essential for the study of the liberal arts.[1] There was no time for artistic presentation and literary eloquence. This was a grave loss, but the achievement was there all the same. The main ideas of the earlier masters—the dignity of man, the intelligibility of the universe, the nobility of nature—not only remained intact, but were fundamental concepts in the intellectual structures of the thirteenth century.

These concepts were so much taken for granted that they no longer seemed to call for poetic expression. They were introduced as a matter of course into the most technical discussions on the most unlikely subjects. I have in front of me a highly abstract argument about the Incarnation, written by the first great Oxford master, Robert Grosseteste, about 1230.[2] If we compare it with

[1] I refer here to the two volumes of texts put together by Thierry of Chartres, formerly in the library of Chartres cathedral. They were destroyed in the last war, but happily not before they had been microfilmed.
[2] *De cessatione legalium*, ed. D. J. Unger, *Franciscan Studies*, 1956, xvi, 1–36.

Anselm's great treatise on the same subject, completed just a hundred and thirty years later, we see the great difference that the scientific humanism of the intervening period had made. Anselm is far superior in literary grace, but Grosseteste is inspired by a much more profound humanism. Anselm had argued that the Incarnation was necessary because man had sinned beyond the possibility of redemption by any other means, and that God necessarily became man, not because of any quality in man, but because of his otherwise total ruin. For Grosseteste the picture was quite different. He too saw God's Incarnation as necessary for man's salvation. But it was not man's sin that made it necessary: it was necessary for the completion of man's nature, and it would have happened if man had never sinned. It was therefore not a last desperate throwing of God's final reserves into a battle that was almost lost. It was a final act in the unfolding drama of creation: it made Man and Nature complete, and it bound the whole created universe together in union with God.

Whether this is good theology or good science I do not know. But it is certainly profoundly humanistic in a way that Anselm's argument is not. It is filled with a conception of a human dignity so exalted that God could not stop short of Incarnation, and of a natural order so sublime that it required to be completed by a God-perfected man. This is the final step in scientific humanism. It was not a step that was generally taken by Grosseteste's contemporaries, but a large body of the theological work of the thirteenth century displays a similar faith in man and nature. Indeed the chief objection that can be brought against scholastic theology is not its lack of humanism, but its persistent tendency to make man appear more rational, human nature more noble, the divine ordering of the universe more open to human inspection, and the whole complex of man, nature and God more fully intelligible, than we can now believe to be plausible. But— regarded simply as an effort to comprehend the structure of the universe and, in the striking image of William of Conches, to demonstrate the dignity of the human mind by showing that it can know all things—this body of thought is one of the most ambitious displays of scientific humanism ever attempted.

From this point of view, the two *Summae* of Thomas Aquinas mark the highest point of medieval humanism. They are the most successful realization of the programme of study roughly sketched in our second chart. The reader is tempted to say as he reads: 'Of course there are things man cannot yet understand—but not many; of course man is a sinner—but how wonderfully the ravages of sin have been restored by reason, and how easy, how natural, how rational the steps to salvation.' The natural faculties are no longer in ruins. Reason and nature have inherited the world. The work of Thomas Aquinas is full of illustrations of the supremacy of reason and nature. His judgements nearly always give the natural man rather more than his due. He reversed the ancient opinion that the body is the ruined habitation of the soul, and held with Aristotle that it is the basis of the soul's being. Everywhere he points to the natural perfection of man, his natural rights, and the power of his natural reason. The dignity of human nature is not simply a poetic vision; it has become a central truth of philosophy.

Thomas Aquinas died in 1274, and it is probably true that man has never appeared so important a being in so well-ordered and intelligible a universe as in his works. Man was important because he was the link between the created universe and the divine intelligence. He alone in the world of nature could understand nature. He alone in nature could understand the nature of God. He alone could use and perfect nature in accordance with the will of God and thus achieve his full nobility.

## VI

There was thus in the twelfth and thirteenth centuries a continuous and uninterrupted reassertion of the claims of human dignity. The intellectual enquiries of the period made God, man, and nature intelligible and coherent; the area of the natural world was enlarged at the expense of the supernatural, and the pressure of the unknown which had weighed heavily on many parts of life was lightened. So far we have examined these changes only in relation to their effect on religious and intellectual attitudes, but there is another area which needs to be examined—the area of practical activity in government and society.

Governments were very quickly affected by the new intellectual outlook of the twelfth century. In the eleventh century the anointed king, who received divine sanction at his religious institution and exercised authority as the vicar of Christ, was a commanding figure. Even if his practical authority was very limited, he represented in his visible and symbolic adornments the majesty of God on earth. This gave a dignity to human government, but it was a dignity that came from no human source.

In the twelfth century all this was changed. Government by ritual came to an end, and government by administration began. Rulers grew in real power, but they were cut down to human dimensions. Coronations of course continued, but their religious significance ceased to count in political discussion. We hear much of oaths and fealty and homage, and later of the common good and the rule of law; but the royal unction, the ring, the sceptre, and the vestments sank into political insignificance. With the disappearance of these supernatural sanctions in government, the way was open for the development of purely human concepts, like 'the common good', the 'political community', 'the majority opinion'. It was in the thirteenth century that these ideas became part of the political equipment of Europe. The English *Magna Carta* of 1215 is worth reading in this context. It is far removed from any idea of a semi-sacerdotal kingship. It stands at the threshold of a philosophy of the state. It speaks the language of common rights, common law, of things which all free men may demand, of legalised resistance. On this foundation it will not be long before the community is seen as the source of the ruler's powers, and a completely natural theory of the state has been developed.

The change of emphasis from the supernatural to the natural in human government can be seen in law as well as politics. Until the twelfth century the basic legal procedure was an appeal to a supernatural judgement. For most people and for most occasions the due process of law meant the priest administering the sacrament, exacting an oath, praying over the cauldron, or the hot iron, and calling for a divine discovery of the malefactor. It was with reluctance that men turned to merely human expedients, to rules of evidence and experiments with juries. Fallacious human expedients were a poor substitute for the certain judgements of God, but they prevailed. Men in country-districts were very reluctant to let the supernatural go. They must have felt very defenceless against marauders and secret slayers when they had no remedy but the witness of neighbours and the verdicts of corruptible juries. The world must have seemed to countrymen a cheerless place without the finger of God and the testimony of the saints in their law-suits; but they had to face it.

The awe-inspiring and religiously edifying ordeals were on their way out in the middle of the twelfth century; they were right out a century later. Scholars can mark the stages of decline; revival of Roman law on the Continent, the appearance of juries in England, the Lateran Council of 1215 which forbade priests to take part in ordeals. But these stages are simply the symptoms of a great change of mind—the change from a supernatural to a natural view of human society.

At this point caution is necessary. Society does not become more attractive by becoming more human in its inspiration. Oppression keeps pace with the growth of freedom. As more human activities are released and pronounced legitimate, the strong are supplied with more legitimised areas of activity and reasons to justify their power; the warlike can speak more convincingly about the justice of their cause. Good words like liberty, social usefulness, and necessity are adapted to cover every kind of self-seeking. These are the penalties of humanism. One cannot have it both ways. Either the world is a highly restrictive place where men go about in fear of indulging almost any kind of human impulse, or it is a place where the strong are not only active but confident. They can deprive the poor even of the satisfaction of being right. In an expanding world the remedies for new evils never keep pace with needs of the oppressed; but if they do little for those who suffer, they do much for the theory of society. The problem of encouraging growth, and yet regulating it, first began to be taken seriously in the twelfth century when the old restraints and prohibitions began their long retreat.

In a general way, the social ideas of the earlier age had been based on authorities which had their ultimate sanction in biblical precepts very discouraging to growth. I have already quoted some of the precepts which were held to prove that trade was wrong, profit wrong, property wrong, usury of course wrong. These propositions could comfortably pass for the social ideals of a primitive, immobile society, and they remained reasonably intact until the twelfth century. Of course they were often broken, but as ideals they called for no reservation. Then about 1140 we find signs of a great change of mind. The change was not very conspicuous at first. It took the form of dissecting the traditional texts, and some of them were very resistant to dissection. This was work for lawyers, men who had the practical task of distinguishing between licit and illicit activities for the guidance of the ecclesiastical courts. They were not men who moved in a hurry; but in the end they moved far.

Let us look at one or two of their problems and the way they were handled. In the first place: property. There can be no doubt that an adequate view of property is one of the first essentials for a fully developed society. If the individual's rights are too restricted, the result will be a restriction of personal life. But if there is no restriction, the result will be oppression and injustice. And if theory diverges too far from practical reality, the result will be that theory is simply ignored. Where do the Middle Ages stand in this respect?

By and large the answer is fairly plain. Down to the twelfth century there was a very meagre theory of property derived from the Bible and the Fathers. The Bible seemed to demand two things: first that men should have a great indifference to property, and secondly, that all property should be held in common. The first of these points requires no elaboration, the second is rather more recondite. The theory of ideal communism was based on the account of the life of the early Christians in the Acts of the Apostles. 'No one said that anything he possessed was his own, but they had all things in common'. From this it was universally concluded in the early Middle Ages that all private property had the nature of sin, and that in a perfect state there would be no such thing. When St. Benedict included in his Rule the provision that all things were to be held in common, he was expressing not just an ideal for a religious society, but the ideal for all society.

This was still the ideal in 1140.[1] At this point the lawyers got to work on the texts. They were faced with the biblical descriptions of early Christian communism and with other texts emphasizing that everything in the world was for the common use of all. Then they began to make distinctions. They discovered that common *use* was compatible with private *ownership*; that private ownership had the virtue of ensuring stability and orderly administration; that common use was intended simply to serve in an

[1] For a selection of texts expounding the traditional doctrine of the iniquity of private ownership c. 1140, see Gratian's *Decretum*, Dist. 1, c. 7; Dist. 47, c. 8; C. 12, q. 1, c. 2.

emergency as a residual safeguard for human survival. These ingenious and worldly distinctions had many advantages for a society which was becoming increasingly complicated and commercial. When they were subjected to the active polishing of legal minds, the biblical precepts which discouraged growth began to wear very thin.

Quite soon—in the first half of the thirteenth century—Aristotle's *Ethics* and *Politics* arrived in the West to reinforce the distinctions drawn by lawyers. These works cleared private property of the last taint of sin; and the distinctions already drawn by lawyers made it easy to accept the Aristotelian view that private property is naturally good and necessary for the good life. Gathering all these strands together, Thomas Aquinas produced a comprehensive defence of private property. He elaborated its natural necessity and virtues, and attempted to attach Christian safeguards to its practical exploitation. These safeguards defined the legitimate motives for seeking temporal gain and drew the boundaries of legitimate appropriation. The ancient ideal Christian communism was reduced to a counsel, literally, of despair: 'he who suffers from extreme need can take what he needs from another's goods if no one will give to him.[1]

This compromise is very typical of the attitude that had grown up since 1140: nature forms the base, religion provides—can one say?—the frills. It is almost this, for Europe accepted the defence of property with zest; but when it came to common use I do not know that any thief escaped conviction by pleading extreme need. Property was grounded in nature, common use in divine command. The more it was studied the more nature grew in size and solidity, for it was capable of indefinite elaboration. The supernatural apex was destined to disappear further and further into the clouds, because it was difficult to frame rules and sanctions for its practical application.

There were those who fought against this worldly trend and continued to support the stark ideal of a propertyless perfection. But they were swimming against the tide. The last defenders of this social conservatism were found in the Franciscan Order, and they were condemned in 1323 by Pope John XXII who declared

---

[1] *Summa Theol.* 2, 2, q. 32, art. 7, ad 3. The fullest statement of the case for private property is in *Summa Theol.* 2, 2, q. 66, art. 1, 2 and 7. In its main outline this statement follows Aristotle, *Politics*, ii, 5, 8.

the doctrine of the complete poverty of Christ and his disciples heretical. This was the end of the long road from Biblical Christianity to the acceptance of the natural man with his urge for ownership.[1]

Many other social values followed the same road at the same time. On the question of trade, the lawyers of the mid-twelfth century were still quoting the old biblical texts and interpretations to the effect that trade is no fit occupation for a Christian, that it is wrong to buy an article hoping to sell it unchanged at a higher price, that profit is sinful, that it is wrong to vary the price according to the demand.[2] Once more the lawyers got to work. They moved more slowly here than in the case of property, partly because merchants were socially unpopular, and partly because Aristotle agreed with the biblical commentators in thinking trade inconsistent with virtue.[3] But even here the lawyers moved in the end. They set about determining the elements of a just price, and in so doing they laid the foundations of economics. They examined the motive of profit and determined the extent to which it was morally justified. They analysed interest, and attempted to distinguish usury from risk-bearing investment. They discussed the place of merchants in society, and gave them a grudging, but still a distinct, recognition as necessary instruments of social well-being.[4]

Here as elsewhere Aristotle was at once a stimulus and a barrier. He was a stimulus in encouraging the formulation of a general theory of social classes much more elaborate than the old classification of *aratores*, *oratores* and *bellatores* of earlier centuries;

[1] The Franciscan Order is especially interesting for the history of social doctrines because it exhibits in a period of a hundred years a development spread over several centuries in western society as a whole. The final stages of the retreat from the doctrines of the sinfulness of private property, which was not effected without the most violent opposition, are conveniently described by J. Moorman, *The Franciscan Order from its Origins to 1517*, 1968, 307–19.

[2] The texts quoted in Gratian's *Decretum*, Dist. 88, originally dealt only with the prohibition of trading by the clergy, but at a very early stage in the development of this text two chapters (cc. xi and xii) were added containing biblical texts and interpretations violently hostile to trade in any form.

[3] See especially Aristotle, *Politics*, vi, 4; vii, 9. Thomas Aquinas makes a meagre provision for merchants in society in his *De Regimine Principum*, ii, 3, but he makes some interesting concessions to commercial practice in *Summa Theol.* 2, 2. q. 77.

[4] For an analysis of later medieval views on some of these problems, see R. de Roover, 'The concept of the Just Price: theory and economic policy', *Journal of Economic History*, 1958, xviii, 418–434; A. Dumas, 'Intérêt', *Dictionnaire de Droit Canonique*, 1953, v, 1475–1518; J. T. Noonan, *The Scholastic Analysis of Usury*, 1957.

but he was a barrier in the confirmation he gave to the prejudices of aristocratic and agrarian society. Nevertheless, the social theories which developed under Aristotelian influence—with all their limitations and fallacies—were the first serious attempts at comprehensive social and political thought in western Europe. For the first time for many centuries nature and natural virtues were seen to provide a general framework for human society. Nature brought freedom, and with freedom the strong grew stronger. Just as no thief escaped the gallows by pleading the apostolic privilege of the common purse, so the 'just price' was more effective in keeping down the price of labour after the Plague, than in restricting the rising price of corn after a drought. This was part of the price of humanism.

A similar development took place in thinking about war. The Bible was indeed a somewhat ambiguous guide on this subject, but there could be no doubt about the direction in which it pointed: 'he who takes the sword shall perish by the sword', 'thou shalt not kill'. The thought of the early Middle Ages sought to follow this pointer. The only war which was thoroughly approved was the holy war against invading paganism. To this, no doubt, could justly be added bloodshed in self-defence, or in defence of the church or of widows and orphans, but the limits of legitimate violence were narrowly drawn. Even in a cause so well authenticated by papal approval as the Norman Conquest of England the bishops of Normandy laid down a severe code of penances to atone for the blood shed in the great battle, and they were not very different from the penances imposed for acts of plain murder.

By 1140 this pattern was beginning to change. Gratian, the great canon lawyer of this date, still showed a strong inclination to keep legitimate warfare within traditional limits.[1] The only war his book explicitly approved was war against heretics waged by episcopal authority under papal direction; he said nothing about the wars of secular rulers for the maintenance of secular rights. Yet we can see a hint of the distinctions which were to transform the discussion of all social questions in his dictum that biblical precepts about turning the other cheek were to be fulfilled in the preparation of the heart and not in bodily ostentation. In other

---

[1] Despite its very limited range, the long section on war in Gratian's *Decretum*, c. xxiii, is the first serious discussion on problems of war in medieval Europe.

words, Christians were to think one thing and do another; what else indeed in western society can they do? Once this was understood the way was open for that further distinction which led Thomas Aquinas to say that he who takes the sword at the command of the ruler does not *take* the sword, but only *uses* what has been committed to him. St. Thomas's doctrine of the just war is capable of very subtle elaboration, but it leaves decisions of war or peace wide open to the judgement of the secular ruler. Although he draws on an assortment of biblical and patristic texts, his conclusions are wholly secular and could equally well have been drawn from Aristotle or from natural reason.[1]

There is here however a possible misunderstanding I must guard against. In pushing back the area of the supernatural no medieval thinker intended to dispense with it altogether. On the contrary, we have seen that the existence of the supernatural was held to be necessary for the completion of nature. When everything possible had been done to perfect the natural order, there still remained (as Grosseteste had said) the need for a unifying principle which only the God-Man could provide. At the end of all, the union of natural and supernatural was the culmination of medieval humanism. This union found its noblest expression in the concluding pages of Dante's *De Monarchia*:

> Man is a mean between the corruptible and the incorruptible. Just as every mean partakes of both extremes, so man has a dual nature. And since every nature is ordained for a definite end, it follows that man has two ends—on the one hand the happiness of this life, which consists in the exercise of his human power and is symbolized by the terrestial paradise which we attain through the teachings of philosophy and the practice of the moral and intellectual virtues; and on the other, the happiness of eternal life which consists in the enjoyment of the vision of God, to which man cannot attain except by God's help.[2]

Here we have a statement of the autonomy of the natural order, which is the essence of medieval humanism. Here reason rules: it

---

[1] The essential discussion on war in Thomas Aquinas is *Summa Theol.*, 2, 2, q.40, art. 1, which may be supplemented by the article on the killing of malefactors, *S.T.* 2, 2, q.64, art. 3.

[2] *Monarchia*, iii, 16.

makes the universe intelligible; it makes man free. It also makes him seek his eternal satisfaction in something beyond reason. By reason we can see at once the autonomy of nature and the necessity for that which is above nature.

This is not quite the humanism of the Renaissance, and it is far from the humanism of today; but whether we consider its inherent grandeur or its influence on the future, it has a good claim to be considered the most important kind of humanism Europe has ever produced.

## VII

Many reasons may be given for rejecting the kind of humanism we have been considering. We may disagree with its theological basis, or its belief in the intelligibility of the universe, or the central position accorded to man, or the optimism about man's rational powers. But it is at first sight puzzling that men who had no quarrel with God or with reason, and who sought to glorify man, should have denied that the ways of thinking I have described had any claim to be called humanistic. Anyone who knew anything about the world of the eleventh century would have had to agree that the dignity of man, the intelligibility of the world and of God, and the application of reason to practical affairs had made such progress in the twelfth and thirteenth centuries that they had become the central features of all thought and experience. Why then did these two centuries come to seem in retrospect so hostile to humanistic values?

I think the main explanation to this puzzle lies in the early fourteenth century. Europe then entered a period when the optimism which had buoyed up the efforts of the previous two centuries was abruptly destroyed: the flow of new intellectual materials came to an end; the forward movement in settlement and expansion came to a halt; the area of disorder in the world was everywhere increasing; everything began to seem insecure. Until this time it had seemed that, however horrible the present might be, the future was likely to be better. It was reasonable to believe that all the new information about the universe could be fitted into one grand universal plan, and it was not unreasonable to think that the papal, or perhaps the imperial, system of universal authority would in time bring universal peace. There was very little ground for thinking that the universe and God might after all be beyond the reach of reason, and humanly speaking chaotic.

But quite quickly this whole situation changed. It does not need a dramatic disaster to change the intellectual outlook of a generation. It only needs a slight change of direction, the end of expansion, the drying up of sources of information, a series of small setbacks, a persistent sense that nothing is going well. Petrarch, who above all stood for a new kind of humanism in the mid-fourteenth century, had reason to be disillusioned with the achievements of the last two centuries. The kind of intellectual and practical order at which men had aimed suddenly seemed quite unattainable:

> Turn where you will, there is no place without its tyrant; and where there is no tyrant, the people themselves supply the deficiency. When you escape the One, you fall into the hands of the Many. If you can show me a place ruled by a just and mild king, I will take myself there with all my baggage. . . . I will go to India or Persia or the furthest limits of the Garamantes to find such a place and such a king. But it is useless to search for what cannot be found. Thanks to our age, which has levelled all things, the labour is unnecessary.[1]

The hopes of the past had to be buried. But such hopes are never buried with simple quiet resignation: they have to be buried with scorn and derision and a sense of betrayal. Hence the clerical schools with their formalised procedures and legalistic distinctions came to be seen, not simply as the agents of a great failure, but as the promoters of a great enslavement.

All systems of thought have some pervasive weakness built into their structure, and the weakness is all the more ineradicable when it forms in some sense the strength of the system. The characteristic weakness of medieval scientific thought was its dependance on *auctoritates* and *sententiae*. These were the bricks from which the system was formed; they provided the material for argument and the foundations for the most daring conclusions. But they also defined limits beyond which the system could not develop. So the moment of stasis was bound to come sooner or

---

[1] Petrarch, *Invectiva contra quendam magni status hominem sed nullius scientie aut virtutis*, ed. P. G. Ricci, 1949, p.15.

later. This is not a phenomenon peculiar to medieval thought or to scholastic processes of argument; it is a universal phenomenon in the development of every system; but the moment arrived in the Middle Ages with a peculiarly paralysing effect because it arrived without warning.

As soon as men lost confidence in the system and its aims, the details all appeared intensely repellent. No books have ever been written that give less invitation to study by their physical appearance than the manuscripts of the medieval schools; their illegible script, crabbed abbreviations, and margins filled with comments even less legible than the text, invite derision. As soon as men lost confidence in the end toward which this whole apparatus of learning moved, the adjuncts were bound to seem barbarous and inhumane. They had no beauty of style or vivacity of wit to support them.

Hence, as the residuary legatee of the scientific and systematic humanism of the twelfth and thirteenth centuries, a new kind of humanism came into existence. It was the product of disillusion with the great projects of the recent past. When the hope of universal order faded, the cultivation of sensibility and personal virtue, and the nostalgic vision of an ancient utopia revealed in classical literature, remained as the chief supports of humane values. Instead of the confident and progressive humanism of the central Middle Ages, the new humanism retreated into the individual and the past; it saw the aristocracy rather than the clergy as the guardians of culture; it sought inspiration in literature rather than theology and science; its ideal was a group of friends rather than a universal system; and the nobility of man was expressed in his struggle with an unintelligible world rather than in his capacity to know all things. When this happened the humanism of the central Middle Ages came to be mistaken for formalism and hostility to human experience.

# 5

## HUMANISM AND THE SCHOOL OF CHARTRES

I

There are few institutions which have been praised more consistently than the school of Chartres. It has won everybody's sympathy and admiration: their sympathy because it has been seen standing for a humanistic ideal soon to be overwhelmed in a rising tide of law and theology, which most men in their hearts do not much like; and their admiration because it has been seen as the chief medieval exponent of a general literary culture in a world of growing specialization. It went out in a blaze of glory. There was no slow decline from height to height, but after standing on a pinnacle for fifty years, it suddenly sank into obscurity, and was never heard of again, except by diggers for curious facts. It has been praised for many things: as an almost solitary advocate of Platonism before Aristotle quenched all the poetry in philosophy; as a mother of art, eloquence, and style before the study of the ancient authors was crowded out of the academic curriculum; for its touch of paganism in a world becoming ever more closely regimented in the paths of orthodoxy; finally, if we feel no enthusiasm for paganism, there has in recent years been the pleasure of discovering that the apparent paganism was after all orthodox Christianity. So everyone has been pleased and the reputation of Chartres stands higher now than it has ever done.

This whole triumphal march of reputation has been accomplished in little over a hundred years, and it epitomises the rise of medieval studies in general during this period. The authors of the volume of the *Histoire littéraire de France* which appeared in 1814 knew nothing, or almost nothing, of the school of Chartres. They still lived in an atmosphere in which almost everything scholastic was centred on Paris, and they bluntly assigned to Paris the teaching activities of the two brothers, Bernard and Thierry, who were soon to be acclaimed as the chief luminaries of the

school of Chartres. Even in 1850 the young Barthélemy Hauréau
in his prize-winning essay on medieval scholasticism had time for
only a passing glance at Chartres. But the tide was turning. In
1855, another young man, L. Merlet, who was to make a notable
contribution to Chartrian studies, published a collection of letters
which demonstrated for the first time (as he claimed) the prosperity of the schools of Chartres in the early twelfth century.[1] And
in 1862 the same line of thought received an important extension
from the argument of C. Schaarschmidt that the schools of
Chartres were sufficiently important in 1138 for John of Salisbury
to leave Paris in order to spend three years there listening to
William of Conches.[2] Thus two of the greatest names of twelfth
century scholarship were added to the Chartres roll of honour.
Bernard (surnamed Silvestris) and Thierry of Chartres were joined
by William of Conches and John of Salisbury, and the four names
became the corner-stones of the School of Chartres.

These articles and suggestions belong to the prehistory of the
school of Chartres. Its modern history begins with the appearance
of R. L. Poole's *Illustrations of the History of Medieval Thought
and Learning* in 1884. This brilliant work of a young scholar
contained a chapter entitled 'The School of Chartres' in which the
phrase was first used in its modern sense to describe something
that was at once an institution and a way of thought. This chapter
did more than anything else to give a character and outline to the
history of the school. Despite many errors, which Poole himself
was foremost in correcting, his general characterization has never
seriously been questioned. The main drift of the story he told may
be summarized in his own words. After describing the eminence
of the school under Bishop Fulbert who died in 1028, he says that
shortly before 1115

the school emerges again into notice under the rule, first, it
should seem, of Theodoric and then of his brother Bernard,
and thence forward, down to near the middle of the twelfth
century, it enjoyed a peculiar distinction, continually growing
until it became almost an unapproached pre-eminence, among
the schools of Gaul.

[1] L. Merlet, 'Lettres d'Ives de Chartres et d'autres personnages de son
temps', *B.E.C.*, 1855, 4th ser., i, 443–71.
[2] C. Schaarschmidt, *Johannes Saresberiensis*, 1862, pp. 14–23.

This pre-eminence Poole ascribed to the combined efforts of Theodoric 'who boldly pushed the principles of realism to their furthest issues', and Bernard Sylvester his brother and successor as chancellor, 'a devout Platonist', 'a humanist', and a scholar who 'with a frank vigour' 'portrayed the cosmogony according to a scheme compatible only with some form of pantheism'. Under these men, using the methods rather 'of a university than a school' Chartres attracted perhaps not so many pupils as some other schools, but a 'distinctly higher class of students than Melun or St. Geneviève or the Petit Pont at Paris'. As evidence of this he adduced John of Salisbury's willingness to quit Paris 'after two years under famous dialecticians at Paris' to spend three more years under the masters at Chartres. These masters included such men as William of Conches, 'Platonist, cosmologist and grammarian, whose writings are a good sample of the freedom of thought that issued from the classic calm of Chartres', Richard l'Evêque, 'whose virtues as a man and a scholar are celebrated in no ordinary terms' and Gilbert de la Porrée.

If Poole provided the eloquence and the vision, it was left to the Abbé Clerval to fill in the details eleven years later. His *Ecoles de Chartres au Moyen-Age* which appeared in 1895, is one of the most influential books of local history ever written. Clerval, besides being professor of ecclesiastical history in the local seminary, was librarian of the town, and he was the first to use the manuscripts of Chartres to illustrate the history of the school. Their use made it possible to give the schools a substantial existence and an atmosphere which only a local historian could have created. The study of the manuscripts, and the contemporary studies of the art and architecture of the cathedral, made Chartres a symbol of the intellectual life of the twelfth century. Clerval wrote of the masters and pupils, the studies and organization of the schools, as if the whole scene were present to his eyes. He developed the theme which Poole had first announced. The schools of Chartres from the eleventh century onwards 'constituaient une véritable academie; leur organization persévère et se développe. La valeur de leurs chanceliers et de leurs écolâtres, dont la suite se continue avec une gloire ininterrompue, l'importance et l'éclat de leurs doctrines théologiques ou philosophiques, en font des écoles à part, ayant leur cachet et leur individualité particulière.' After 1150 this glory was suddenly eclipsed by the rivalry of Paris, which 'malheureusement ne tardera pas à exercer sur les écoliers chartrains une irrésistible attraction.' But for half a century Chartres had stood on a pinnacle of fame and influence, and Clerval was able to describe the life of the schools during this period of greatness in much detail. The account he gave may be summarized thus:

Under Ivo (d. 1115) the bishop himself taught, but his successors, being too occupied by external duties, were brilliantly replaced in this task by chancellors and masters whom they appointed. Teaching in the schools was the chief duty of the chancellor and the masters whom the chancellor chose in concert with the bishop. These masters of the schools were men of great weight and dignity, the advisers of the bishop in theological matters, and aspirants to the chancellorship at Chartres and to bishoprics elsewhere. The best of these masters rose to be chancellors of Chartres. At the beginning of the century the chancellor Wulgrin had Bernard as his assistant master. When Bernard became chancellor he was assisted by Gilbert and Thierry. When Gilbert and Thierry in their turn became successive chancellors they were assisted by Guy, Hugh, Ivo, Payen Belotin, Garin, Odo, Robert le Petit, William de Modalibus and Rainald. Masters so famous as these 'ne pouvaient manquer d'élèves'. Those of Bernard indeed formed 'une véritable colonie', but almost equally plentiful were the pupils of his successors. They were bound together by an 'ésprit de solidarité' which gave the school a unity and cohesion both in its institutional life and in the literary and philosophical principles which guided its teaching.[1]

Such was the picture drawn by Clerval, and in its main outline it has won universal acceptance. It gained the scholarly approval of R. L. Poole, who completed and corrected some of the details in a masterly article which appeared in 1920.[2] This article has all Poole's usual lucidity and sobriety, and its caution rather strengthened than weakened the general outline given by Clerval.

Until this point everything had developed very smoothly, but nothing had been done to add to the intellectual content of the school's activity. Indeed, in the intellectual sphere, the school had

---

[1] The names and details quoted above will be found on pp. 143–179 of Clerval's book.

[2] 'The Masters of the Schools at Paris and Chartres in John of Salisbury's time', *E.H.R.*, 1920, xxxv; reprinted in R. L. Poole, *Studies in Chronology and History*, 1934, 223–47.

suffered a substantial loss for which Clerval deserves the credit. The early reputation of the school—that is to say its reputation from about 1850 to 1890—had been built on the supposition that Bernard the Chancellor of Chartres was the same man as Bernard Silvestris who wrote the considerable work of Platonic cosmology called *De Mundi Universitate*. So long as this identification stood, one could believe many things about the Platonic tradition at Chartres. But Clerval showed that Bernard Silvestris was a master of Tours and had nothing to do with Chartres, and later work has entirely borne out this conclusion.[1]

It is strange that this loss did not much affect the now triumphant reputation of the school of Chartres, though it was not until 1938 that any substantial attempt was made to fill the gap. In this year J. M. Parent produced a book which initiated a new age in Chartrian studies—the age of the systematic publication of the lecture notes of the masters in whom we are interested.[2] Until this time almost nothing that came from their classrooms had been printed. Since 1938, with the exception of the war years, there has been a steady stream of studies and editions which have brought the work of the masters to life. For the first time we begin to be able to see them at work in their lecture rooms. Yet it is remarkable how little the earlier picture of the school of Chartres and its masters has so far been altered by these revelations. The role of Bernard Silvestris has been quietly filled by Thierry and William of Conches, but the accents remain unchanged. Recent accounts of the programme and ideas of the school of Chartres and of the special character of its attempt to reconcile Platonism and Christianity simply give a new documentation to the judgment formed by R. L. Poole as a result of studying the work of Bernard Silvestris; they do not substantially change it. The same may be said of the flow of publications since the war, which have brought to light a new range of texts and a new generation of scholars to carry on the work of Clerval and Poole.[3]

---

[1] *Les écoles de Chartres au Moyen Age*, pp. 158–162. R. L. Poole (retracting his earlier opinion) sums up the evidence in *Studies in Chronology and History*, pp. 228–35.

[2] J. M. Parent, *La doctrine de la Création dans l'ecole de Chartres*, 1938.

[3] The most notable of these publications are mentioned below, pp. 80–1, in discussing the work of the masters chiefly associated with the school of Chartres.

## II

The picture of the school of Chartres both as an institution and as the source of a scholastic programme, which has emerged from all these labours, is certainly very impressive and quite unusually coherent. This is largely the result of the confidence with which later scholars have been able to use the work of their predecessors. Recent workers concentrating on the scholastic programme have taken the institutional framework built up by earlier scholars more or less for granted. In working on the large connections of thought and outlook represented by the masters associated with Chartres they have been able to assume that the base is firm. Chartres with its schools is, so to speak, the launching pad from which the philosophical missiles are projected into outer space. The routine is well-established. The labours of earlier scholars have made the preparatory stages almost accident-proof, and after a brief count-down—Bernard, Thierry, Gilbert, William —we are off into a state of weightlessness among the Platonic Ideas. But before we lose sight of the earth we may ask, how secure is the foundation from which we have been launched on this journey? In other words, what do we know about the school of Chartres?

The answer to this is: remarkably little; much less than is generally supposed. Let us ask first about the organization of the school; then about the masters who taught there; and finally about the pupils who studied there.

First, the organization. It is certain that there was a school of some kind at Chartres. But this in itself tells us little. Schools existed in cathedral cities and other important centres all over Northern France and England at this time, and the letters pub-plished by Merlet in 1855, which first drew attention to the school at Chartres, tell us as much about schools at Laon, Le Mans, Orleans, and Châteaudun as about the school at Chartres. They tell us, that is to say, that there was a master with pupils at each one of these places; but about the level of instruction or size of the enterprise in any of them they tell us nothing at all. Secondly we may be sure that the chancellor of the cathedral had a general responsibility for the school—that is to say he probably appointed a schoolmaster. But we cannot assume, as Clerval did, that the supervision of the school was a main part of his duties, or that he himself taught in the school. He may have done so; but the existence of a famous man as chancellor of the cathedral cannot be accepted as proof that this famous man was teaching in the school —any more than the appearance of a famous master among the witnesses to the bishops' charters can be accepted as proof that this master was teaching in the school. There are many cases where it is clear that this deduction cannot be drawn. Consequently each case must be examined in the light of the available evidence. The chancellor had many duties besides making provision for a school. He had to conduct the correspondence of the chapter, look after the library and archives, administer the property attached to his prebend, and live as befitted a dignatory of the church. His own learning cannot be taken as an index of the learning of the school: many cathedrals had learned chancellors without having famous schools, and vice versa.

It would be unwise to attempt to settle the question on negative evidence. We may simply note that on the only occasion when we have positive evidence of a chancellor of Chartres teaching in a school in the first half of the twelfth century, he was teaching not at Chartres but at Paris. This was Gilbert de la Porrée, whom John of Salisbury heard lecturing at Paris on Mont S. Geneviève in 1141.[1] He had been chancellor of Chartres since 1126 and it is generally assumed that he had given up his chancellorship in order to lecture in Paris. There is no evidence to support this supposition. But, in any case, the fact that Gilbert went to teach in Paris suggests that he did not find sufficient scope for his teaching in Chartres. Whether he went to Paris while he was still chancellor of Chartres, or resigned his chancellorship in order to teach in Paris, it is hard to reconcile his appearance in Paris with the generally accepted account of his presiding over a great and famous school at Chartres.

But after all, it may be said, what counts in a school is not the head but the masters and the quality of the teaching, and the pupils. What do we know about these?

Clerval has provided us with a long list of masters who taught at Chartres during the first half of the twelfth century: Bernard, Gilbert de la Porrée, Thierry, before they became successive chancellors; Guy, Hugh, Ivo, Payen, Belotin, Garin, Odo,

---

[1] *Metalogicon*, ii, 10, ed. C. C. J. Webb, 1929, p. 82.

Robert le Petit, William de Modalibus and Rainald. To this list most scholars would be prepared to add William of Conches.

Faced with this impressive list, it is important to begin by stating that the only evidence for some of these names is their appearance with the title *Magister* in lists of witnesses of the bishops' charters. This is quite unsatisfactory. So far as I can discover the only man on the list for whom there is quite convincing evidence of a teaching career at Chartres is the first one, Bernard. Bernard appears in a list of canons at Chartres of 1119–24 as *magister scolae*, and he is evidently the master referred to as 'Master B'. in the letters printed by Merlet.[1] John of Salisbury has left a magnificent account of Bernard's teaching, which he must have had from men who were Bernard's pupils. The evidence which connects Bernard with the school of Chartres in his day is very solid, and it makes the contrast with the period after Bernard all the more striking. After about 1120, for the next thirty years, the connection of every master or pupil with the school of Chartres is conjectural. We must not put the matter too strongly. There *must* have been a master, and there *must* have been pupils at Chartres. But this is something that can be said about many cathedral schools. We need more evidence than this for the special distinction of the school of Chartres, and evidence is—to say the least—hard to find: much harder than it is at Paris or Laon.

To test this assertion we may leave aside for the moment the minor characters mentioned by Clerval and concentrate on the three men who have done most, after Bernard, to make Chartres famous. They are Thierry, Gilbert de la Porrée, and William of Conches—undoubtedly three of the most important writers of the period. What is their common connection with Chartres?

First of all Thierry. Clerval established the now traditional account of his career: he was the brother of Bernard of Chartres;

---

[1] The most important document for Bernard's career as a teacher at Chartres is printed in R. Merlet and A. Clerval, *Un manuscript chartrain du XIe siècle*, 1893, pp. 195–6: it is an oath taken by the canons of Chartres, including *Bernardus scolae magister*, at some time between 4 November 1119 and 1124, and probably nearer the earlier of these two dates. In 1124 he appears as chancellor in an agreement between the monks of St. Peter of Chartres and those of Nogent (*Cartulaire de S. Denis de Nogent-le-Rotrou*, ed. Ch. Métais, 1895, pp. 240–3). Two years later, in a charter of 27th November 1126, Gilbert (de la Porrée) appears as chancellor, though in another charter of the same day he is called simply *canonicus* (*Cartulaire de l'abbaye de S. Père* (sic) *de Chartres*, ed. M. Guérard, 1840, pp. 263, 267).

while his brother was chancellor he taught at Chartres; on his brother's death about 1126 he went to Paris, but he returned to teach at Chartres as chancellor from 1141 till his death in 1151.

It is rather tedious to analyse these bare and apparently harmless statements; but so much has been built on them, and so much scholastic history in the twelfth century depends on similar chains of reasoning, that criticism has a wider importance than might seem likely. The reputation of Chartres has been kept afloat by a disinclination to niggle; but niggle we must. To begin with: was Thierry the brother of Bernard of Chartres? Apart from this relationship he would scarcely have begun to have a place in the early history of the school. The only evidence comes from Otto of Freising, who tells us à propos of Breton cleverness that there have been three very clever Bretons in his day: Abelard, and the brothers Thierry and Bernard.[1] It is certain that the Thierry referred to here was the later chancellor of Chartres, but it is pure hypothesis to say that his brother Bernard was Bernard of Chartres. Otto does not tell us this. Nor does John of Salisbury, though he has plenty to say about both Bernard of Chartres and Thierry.[2] Nor does Abelard, who is our only other source of information about Thierry's brother. Abelard's evidence indeed points in a quite different direction. He describes Thierry's brother as a very incompetent theologian with an absurd view of the efficacy of the words of consecration in the Mass.[3] It is possible of course that this theologian whom Abelard thought so incompetent was Bernard of Chartres, the great teacher of the liberal arts whom John of Salisbury admired so extravagantly, but we need some evidence before we are persuaded. Besides, there are minor incongruities in the theory which could be insisted on: the fact that John of Salisbury mentions Bernard of Chartres and Thierry in the same sentence without hinting that they were brothers; the fact that Bernard of Chartres died nearly thirty years before Thierry. But why insist on these things? The point is quite unimportant, except that it provided an initial link between Thierry and Chartres, which made Clerval think he had seen Thierry's name as a master of the school of Chartres in some

[1] *Gesta Frederici Imperatoris*, i, 49, ed. G. Waitz, *M.G.H. Scriptores in usum scholarum*, 1912, p. 68.
[2] *Metalogicon*, ed. Webb, pp. 17, 29, 53–81, 93, 94, 124, 136, 205–6 (on Bernard); pp. 16, 80, 191 (on Thierry).
[3] *Theologia Christiana*, *P.L.* 178, 1286.

charters of the time of Bernard the Chancellor.[1] If any such
charter exists, I have been unable to find it. Failing this, there is
not the slightest evidence of a connection between Thierry and
Chartres until he became chancellor in 1141. Nor is there any
evidence that he taught at Chartres while he was chancellor. The
only place where he is *known* to have taught is Paris, and it was
certainly there that he spent the main part of his teaching life.

It would be quite wrong to blame Clerval for misleading us.
Every historian interprets evidence under the influence of his
vision. For Clerval, the most solid thing in the twelfth century
was Chartres, and Chartres was given the benefit of every doubt.
When he wrote, the scholastic world of the twelfth century was
thinly populated, and he did not know, as we now know, how many
men with the same name and similar occupations were apt to be
around at the same time. He therefore easily allowed Chartres to
draw every suitable unattached name into its orbit.

He approached Bernard's successor as chancellor, Gilbert de la
Porrée, with the same preconceptions.[2] Just as every Master B.
was available as Bernard of Chartres, so every Master G. might be
Gilbert de la Porrée. This tendency was already at work in 1855.
Among the letters published in this year by Merlet there is one to
Master B. from his disciple G. The disciple expresses the wildest
enthusiasm for his master: he owes everything to him and can
scarcely endure to be separated from him; he has become a schoolmaster in Aquitaine, but he continues to sigh for his old master,
and so on. Well, it is very likely that Master B. is Bernard of
Chartres. But who is the disciple? Certainly Gilbert de la Porrée,
said Merlet. Poole agreed: 'there can be absolutely no doubt
about its attribution'. Naturally Clerval did not dissent'[3] It seems

[1] *Les écoles de Chartres*, p. 160, Clerval quotes two charters of 1119–1124,
which Bernard witnesses as chancellor, 'tandis que son frère Thierry, dans les
mêmes pièces, s'attribue le titre de *magister scolae*'. Thierry's name, however,
does not appear in the charters to which Clerval refers. Further, Clerval says
(p. 170), that a reference by Abelard (*Hist. calamitatum*, *P.L.* 178, 150) to
Thierry as *quidam scolarum magister* is shown by the context to refer to Chartres.
But so far as I can see the context shows nothing of the kind. These small
errors would not be worth mentioning if it were not that the whole picture owes
so much to trifling errors and weak inferences.

[2] After quoting charters witnessed by Gilbert as canon and chancellor of
Chartres, Clerval proceeds: 'C'est alors (1124–1137) qu'il enseigna avec la
collaboration sans doute de Thierry, et qu'il eut pour disciples; Rotrou, Jordan
Fantosme, Jean Beleth et Nicolas d'Amiens' (*Écoles de Chartres*, pp. 164–5).
For these assertions no evidence is offered.

[3] Merlet, *B.E.C.*, 1855, pp. 461–2; Poole, *Illustrations of Medieval Thought
and Learning*, p. 134n; Clerval, p. 164.

harmless enough, especially since Gilbert de la Porrée probably *was* anyhow a pupil of Bernard of Chartres. But even here the habit of easy attribution paved the way for exaggerations and false conclusions. This attribution helped to suggest that the school of Chartres had a central place in Gilbert's scholastic life. But on a cool view the identification of Gilbert de la Porrée with this raving young admirer of Master B. is quite unlikely.

Our picture of Gilbert's connection with Chartres must be based on quite different evidence, and the small amount of evidence that exists suggests that Gilbert studied grammar under Bernard of Chartres, and then went on to Laon to study theology. It was at Laon that he wrote the first great work which made him famous. The man to whom he submitted it for approval and criticism was not Bernard of Chartres, but Anselm the great master of Laon.[1] It is true that Gilbert became a canon of Chartres by 1124 and chancellor in 1126. He *may* have taught there, but there is a striking absence of pupils who can be shown to have studied under him during those years. His teaching career still needs to be elucidated, but for the moment the only certainty attaches to his teaching in Paris in 1141, and there is some evidence that his influence radiated from this centre.

We turn now to William of Conches. Here again there is a quite strong presumption that he was a pupil of Bernard of Chartres. No contemporary or near-contemporary source actually tells us this, but John of Salisbury twice associates the two names, first when he says that William followed the same method of teaching as Bernard, and secondly when he calls William the richest or most fertile grammarian of his day after Bernard of Chartres.[2] Certainly this is not proof, but in the web of hypotheses from which the school of Chartres has been created, it is as near proof as we can get. Much more important, however, is the question whether William of Conches himself taught at Chartres. If this could be established we should have a perfect case of the continuity of the Chartrian tradition over a period of perhaps thirty years from about 1110 to 1140.

We have now reached the point of central importance for the

---

[1] 'Glosatura magistri Giliberti Porretani super Psalterium quam ipse recitavit coram suo magistro Anselmo causa emendationis'. (Balliol College, Oxford, MS. 36, quoted by R. A. B. Mynors, *Catalogue of the Manuscripts of Balliol College, Oxford*, 1963, p. 26.)

[2] *Metalogicon*, i, 5; i, 24; ed. C.C.J. Webb, pp. 16–17, 57.

history of the school of Chartres. The suggestion, which has been accepted almost without dispute for the last hundred years, is that William of Conches studied at Chartres and then taught at Chartres, and that the great John of Salisbury was one of his pupils at Chartres. The evidence is John of Salisbury's own account of his student days. He tells us that he left England in 1136 and studied logic on Mont Saint Geneviève, in the suburbs of Paris, from 1136 to 1138. Then he left the Mount and followed the lectures of William of Conches and others for three years from 1138 to 1141. Finally in 1141 he returned and studied logic and theology under Gilbert de la Porrée.[1] The great question for us is, where did John of Salisbury spend the years from 1138 to 1141, and in particular where did he hear the lectures of William of Conches?

Until 1848 scholars took it for granted that everything described in John of Salisbury's account of his student days took place in Paris. Then Petersen, the editor of John of Salisbury's *Entheticus*, pointed out that if he *returned* in 1141, he must previously have *left*. This seemed reasonable, and it started a search for the place to which he had gone. Petersen thought that he had returned to England. But then Schaarschmidt hit on the idea that he had gone to Chartres.[2] His main argument was that he could only have written the very full account of the teaching of Bernard of Chartres, which he gives in his *Metalogicon*, if he had been an eye-witness. We know now that the argument is certainly false, because Bernard had died long before John came to France, and he must have got his information from Bernard's pupils, whom he could meet anywhere. By the time this was known, however, the reputation of the school of Chartres was showing its power of surviving the demolition of the evidence on which it was built. Schaarschmidt's other arguments amount to nothing. Nevertheless he succeeded in making it an established doctrine that John of Salisbury went to Chartres in 1138 and studied for three years under William of Conches. It is an attractive hypothesis, but is it true?

If it is true, it is certainly odd that John of Salisbury should

[1] Ibid, ii, 10; pp. 77–82.
[2] See C. Schaarschmidt, *Johannes Saresberiensis*, 1862, pp. 14–22, where the earlier views are discussed and the new solution to the problem of John of Salisbury's whereabouts between 1138 and 1141 is proposed.

not have mentioned the place where he spent three important years, and we may ask whether Petersen did not pose an unreal problem in insisting that John must have left Paris. He certainly left Mont S. Geneviève; but we must remember that the Mount was a suburb of Paris outside the city walls. The sense of John's account of his life would be amply met if he left the Mount to go down into Paris, to the schools by the river, and returned to the Mount after three years. This would fit very well into the other details he gives. For instance, he tells us something, though in a rather confused way, about the other masters with whom he apparently studied during the three years from 1138 to 1141: one of them was Adam de Petit Pont, who certainly taught in the city; another was Thierry, who was certainly teaching in Paris at this time: a third was the Parisian master Petrus Helias. Altogether it is hard to avoid the conclusion that Petersen started a false trail by forgetting that a man could leave Mont S. Geneviève to go, not away from, but into Paris. Schaarschmidt then hit on a popular, but wholly unproved, answer to Petersen's question, and his successors have been only too willing to make the pilgrimage to Chartres.

If this is so, then William of Conches must join Thierry and Gilbert de la Porrée among the masters who can be found teaching at Paris, but so far as we know, not at Chartres. And John of Salisbury must join the many students who studied at Paris but not, so far as we know, at Chartres. And if he goes, who is left? It is very difficult to say.

## III

Apart from the details there are, it seems to me, three general sources of misunderstanding in the traditional account of the school of Chartres. Of these the first, and least important, is the tendency to exaggerate the importance of Chartres as a teaching centre, and to draw into the orbit of Chartres any works which exhibit certain 'humanistic' characteristics and have no other obvious local attachment. The second is the widely accepted conception of a 'humanism' which came into existence, flourished briefly, and was suddenly extinguished in the first half of the twelfth century, especially in the scholastic environment of Chartres. The third is the conception of an 'anti-humanistic' tendency, especially associated with the studies of logic, law, and theology at Bologna and Paris, which were a main cause of the decline of Chartres.

To speak briefly of each of these misconceptions in turn:

1. Chartres was only one of many cathedral schools in northern France whose continuous existence can be observed from the eleventh century onwards. Several of these schools had at some moment in their history one master of more than local significance who drew pupils from a large area. For a time these masters gave their school a wide fame. But we must be careful to distinguish between this short-lived fame, which depended on one man, and the lasting fame of the later universities, which depended on a tradition of scholastic success and a large variety of teachers and students. The cathedral schools existed to serve a limited and local need: their main purpose was to equip the higher ranks of the diocesan clergy with useful learning. Unless an outstanding master created quite exceptional conditions, these schools did not normally draw pupils from far afield. Their resources did not allow for the co-existence of many masters. Their main purpose was to provide fairly elementary instruction at a diocesan level. Accidents of personality apart, they had not the resources of teachers or students to make possible or desirable a permanently higher level of instruction than that of a grammar school.

Yet by the early twelfth century there was a substantial and growing demand for something more than this. Ambitious young men who wished to reach the highest places in government, whether ecclesiastical or secular, needed to be equipped with an advanced knowledge of systematic theology and canon law; they needed to operate easily in the intricacies of highly technical argument. It was quite beyond the resources of a cathedral organisation to meet this need, except in the lifetime of an outstanding master with talents superior to the function for which he was employed. In the period from about 1090 to 1120, by far the most successful of the cathedral masters in meeting the new demand were the brothers Anselm and Ralph at Laon; but even they could not for long found a school capable of surviving at the level to which they had raised it.

Almost within the lifetime of these two brothers it was becoming clear that the only two places in Europe with the special qualities necessary for perpetuating higher studies were Paris and

Bologna. They both provided—for reasons which are far from clear—opportunities for many masters to teach, and for many students to come and go as they wished. From a period quite early in the twelfth century, the number of masters and the wide choice open to students gave Paris a position quite different from that of any other city in northern Europe. In the years between 1137 and 1147, when John of Salisbury was a student, he was able to hear the lectures of ten or twelve masters, of whom six or seven were men of the first importance in their subject. This simple fact gave Paris an overwhelming advantage over every other centre of study in the North. At the same time Bologna, where the schools were fostered as a political and economic asset and had no connection with the cathedral, established a similar lead in southern Europe. Both these cities had freed themselves from the restrictions imposed by the ordinary cathedral school; and Oxford, the next competitor for an international role in the arts and theology, had no cathedral at all.

The framework of a cathedral organization was quite inadequate for the development of permanent institutions of advanced teaching. This fact does not detract from the achievement of those early cathedral masters who won a general fame in their own day. Quite the opposite. It merely explains why they did not found schools of permanent importance. Chartres is unique among cathedral schools in having had *two* masters of international standing separated by a century: Fulbert in the early eleventh century and Bernard in the early twelfth. No other cathedral school can show so much.

Both Fulbert and Bernard are examples of something very rare in the history of scholarship: they were men of the highest intelligence who made teaching their first concern. They were not original thinkers, but they commanded the whole learning of their day and they had the power and impulse to make it accessible to others. There is indeed much more evidence for the number and diversity of Fulbert's pupils than for Bernard's a century later. This may partly be due to chance, for we are exceptionally well informed about the names and occupations of Fulbert's pupils; but I think it is also likely that Fulbert was better equipped to provide what his age required. By contrast, Bernard was in his time somewhat old-fashioned. His type of learning no longer held the imagination or satisfied the ambition of younger men. They were turning elsewhere: to Laon for theology, to Spain for science, to Paris for the multiplicity of masters and the wide range of opportunity. Even when Bernard was at the height of his powers, Laon was vastly more attractive to the ambitious young man than Chartres, and Paris already enjoyed a freedom of scholastic movement that Chartres could never hope to emulate.

Yet Chartres was, and long continued to be, a sweet and pleasant place. The genial liberality of its counts, the lack of tension in its political relations, the freedom of its ecclesiastical society, the wealth and numbers of its cathedral canons, all helped to provide an atmosphere of well-being and learning in the church. In the course of the century it had many learned and distinguished men as bishops, chancellors, and canons; and even in a century of great cathedrals, the cathedral of Chartres must be reckoned one of the finest monuments of the age. All these factors must give Chartres a special place in our mental image of the twelfth century, but when we transfer this glowing image to the *school* of Chartres we must beware. As an institution the school attached to the cathedral suffered from the limitation of most of the cathedral schools. It existed to serve a local need, and when Bernard died it reverted to this, its proper function.

2. The second misconception concerns the 'humanism' of Chartres. 'Humanism' is a word that it is sometimes necessary to use and there is nothing wrong with it except that it stands for many different things. Any study of the seven liberal arts, which were the foundation of all education from the Carolingian age, implies a certain degree of humanism. That is to say, in studying the arts you are studying the human mind and the external world: the human mind and its forms of expression in grammar, rhetoric, and logic; and the external world in the arts of arithmetic, geometry, music and astronomy. The subjects may be extremely circumscribed, but they still have their basis and development in human powers alone. They are therefore genuine humanistic studies, and every cathedral school of the period from the tenth to the twelfth centuries was in its general tendency humanistic. To this range of humanism the school of Chartres certainly belonged.

But was there a special type and intensity of humanism peculiar to the school at Chartres? I think not. There is—to say the least—no evidence that the works of William of Conches and Thierry represented the teaching of Chartres rather than that of

Paris or (for that matter) Tours or Orleans. These works represent a phase in European studies rather than a narrowly localized form of humanism. They are the product of that moment when ancient materials handed down in the West for centuries had been thoroughly assimilated, and masters could write about them with ease and confidence. They are among the last expressions of western scholarship before the deluge of new materials which destroyed literary ease in academic exercises for a long time to come. The problems that now arose were too difficult and complicated for easy reading.

Both William of Conches and Thierry were men who seem to have realized that they had reached the end of the road. They were both keen seekers for new materials, but they had no idea how plentiful the new materials would soon become. They are the last representatives of the generation which had derived its knowledge of the world of men and nature mainly from the tradition of the Latin world—from Ovid and Virgil, from Macrobius and Martianus Capella, from Boethius and Cassiodorus. However eager they might be for new texts, their range of competence scarcely extended beyond the sources that had long been familiar, and two stout volumes could hold all the natural knowledge that Thierry considered really essential from the past. This humanism was certainly not shallow, but it was very limited in its range, and the range was that of contemporaries everywhere in northern Europe.

3. This brings us to the third misconception implied in the traditional account of the school of Chartres—the misconception about the end of the humanism represented by William of Conches and Thierry.

What came to an end in fact was not humanism, but the limitations on humanism imposed by the paucity of ancient sources and the conservation of ancient methods of instruction. William of Conches and Thierry, and all the men of their generation who worked on the same sources, had reached the end of the road because they had reached the end of the available facts. Plato's *Timaeus* may be a marvellous book, but if you read it as a scientific text-book, in isolation from Plato's other works and in total ignorance of the scope of Greek scientific experience, it cannot take you very far. For any further advance new material and new methods of systematic analysis were essential. These two things, new materials and new methods, were brought into the schools in the late twelfth century, and their exploitation was essentially the work of the universities as distinct from the cathedral schools.

## IV

It may not be out of place at this point to review the works of the masters who have generally been taken to represent the Chartrian tradition in the more general context which I have sketched. In this context the works of William of Conches and Thierry appear, not as the products of a brilliant but short-lived tradition of a single school, but as the representatives of a phase in the continuous development of western studies and of medieval humanism. Even Bernard of Chartres, the one great and indisputable Chartrian master of the twelfth century must be seen not as a landmark in the history of a school to which he gave a brief distinction, but as the last great schoolmaster in the late Carolingian tradition. It is with him that our survey must begin.

## 1. *Bernard of Chartres*

Nearly everything that we know about Bernard and his teaching comes from John of Salisbury. What John of Salisbury tells us is that he was a wonderful schoolmaster who developed a method of teaching his pupils Latin which ensured that even a pupil of moderate ability could learn to write and speak Latin correctly within a year. The basis of his method seems to have been a thorough grounding in grammar and composition enforced by a system of daily exercises which impressed the rules on his pupils' minds. What John of Salisbury describes sounds very like the upper forms of a good English public school on the classical side —the formation of character and godliness going hand in hand with a careful attention to the niceties of the Latin language. We must remember that John was writing in the 1150s about a master of the previous generation, and he described his method in detail mainly because it was no longer followed. Even John's own Latin masters, William of Conches and Richard Bishop, who had followed the same method as Bernard of Chartres in earlier days, had given it up because their pupils had insisted on getting on more quickly.

The picture which emerges is of a great teacher, sober, methodical, conservative in his tastes and in his philosophy. His teaching, so far as we can reconstruct it, kept strictly within the framework of the arts as they had been known in Europe since the tenth century. Yet with this conservatism of outlook and aim Bernard had a power of crystallizing points in rough but memorable verses and pithy sayings by which a schoolmaster is remembered. In an unobtrusive way Bernard was the main hero of John of Salisbury's survey of the learning of his day. He stood for the literary and moral virtues which John most admired. Perhaps John himself would have liked to be a master such as he imagined Bernard to have been, but by his day the prospects for an exponent of this kind of learning were not good, and John had to content himself with being an administrator.

## 2. *William of Conches*

The first thing to be noticed about William of Conches is that his scholarly career falls into two fairly distinct parts. He was one of those men who do their best and most original work when they are young. He lived till 1150 or later, but already by about 1125 he had produced one work of first-class importance which he never substantially added to or improved. This was his *Philosophia Mundi*. It was the first attempt in the West to give a systematic account of the whole of nature on the basis of a few simple scientific ideas. I am not here forgetting the work of John Scotus Erigena two and a half centuries earlier, nor that of William's contemporary Honorius Augustodunensis. Nor am I forgetting the illustrated English scientific manuscripts contemporary with the *Philosophia Mundi*, which describe the world in a basically similar way.[1] But Erigena's work is primarily a work of mystical theology, the scientific survey of Honorius Augustodunensis is an encyclopaedia pure and simple, and the English scientific manuscripts, beautiful though they are, are too jejune for serious intellectual study. Only William's is a work of systematic science, that is to say a work in which the details are subordinated to a general scientific plan.

The scientific ideas of William of Conches were not his own. They came partly from the *Timaeus*, with elaborations drawn from Macrobius and Martianus Capella, and partly from Galen through

[1] See below p. 165 and Plates IV–VI.

the recent translations of Constantine the African. What William of Conches provided was organizing power and lucidity. It has been said that William of Conches read the *Timaeus* through the eyes of Macrobius, but this (I think) is to put the cart before the horse. Many men had lost themselves in the intricacies of Macrobius. What William had the power to perceive was that these intricacies could be reduced to order if seen through the eyes of Plato, and that the same simplifying process could be extended through the whole field of human biology with the help of the great Arab physicians whose work had only recently become available in Latin. He went back to the fountainhead. Until the scientific works of Aristotle were translated into Latin, a strong interest in natural science ultimately led back to Plato because he was the source, directly or indirectly, of all general scientific ideas. William of Conches wrote before Aristotle was known as a scientific teacher, but he illustrates very well the reasons for Aristotle's later scientific supremacy and Plato's decline: Plato provided very few facts. William of Conches was already stretching out for more facts. He did not know the potential abundance of Aristotle; but he seems to have been the first to recognize that medical works newly translated from Arabic could help to complete Plato's picture of the universe. In this way he provides an early example of the restless search for new materials which would soon transform the scientific outlook of the West.

William of Conches was not alone in his interest in the workings of nature. His *Philosophia Mundi* has many indications of the existence of widespread discussion. The rapid diffusion of his work confirms this impression. It was being read in Constantinople in 1165. By this date—apart from the two version by the author himself—there were two other versions almost certainly made by others. In one form or another there are a hundred and forty manuscripts of the work now in existence. They mostly come from the twelfth and thirteenth centuries, and they demonstrate William's success in summing up the science of the pre-Aristotelian age.[1]

The *Philosophia Mundi* was the best expression of the scientific interests of a whole generation seeking for an orderly description

[1] These statistics are based on A. Vernet, 'Un remaniement de la *Philosophia* de Guillaume de Conches', *Scriptorium*, 1947, i, 252–9. The evidence for the work having reached Constantinople by 1165 is to be found in the *Liber thesauri occulti* of Paschalis Romanus, ed. S. Collin-Roset, *A.H.D.L.*, 1963, xxx, 111–198.

of the universe. The long effort to build up the image of the school of Chartres has accustomed us to suppose that Chartres must somehow lie behind the interests displayed by William of Conches. This is far too narrow a view. William of Conches was not the representative of a school but of a generation. He is a bridge between the meagre scientific resources of the early Middle Ages and the massive influx of new material which began almost as soon as he had written his great work.[1]

## 3. *Thierry*

Thierry was the complete teacher of the liberal arts of his day. He has left nothing that is not a record of his lectures—on Boethius' *De Trinitate*, on Cicero's *De Inventione* and on Genesis Chapter I.[2] We must not be misled by the theological appearance of some of the titles: Thierry was not a theologian, though he illustrates the tendency for teachers of the arts at this time to be drawn into theological controversies. He was essentially a teacher of the arts. His collection of texts on the seven liberal arts, his *Heptateuchon*, is the best monument we have of the complete arts course before it was drowned in the flood of new material and new interests in the late twelfth century. His preface to this collection is a noble statement of the aims of an old-fashioned master of the liberal arts.[3] He wished, he says, to join together the trivium and quadrivium so that the marriage might bring forth a free race of philosophers. He attached special importance to scientific subjects, or, as he would say, to the subjects of the quadrivium. One of Abelard's biographers tells us that Abelard heard him lecture on the quadrivium, and went to him for private instruction

[1] It may be useful here to list the most important of the texts of William of Conches's lectures which have been edited or analysed in recent years: glosses on the *Timaeus*, ed. E. Jeauneau, 1965; glosses on Boethius *De Consolatione Philosophiae*, J. M. Parent, *La doctrine de la Création dans l'école de Chartres*, 1937, 124–36; glosses on Priscian, E. Jeauneau in *R.T.A.M.*, 1960, xxvii, 212–47; glosses on Macrobius, E. Jeauneau, 'Gloses de Guillaume de Conches sur Macrobe: note sur les manuscrits', *A.H.D.L.*, 1960, xxvii, 17–28.

[2] Thierry's commentaries, lectures and glosses on Genesis and Boethius *De Trinitate* have been printed by N. Haring in *A.H.D.L.*, 1955, xxii, 137–216; 1956, xxiii, 257–325; 1958, xxv, 113–226; 1960, xxvii, 65–136. Some of the glosses on Cicero's *De Inventione*, including an interesting preface are printed in W. H. D. Suringer, *Hist. critica scholasticorum latinorum*, 1834, i, 213–53, and there are further extracts in M. Dickey, 'Some commentaries on the *De Inventione*', *M.A.R.S.*, 1968, vi, 1–41.

[3] The contents of this collection of texts were first analysed by Clerval, *Ecole de Chartres*, pp. 220–248. The Prologue is printed by E. Jeauneau in *Medieval Studies*, 1954, xvi, 171–5.

in mathematics, but he soon found the subject too difficult.[1] Whether or not this is true, Thierry's lectures on Genesis and Boethius are full of scientific interest. The view of the universe which they present is very similar to that in William of Conches' *Philosophia Mundi*. They used the same sources and approached the study of the world and its constituent parts in a similar way.

Thierry was certainly a great teacher. Men dedicated their books to him and were glad to say that they had been his pupils.[2] He was sharp-tongued, independent, careless of popularity, and he attracted men who spoke of him with that exaggerated admiration which is the supreme reward of the teacher. Like William of Conches he had mastered the past, and he thought he saw further than the greatest scholars of antiquity, not because he had anything new to contribute, but because he could survey the whole field. Yet he too felt the need for new texts, and his *Heptateuchon* shows that he was touching the fringe of the great new discoveries of ancient writings.

At the moment when the old learning was assimilated, the old boundaries were beginning to break down. Every master of note at this time shows a tendency to break out in one direction or another—into theology, law, or natural science, and into specialised fields of independent study like logic or grammar. Some masters broke out more reluctantly than others, but they all did so to some extent. They had to, if they were to survive. It must often, then as now, have been difficult for a master to reconcile his private interests with those of his pupils, and the latter in the end always prevailed. William of Conches had to adapt his teaching to his pupils' demands, and Thierry's works also illustrate the strength of the pressure from below which drove the masters on. We have three versions of his commentary on Boethius's *De Trinitate*, just as we have of the *Philosophia Mundi*, and I think it is very likely that two of them are the work of pupils who developed their master's teaching in different ways. These are just a few of the signs that the whole field of learning was in a state of upheaval

---

[1] See V. Cousin, *Ouvrages inédits d'Abelard*, p. 471. R. L. Poole discusses the story, *Illustrations of Medieval Thought and Learning*, p. 363; see also Clerval, p. 192.

[2] See Bernard Sylvestris, *De Mundi Universitate*, ed. C. S. Barach and J. Wrobel, p. 5; and Clerval, *Enseignement des arts liberaux à Paris et à Chartres ...... d'après l'Eptateuchon de Thierry*, 1889, for Hermann of Carinthia's dedication to Thierry of his translation of Ptolemy's *Planisphere*.

largely caused by the multiplication of students who would pay only if they got what they wanted.

The three masters of whom I have spoken all had sufficient power to leave the stamp of individuality on their works. But we must not exaggerate either their isolation from the general current of thought or the importance of their achievement. All their thoughts were old thoughts. They had the strength to make old thoughts live again, but they could not add to them. They had the strength to form this exiguous material into an intelligible whole, but they could not break far out of an ancient framework of knowledge. To gather new material, to systematize the new as they had systematized the old, to reach out to new patterns of thought, and to fill the vast empty spaces of ignorance, were tasks that belonged to the future. These tasks were beginning to be undertaken in the times of William of Conches and Thierry, and it was out of them that the complex system of studies of the mediaeval universities grew. These studies were not a reaction against humanism, Chartrian or otherwise; they were the necessary and inevitable development of whatever Thierry and William tried to do. This development required the labours of many men; and the places where many masters and students could assemble had advantages which grew more conspicuous from year to year. In intellectual productivity, as in any complex process, numbers are important because they make specialization, competition, and the growth of new techniques both possible and easy. In these respects Chartres, even in the first half of the twelfth century, could not compete with Paris. Hence Thierry, Gilbert de la Porrée, and (as I think likely) William of Conches all gravitated to this centre, and in so far as they represent a school at all, it is the school of Paris rather than that of Chartres.

## V

We may, however, finally ask why, if the foundations of what I may call the legend of Chartres were as insecure as I have suggested, they have seemed so firm to such excellent scholars as Clerval and Poole, and to all those who have accepted their conclusions. I think there are several reasons, both personal and general. Of the two great founders of the legend, R. L. Poole had formed his views of the school of Chartres when he believed that

Bernard Silvestris was the same man as Bernard of Chartres. This provided the school with a very solid foundation. He had also noticed the general coherence between the work of Bernard Silvestris and Thierry of Chartres whom he wrongly believed to be his brother, and between Bernard Silvestris and William of Conches, whom he wrongly believed to be his pupil. He also believed that it had been demonstrated that William of Conches taught John of Salisbury at Chartres. The chain of evidence connecting these men and their habits of thought with Chartres seemed unbreakable. Yet not one of these links is firm, and most of them are demonstrably false. In part Poole recognized this when he returned to the subject nearly forty years after writing his first book. But he was unwilling (as we all are) to alter his views more than was strictly necessary, and though he saw the weakness of some of Clerval's new arguments, he was willing to accept the support which Clerval provided for the main conclusions of his early work without thinking them out afresh.

As for Clerval, we must remember his circumstances. He was Professor of History at the Seminary at Chartres and deeply concerned in building up the new centre of clerical learning, of which the pupils are such a conspicuous feature in the cathedral close today. It was very easy for him to think of the twelfth century schools as a prototype of what he saw about him. He was encouraged to do this by the manuscripts in the library, which he was the first to use to reconstruct the history of Chartres. He saw Thierry's *Heptateuchon*, and he reconstructed from this and from other volumes of that impressive library a course of studies which he characterized as Chartrian. It was easy for him to forget that the *Heptateuchon* was probably a monument of Thierry's teaching at Paris, and that its connection with Chartres was in a sense fortuitous. It was easy also to forget that the texts of the *Heptateuchon* were in the main the texts of a whole generation of masters and not of Thierry alone. The imaginative impact of these books on Clerval was very great. It was fatally easy for him to see everything centred on Chartres, to make easy identifications of Masters B. and G. with Bernard or Gilbert (or if necessary William), and gradually to build a system held together by a logic of its own. Sometimes he was demonstrably wrong; but more often he erred simply by giving Chartres the benefit of every doubt. The cumulative effect of building multiple benefits of this kind into a system is very great. It is also very impressive because it conflicts with no obvious rules of evidence. The system stood because, in the nature of the case, it could not conflict with many known facts. I think it has now begun to conflict with some of the facts, and the time has come to take the pieces apart again.

# 6

## THE LETTERS OF ABELARD
## AND HELOISE

### I

The letter-collections of the twelfth century have a special place in the history of medieval correspondence: they are distinguished by their learning and by their vivacity; they are the source of much of our knowledge of the religious, philosophical, legal and moral thought of the period; and many of them convey an impression of the writer's personality which we shall look for in vain in the letters of the next century. The letters of the thirteenth century are narrower in their range of interest; they are largely letters of inflated propaganda or trivial detail; and they are almost always over-loaded with rhetorical verbiage and the spongey adornments of epistolary style. Twelfth century letter-writers were lucky in their moment. Many sciences were still relatively immature, and important matters of scientific interest could still be dealt with adequately in the form of letters. I am reminded of the letters of Alexander Pope or Gilbert White six hundred years later. Some of the conditions that prevailed in the twelfth century had by then returned, and Gilbert White could communicate observations of the first importance in letters that anyone can read with pleasure. He could have done the same thing in the twelfth century, but not in the thirteenth; in the eighteenth but not in the twentieth. Learning moves on, and significant arguments or observations come to require a more technical treatment unsuitable for a letter—suitable only for a treatise or a lecture.

The learning of the twelfth century could more easily be given literary form than the learning of the thirteenth century. Consequently a high proportion of the letters of the earlier period were intended to be read as learned works. Even the act of writing a letter was an exercise in a learned science. Like other branches of the liberal arts the science of letter-writing underwent a vast development in the twelfth century. The rules of style and organization of material were elaborated and exemplified in a heap of epistolary models and treatises. No letter of the time should be read without remembering the rules. The rules might not always be kept: it was one of the higher branches of the art to know when and how they could be broken; but they are never wholly disregarded. The appearance of naturalness is deceptive if this is taken to mean that there were no rules; but in the best writers of the twelfth century the rules arc not obstrusive. It is only later that formality and rhetoric become burdensome, so that even Dante's letters cannot be read without disgust at their far-fetched artificiality. In the twelfth century art and learning still had the appearance of nature.

There is another characteristic of twelfth century letter-collections which must be mentioned before we turn to the letters of Abelard and Heloise. Nearly all important writers kept copies of their own letters, and it was from these that letter-collections were made. This means that we can seldom be sure whether the text that we have is the same as the text that was actually sent. In the few cases where comparison can be made there are nearly always some differences: they may be small or large, but they are sufficient to show that eminent letter-writers sometimes corrected their own drafts even after the letters had been dispatched. This was a perfectly permissible practice, because the readers of letter-collections were interested in the style and learning of the writer and not in the letters as historical documents. Moreover they were rarely interested in the replies to the letters. Those who made the letter-collections we now possess must very often have had many replies to the letters at their disposal; but they nearly always ignored them. A collection of letters was essentially a memorial to the learning of a single man, so it is nearly always very one-sided. Since it deals with a wide range of subjects which have arisen more or less by chance, the normal collection may be looked on as a work of loosely organized learning held together within a framework of a highly developed epistolary art. What it lacks in logical arrangement is made up by its intellectual and stylistic unity.

If we turn to the letters of Abelard and Heloise with these considerations in mind, we see at once that in some respects they conform to the type of letter-collection I have described, but in other ways they diverge very markedly from it.[1] On the one hand

---

[1] The most easily accessible edition of the whole correspondence of eight

they are works of learning which follow the rules of contemporary letter-writing. But, far from being one-sided, both sides of the correspondence are represented, and they are so arranged that they tell a single story ending in a climax or (as some might think) anti-climax. They must be read straight through if they are to be understood. This is so unusual in the letter-collections of the twelfth century that it has aroused the suspicion of literary invention. In itself this suspicion is not unreasonable. There was a strong appetite in the twelfth century for dramatic confrontation, and several spurious epistolary dialogues had a wide circulation.[1] It was not beyond the bounds of reasonable possibility that the letters of Abelard and Heloise should have belonged to this literary genre. And even if they have a genuine foundation, it would be no surprise to find that they were extensively altered when they were collected for publication.

Both these possibilities have been widely discussed, and it is not my intention to add to the body of critical learning on this subject.[2] For the moment I wish only to look at the correspondence as a whole, and (on the supposition that the letters are genuine) to examine some of their details in the light of the literary habits of the age. As for the genuineness, that is a question that will arise in due course as the correspondence unfolds.

## II

The letters, if they are genuine, must all have been written between about 1132 and 1135, when Abelard was abbot of a miserable monastery at St. Gildas in Brittany, and Heloise was abbess of the prosperous and well-regarded convent of the Paraclete near Troyes in Champagne. He was then a man in his

letters is *P.L.* 178, 113–326. There is a modern edition by J. T. Muckle and T. P. McLaughlin in *Mediaeval Studies*, 1950, xii, 163–213; 1953, xv, 47–94; 1955, xvii, 240–281; 1956, xviii, 241–92. For a critical edition of Abelard's first letter, see J. Monfrin, *Abelard, Historia Calamitatum*, 1959.

---

[1] In particular, the spurious correspondence of St. Paul and Seneca, and of Alexander the Great and Dindymus. The first of these is several times cited by Abelard in his works.

[2] It is sufficient to mention here on the one hand the all-out criticism of B. Schmeidler, 'Die Briefwechsel zwischen Abelard und Heloïse, eine Falschung?' *Archiv für Kulturgeschichte*, 1913, xi, 1–30; 'Die Briefwechsel zwischen Abelard and Heloïse dennoch eine literarische Fiction', *Revue Bénédictine*, 1940, lii, 85–95; and on the other side, the replies of E. Gilson, *Héloïse et Abélard*, 2nd ed. 1948, and J. T. Muckle, *Mediaeval Studies*, 1953, xv, p. 57.

middle fifties, she a woman twenty years younger. But the love affair with which the letters are mainly concerned had taken place some fifteen years earlier, between about 1117 and 1119. The events of these years require here only the briefest recall: Abelard's seduction of his young pupil in her uncle's house, the birth of their child, Abelard's mutilation at the hands of the uncle's hirelings. Then in an agony of shame and despair Abelard constrained Heloise to become a nun at Argenteuil near Paris, while he became a monk at the royal monastery of St. Denis. It was all over by 1119.

After this date Abelard and Heloise went their separate ways. Abelard quarrelled with the monks of St. Denis and experienced his first condemnation at Soissons in 1121. He escaped from these troubles to a hermitage near Troyes which he called the Paraclete, and here for a few years from 1122 to 1125 he rose to new fame as a teacher. Then, by one of those ill-judged decisions which punctuated his career, he accepted the abbacy of the distant and ill-favoured abbey of St. Gildas in Brittany, and he and his monks settled down to make each other miserable. Meanwhile Heloise had risen to be prioress of Argenteuil; but she too became a wanderer when the monks of St. Denis found reason to eject the nuns from their convent. Abelard heard of the outrage of his old enemies and hastened to give his old hermitage of the Paraclete to the nuns, making Heloise their abbess. For the next few years, from about 1129 to 1132, he found some relief from his own monastic misery in visiting the nuns and helping them to organize their lives. Things were in this state when the correspondence begins.

The first letter in the collection is Abelard's. It is very long, and it contains the best autobiography written in the twelfth century. It is the autobiographical content which gives the letter its value for the modern reader; but in the context of the correspondence which it introduces there are two formal features of the highest importance. In the first place it was not addressed to Heloise, but to some unnamed clerical friend who was in trouble. Secondly, it was a letter of a well-defined rhetorical type known as *consolatoria*. This was one of the types of letters recognized by the masters of the epistolary art, and the arguments to be used in such a letter were well known. It was necessary to say something like this: 'your misfortunes, however great, have all happened to other and better men'; or 'these troubles will prove to be a blessing in disguise'; or 'your tribulations are a judgement upon sin'; or 'these things are sent to try us'; and so on. This was all so well understood that the main interest of letters of this kind lay in the skill with which the writer chose and deployed his limited range of arguments. Abelard concentrated on the first of these arguments: 'Take comfort; my troubles have been much worse than yours'. Into this theme he poured the bitterness of half a lifetime, and what emerged was an autobiography; but it was an autobiography written for a special purpose and as an illustration of a single theme. We must not be misled by the brilliance of the result into forgetting the rhetorical theme which is its sole justification.

No doubt it is tempting to say that the occasion and the argument were merely excuses for Abelard to satisfy his urge for autobiographical self-disclosure. No doubt, in the miseries of St. Gildas, he was glad to have an excuse for working off some of his bitterness in writing. But the form determined the scope and nature of his autobiography, and when it fell into Heloise's hands she took the formal excuse quite seriously. In any case the form of the letter required that the autobiography should be purely and simply an account of his own misfortunes. Of these Abelard distinguished seven, and all that he tells us of his life is hung on those seven pegs. They are, in chronological order:

1. His persecution by his early masters William of Champeaux and Anselm of Laon.
2. His mutilation at the instigation of Heloise's uncle.
3. The unjust condemnation of his first theological book at the Council of Soissons in 1121.
4. His persecution by the monks of St. Denis.
5. His persecutions at his hermitage.
6. His persecutions at St. Gildas.
7. The persecutions which arose from his relations with Heloise and her nuns at the Paraclete.

From a formal point of view Heloise appears merely as a cause of two of the seven persecutions. The famous love-affair was no more than the prelude to one, and in retrospect not the greatest, of these misfortunes. But Abelard allowed himself a wide liberty of expansion. Three of his persecutions, especially the first, second and seventh, provided the occasion for very long digressions which might interest the clerk to whom the letter was addressed. In the first of these Abelard gave his own account of the state of theology and learning in his youth; in the second he recalled at length and with many *auctoritates* the objections which Heloise had urged against marriage; and in the last he discoursed on the great advantage possessed by a eunuch as an instructor of women. As for romance, regret, nostalgia, affection, sympathy, or anything of the sort in his relation with Heloise, there is not a trace. His motive in his affair with Heloise is revealed as undisguised lust: he had picked on her because he wanted a woman but could not hope for a lady or tolerate a whore, and he found in the beautiful niece of his landlord an easy prey. Abelard portrays himself throughout as half-beast, half-monk, sinking through sensuality into the filth of carnal sexuality; but rising through philosophy and bodily mutilation to the stature of a spiritual man. Rhetorically therefore we pass from the *locus* 'worse misfortunes than yours have happened to me' to a mixture of historically less interesting, but morally certainly more elevated, indications that 'these things were a judgement upon sin' and that 'they have proved a blessing in disguise'.

For the reader who expects romance, the disillusionment could scarcely be more complete or the picture of Abelard less attractive. No doubt he told the truth, but the disconcerting thing is that he does not seem to be ashamed of the truth. For this there are two explanations. In the first place it was necessary for the argument of a *consolatoria* that the disaster—the mutilation—should be a just retribution for evil-doing, and that it should prove a blessing in disguise. And secondly, the minds of both Abelard and Heloise seem to be untouched by the ideals of romantic love which emerged in the next generation: they were both guided by a more ancient tradition that spoke to them either of the love of God or the love of virtue, but not yet of the tender courtesy of sexual passion.

Abelard saw himself as a modern St. Jerome: a man whose past irregularities had been corrected by Christian philosophy, an inheritor of both pagan and Christian learning, a wanderer pursued by animosities and consoled by the affection of his pupils, and finally as the spiritual director of pious women. At the time when he wrote his first letter this final Jerome-like phase of his career had only just begun, and it is possible that Abelard thought it had gone far enough. He shows no sign of wishing to involve himself more deeply in the vocation of a spiritual director of nuns. On the contrary, he counted it among his misfortunes that it had already brought on him a new odium. But as we shall see, he was gradually forced to make the directing of the religious life of his nuns the chief employment of the years from 1131 to 1135. These are years of scholastic inactivity. They are also the years when the new St. Jerome emerged.

Despite the unromantic mould in which Abelard's account of his relations with Heloise is cast, his letter has probably never been read without stirring feelings of romantic attachment to Heloise, of which Abelard himself seems singularly free. In Abelard's tale there is only one calamity that moves us, and it is not his. The formal purpose of the letter is frustrated by the vivid impression of the personality and tragedy of Heloise. Abelard can scarcely have intended it to produce this result—it is a result of a romantic view of love which neither he nor Heloise shared. Abelard was proud of Heloise—but as a pupil, not a wife. The two points on which he dilated at greatest length were her arguments against matrimony after the birth of her child, and the words with which she assumed the veil after the catastrophe.

The arguments which Abelard put into the mouth of Heloise are a remarkable *tour de force*. Heloise is represented as objecting to matrimony on two grounds: first, that her uncle would not thereby be placated as Abelard supposed; secondly, that marriage was no life for a philosopher. On the second of these points Abelard sets out at great length the illustrations that Heloise had given him of the indignities of married life—the screaming children, the nursery songs, the general uproar. In a word, she would rather be his mistress, and have infrequent joys, than be the wife of a frustrated philosopher. Abelard fills out these arguments with a string of quotations from Jerome, Cicero, Josephus, Seneca, Augustine and St. Paul. Arguments of this kind gained a wide popularity in the twelfth century, and similar diatribes can be found in the writings of John of Salisbury, Peter of Blois, Walter Map and his commentators.[1] They are the semi-serious

---

[1] John of Salisbury, *Policraticus*, viii, 11 (ed. Webb, ii, 294–306); Peter of Blois, Ep. 79 (*P.L.* 207, 243–7); Walter Map, *De nugis curialium*, iv, 3–5 (ed. M. R. James, pp. 143–59; the medieval commentaries are listed on pp. xxxi–xxxviii).

entertainments of learned clerks. It would appear very likely that the majority of the literary quotations were supplied by Abelard as he developed this theme in writing to his friend. We can easily imagine a high-spirited woman using the arguments that Abelard recalls, but even a learned one would scarcely bother with quotations at a moment of deep personal crisis. Yet even if Heloise did not supply the quotations, she never repudiated them. There was a literary background to her thoughts and actions which was an essential part of her personality.

This comes out most clearly in the second important detail which Abelard reports of her conduct. To a modern reader the most repellent incident in Abelard's career was his insistence, after his mutilation, that Heloise should become a nun at Argenteuil before he became a monk at St. Denis. With a shamelessness that only a complete absence of romantic chivalry could excuse he recalls the scene: Heloise stood in the church at Argenteuil on the threshold of her monastic profession, surrounded by friends who begged her not to destroy herself by this ill-considered step. At length she broke from them with these words:

> Great husband deserving of a worthier bed,
> Has Fate such power to bow so high a head?
> Why, impious female, did I marry thee
> To cause thy hurt? Accept the penalty
> That of my own free-will I'll undergo.

And so she hastened to the altar and took the veil.[1]

Did she really speak these words, or are they a literary embellishment of Abelard? In answering this question we must notice that the quotation is very different from the string of quotations with which Abelard reports Heloise's dissuasion from matrimony. In the first place it is short, and could easily break out in the heat of the moment. Then it is entirely appropriate. The words are those with which Pompey's wife Cornelia greeted her husband after his defeat at Pharsala. Cornelia offered herself as a sacrifice to placate the angry gods. 'Slay me,' she said; 'cast my ashes on the waves: perhaps then your way will be smoother, your enemies less strong, as a result of this sacrifice.' Just so, Heloise at the moment of her profession offered herself to death that Abelard

---

[1] P.L. 178, 136; Monfrin, p. 81. Heloïse's verses come from Lucan, *Phars.*, viii, 94–8.

might live. Long before Abelard had seen himself as the modern Jerome, Heloise had seen herself as the modern Cornelia. Indeed, she was more than Cornelia; for Pompey did not after all slay Cornelia and scatter her ashes on the waves; but Abelard killed Heloise and she willingly made the sacrifice of her life.

## III

It has often been said that if Heloise really spoke the lines that have just been quoted at the moment of her profession as a nun, she was certainly a very great pagan and no Christian. Before we go further, we may stop and consider this proposition and compare Heloise's general outlook with that of Abelard.

Since Abelard's mind is the easier to read we may start with him. Like other literate men of his day, his mind was formed by a literature that was ascetic and largely monastic in inspiration. He despised, hated and feared his sexual impulses. Like other men he gave way to them; and then he gave way to remorse, guilt, and self-contempt. He had been saved from a recurrence of this process by his castration, and he recovered his poise in pride, self-pity, and contempt for his opponents. Whether these are Christian impulses is another matter; but certainly the line of thought that they expressed was based on traditional Christian teaching.

Heloise is more difficult to characterize because she had suffered more; but there is no reason to think that she differed from Abelard in her attitude to sexual appetite. In describing the act of sexual intercourse, whether in marriage or otherwise, she too would use the vocabulary of drains and sewage. Where she differed from Abelard was in her claim that in all her acts she was not moved by lust but by a fixation of her will towards Abelard. It was this that made her voluntarily submit to his will, to his obscenities, to his commands, to his lusts, to anything that he cared to put upon her. Since her will was forced, she was much more radically enslaved than Abelard. She approved her enslavement; but she did not approve the actions to which it led. Moreover, when her mind and her will were free, she thought and felt as Abelard did about the superiority of the celibate life. The whole of her plea from the beginning of the correspondence was for the strengthening of her will and the furnishing of her mind.

If Abelard was half-beast, half-monk, she was half-heroine,

half-nun. It is true that she entered the monastic life without the slightest trace of a true religious motive, but this was certainly not unusual at a time when monastic service was only one of the many forms of service required of individuals to the community. It is much more serious that her love of God seems—as she admits —to have been so entirely overshadowed by her love of Abelard: but for this she could find no remedy, though she sought one.

Abelard was a better Christian than Heloise in being a worse man. Heloise could glory in her heroism: Abelard could not glory in his lusts. Heloise could make Abelard her god: Abelard was never in any danger of making Heloise his goddess. Abelard could renounce the past: Heloise could not. Yet they both despised lust and they both despised marriage as a form of legalized lust. Their age had not yet developed a plausible ethic for the secular life. Outside the monastic ethic there were only fragments of a classical ethic, difficult to combine in a coherent system, and still more difficult to combine with the needs of secular activity whether in government, or trade, or marriage. Those who lived in the world were bidden so far as possible to be monks, and to make up the balance by supporting monks. Both Abelard and Heloise accepted this teaching. Their states of mind were very different, but in the end they had only one central code of conduct to fall back on—the code of monastic Christianity.

## IV

It was convenient for Abelard to think that Heloise's case was the same as his own—perhaps indeed he could not imagine that it could be different. He supposed that, once the occasion and possibility for satisfying her lust or submitting to his own were removed, there would be nothing left except a desire for monastic virtue. And since, unlike him, Heloise had no enemies, and since her life was exemplary and well-regarded by all, he felt justified in assuming that by 1131 she had changed from the girl who became a nun in a mood of heroic despair and self-immolation, and had become a mature and devout nun. To all appearances he had ample grounds for this supposition. As he described her to his clerical friend she was one whom 'the bishops of the neighbourhood love as a daughter, the abbots as a sister, the laity as a mother; whom all admire for religion, prudence, and an incomparable sweetness of patience in everything. Rarely permitting herself to be seen, she has shut herself in her chamber in holy meditation and pious prayer; yet the more she has retreated from the world, the more the world has sought her presence and spiritual counsel'.[1]

It was a comfortable picture, and in the circumstances perhaps not unreasonable, except that Abelard, the great questioner of other men's assumptions, had never exerted himself to find out whether it was true.

The letter which contained this picture of herself fell into Heloise's hands by chance. At least that is how it is represented in the letter which she addressed to Abelard when she read it. In form, her letter was an *epistola deprecatoria*. Like the *epistola consolatoria* to which it was a reply, this too was a well-defined type of letter. Its function was to convey a request, and the art of the writer was shown in the skill with which the request was supported. The kind of argument to be employed in it was the subject of scholastic instruction. In the first place it was necessary to show that the request was reasonable; then that it was within the power of the recipient to grant it; and finally that the writer deserved to receive what was asked. What Heloise asked was that Abelard should give her some consolation commensurate with that which he had given his clerical friend. It was not difficult for her to show that this request was reasonable and within Abelard's power, and that she deserved to receive what she asked. But she too—like Abelard—while observing the rules of rhetorical propriety poured into the letter the experiences of fifteen blighted years.

Here again the result is autobiography at a high level of interest and passion, but once more it is autobiography that keeps strictly within the limits imposed by an epistolary type. What she said was briefly this: 'You have written a very long letter of consolation to your friend, having already, as you say, spoken words of consolation to him. Why have you never spoken words of consolation or written a letter of consolation to me in my sorrow? Whose sorrow could be greater than mine? Whose claim on you more urgent? I destroyed myself at your command. I cut myself off from you for ever to show that I belonged to you alone. In the days when we lived in sin, you wrote plenty of songs about me—and now, have you no words, no letter for me? Can it be true, as everyone says, that you

[1] *P.L.* 178, 172–3; Monfrin, p. 101.

didn't love me, but only lusted for me, and have forgotten me when you can lust no more? At least send me some words—you have plenty at your command—to console one who entered this harsh monastic life not for the love of God, but at your command.'

This is not the kind of letter that any man would like to receive, but Abelard's reply does not show him unduly disturbed by it. He could take refuge in two considerations. In the first place, the rules of *deprecatio* required that Heloise should make out the best possible case for the granting of her petition. Besides, rhetorically her arguments left him with an easy reply: 'I have not given you what you ask because you—holy, pious, prudent, filled with divine grace, etc.—have no need of such a letter or such words from me. Rather it is *I* who need *your* prayers.' And so he attempted to cool the flames of indignation by a prosy homily on the great benefits of prayer, especially the prayers of pious women, and he enclosed a litany for the community to say on his behalf. It is sad stuff, but as a literary reply to an *epistola deprecatoria* which the recipient regarded as unreasonable, it was a subtle and flattering rejoinder. If the letters were only examples of epistolary art skilfully displayed this letter would have ended the correspondence in a flood of unexceptionable commonplaces. Equally, if Abelard had been right in thinking that Heloise thought as he did, he would have left her with nothing more to say.

But his assumption was wrong, and Heloise's next letter set out to leave him in no doubt on this point. The letter can be fitted into no rhetorical category. It asks for nothing except that Abelard shall understand the bitterness of her heart and drop the pretences of pious convention and comfortable subterfuge. Abelard must be made to understand her condition, and she left him without any possibility of doubt:

> The lovers' pleasure which we enjoyed together were so sweet to me that they can neither displease me nor fall from my memory. Wherever I turn, they are before my eyes with all their desires. They appear to me in dreams. In the solemnities of the Mass when prayer should be most pure, the obscene images of those pleasures hold my most miserable soul in such captivity that I pay more attention to those defilements than to prayer. I ought to deplore what we did,

but I sigh only for what we have lost. And not only what we did, but the times and place where we did it are so deeply imprinted with your image in my mind, that I relive it all again, asleep or awake, and I sometimes reveal my thought in the movements of my body and in words which break out unexpectedly. How truly wretched I am, and how well may my groaning soul say 'O wretched woman that I am, who will deliver me from the body of this death?'[1]

There is much more of a similar kind, but this will suffice to show the fixation of Heloise's mind and will after fifteen years of separation, and her sense of hopelessness in her struggle for freedom.

## V

Critics have been worried by two main features in the exchange of letters to this point. The first is a matter of fact; the second of psychology.

The question of fact was first raised by B. Schmeidler in the course of his thorough attack on the authenticity of the correspondence as a whole. He argued that Heloise's complaint that she had received no letter or words of consolation from Abelard since the time of their conversion to the monastic life could not be strictly true because there must have been a great deal of personal contact and consultation at the time when Abelard established the nuns at the Paraclete. This of course is true, but only a very solemn critic would think the point very serious. Fr. Muckle, the latest editor of Heloise's letters, has effectively answered the criticism by pointing out that Abelard could have done everything necessary for Heloise and her nuns without satisfying her need for *personal* consolation.[2] In fact, I think we can go further and say that Abelard *could* not give her what she needed so long as he persisted in thinking—as his letter shows he did—that her state of mind was the same as his own. Even when he remembered the words with which Heloise had taken the veil, he could reflect that his own motives at that time had not been any more satisfactory: 'the confession of shame rather than love of the monastic life

[1] *P.L.* 178, 196–7.
[2] *Mediaeval Studies*, 1953, xv, 56–8.

drove me to seek the shadow of the cloister' he told his clerical friend. Of course we know that Heloise's quotation from Lucan meant much more than this, but in all literary quotations there is a wide area of tolerance. Not everyone who says 'To be or not to be' is contemplating suicide, and Abelard may have appreciated the reference to Pompey without supposing that Heloise was a veritable Cornelia.

Abelard's inability to give Heloise the sympathy she needed was therefore much more radical than Fr. Muckle supposed, but he is certainly right in his rejection of Schmeidler's theory that the letter was self-contradictory. Fr. Muckle however, now raises a further objection on his own account. He thinks that, though the letters are genuine in the main, the text must have been seriously altered. His objection is to the state of Heloise's mind revealed in her letters: 'Her whole religious life,' he says, 'has been almost entirely a tissue of hypocrisy, not devotion to God. . . . No expression of repentance escapes her lips but on the contrary she nurses her infatuation . . . she has lived with a false front and played the part of a hypocrite so successfully that not even Abelard has penetrated it. . . . Then too, her letters picture Heloise . . . as a woman of sensual mind, serving Abelard, not God, or as she herself puts it, being such a hypocrite as to fool even Abelard himself.'[1] He finds it incredible that a woman capable of saying the things I have quoted from her letter should have lived for twelve or fourteen years as a nun, prioress, and abbess, not only without scandal, but with the applause of competent judges, and with manifest success. Further, he thinks that if she had written such things, Abelard would have been bound to reprove her a good deal more harshly than he did. Therefore he concludes that Heloise's letters have been contaminated by later insertions. As I have already remarked, it was not unusual in the twelfth century for letters to be extensively altered when they were prepared for publication. But before we agree that it happened in this case, we must ask whether there is any force in the objection that has been raised.

Fr. Muckle's objections to Heloise's self-revelation involve judgements of a peculiarly precarious kind. To judge the spiritual state of contemporary people from their actions is immensely difficult; in the past it is impossible. We are required to assume

[1] Ibid. 59–64.

that the actions and states of mind of a nun in the twelfth century
can be assessed by standards that are applicable (if they are
applicable at all) in the twentieth century. This is a point on
which everyone must form his own judgement. To me the
tensions and obsessions of Heloise's mind seem quite compatible
with, seem even to provide an impulse towards, a severe and
exacting discipline in her practical life. Besides, even at the level
of textual interpretation we may doubt whether the offending
passage from Heloise's letter can reasonably be called the work
of a 'hypocrite', or 'woman of sensual mind', 'nursing an infatuation'. Unless the quotation from St. Paul with which the passage
ends is to be reckoned among its hypocrisies, it shows very clearly
that she looked on her state of mind as a torment. She saw no
possibility of fighting against it, but she did not luxuriate in it.
The final words of the letter are especially revealing in this
respect. She asked Abelard to stop treating her as the victor in a
spiritual battle, who needed only a little pious advice, and to treat
her as an invalid with a desperate disease:

> I do not seek the crown of victory. It is enough if I avoid
> danger. This is safer than engaging in battle. In whatever
> corner God will place me, it will suffice; when everyone has
> sufficient, there is no room for envy. This is my plan, for which
> I can claim the authority of St. Jerome: 'I confess my weak-
> ness; I do not wish to fight in hope of victory, lest I lose
> whatever victory I may have.' Why should I leave port to
> chase uncertainties?[1]

Certainly these are not the words of a *pagan* heroine.

## VI

Abelard was roused at last. He could no longer pretend that
Heloise's state of mind was the same as his own. What she had
now given him was no *petitio consolationis* that could be shown to
be unnecessary, but the proof of present desolation and need. He
took her seriously, and his next letter engages our sympathy as
none of his earlier ones have done. He sent Heloise an exposition
of the manner in which the whole business from the beginning of

[1] Ibid., 198.

their association to their entry into the monastic life was to be regarded from a strictly monastic—and in the circumstances that meant quite simply a Christian—point of view. To penetrate or understand the state of Heloise's mind was not within his capacity, and he did not try to do this. But he dropped the note of cheerful optimism which had so incensed Heloise in his previous letter and he faced the prospect of a long struggle towards peace. 'Vale in Christo, sponsa Christi, in Christo vale, et Christo vive': these last words of his letter are subtly but decisively different from the clever lines of his previous exordium:

'Vive, vale, vivantque tuae valeantque sorores,
Vivite, sed Christo, quaeso, mei memores.'[1]

Heloise, for her part, did not argue. She obeyed, but she imposed on him a heavy task. She said, in effect: 'At least give me something else to think about than my own passions.' In particular she asked for an account of the origin of the monastic life for women, and for a detailed rule for their lives. This letter is Heloise's longest contribution to the correspondence. It contains a long, sharp-witted criticism of the Benedictine Rule as it appeared to an intelligent and learned woman who for fifteen years had lived under it with a divided mind.

Abelard did what she asked, and much more. This fact gives him his greatest claim—not to fame, for that is his due on quite other grounds—but to our personal regard. The correspondence ends with two very long letters—much longer than all the rest put together—in which he sent the desired Rule and History of the Order. They are by no means readable, and they are seldom read. They have no personal interest. They must have cost him much dreary toil; but they bring the story to the only possible end that is not despair. To get the full record of what Abelard did for Heloise, we must add about a hundred hymns, thirty-five sermons, and a substantial series of solutions of Heloise's theological problems. These works, which added little to his fame and influence, must have been the main occupation of Abelard's years of scholastic silence at St. Gildas. Having started as a brilliant expression of early twelfth century learning, rhetoric, and personal vanity, the correspondence ends as a series of monastic documents.

[1] Ibid. 192 and 212.

## VII

It is the transition from the first mood of literary showmanship to the last phase of monastic instruction—a transition made necessary by the persistence of Heloise's self-disclosure—that gives the collection as a whole its human dignity. The last phase has been neglected by later readers, who have read into the earlier letters the emotions and interests that were congenial to their age, but have shrunk from the boredom of the long monastic discourses which bring the correspondence to a close. The letters have been appreciated for their learning, their historical details, their high romantic interest but not often for their monastic instruction. Yet there is some reason to think that it was this instruction that ensured their survival.

It has always been a mystery how and where they survived. Indeed, among all the reasons for doubting their authenticity, the lack of any early manuscripts has been one of the most plausible. There is no evidence of the existence of the letters till about 1280, when Jean de Meung translated them and used them in his continuation of the *Roman de la Rose*. We shall never know very much about the reason for this long silence, but the local and monastic interest of the main body of the correspondence may help to put this problem in its right perspective.

We must begin by turning to the monastery of the Paraclete on the site of Abelard's hermitage near Troyes. Abelard's last two long letters provided the Abbess Heloise with the rules of life and the history of the institution for which she had asked. They were the foundation documents of the monastery. The last words of Heloise's last letter to Abelard were these:

> After God you are the founder of this place. Through God you are the planter of our community. With God you are the institutor of our Order. After you we shall perhaps have another teacher building on another man's foundation, and he may be less concerned for us, or less attentive to us, or less able to help us even if he wishes. Speak to us therefore yourself, and we shall hear.[1]

I do not think there is anything in these words to indicate a change of heart in Heloise. To the end she remained Abelard-

[1] Ibid. 226.

centred. But she is now about to receive the instruction for which she had always asked, and the community was about to become in the fullest possible sense Abelard's creation and the extension of his personality.

We may reasonably suppose that it was Heloise who preserved the correspondence and placed the earlier letters in front of the monastic instructions. They contained the only record of the life of the founder, and they provided an explanation for the foundation of the monastery and its customs. Heloise and Abelard alone can have had copies of both sides of the correspondence, and she survived him in the monastic life for twenty years. The letters dominated her life as they did not dominate Abelard's; indeed they *were* her life, and the basis for the life of the monastic foundation that she did her best to make great. Why should she alter them? She would scarcely alter Abelard's; as for her own, she has not removed her blemishes, and it is hard to see why she should add to them. Nor does she give the impression that she was a woman who easily changed her mind. At the end of the collection of letters, someone—possibly Heloise herself—added additional rules and texts for the discipline of the nuns, and these additions have been preserved in one of the best manuscripts of the letters that we have. In this form the letters remained (as I picture it) at the Paraclete unknown to the outside world till nearly the end of the thirteenth century, when perhaps a chance visitor from Paris or a renewed interest in Abelard brought the correspondence to a wider public and made it part of the world's literature.

## Note on the Manuscripts

A manuscript tradition which begins nearly two hundred years after the composition of the letters cannot be expected to yield any very decisive clues about its starting point. Nevertheless two points stand out. The first is that Paris was the point of origin for the diffusion of the letters in the late thirteenth and early four-teenth centuries. The second, which is more speculative, is that the collection probably reached Paris from the monastery of the Paraclete.

The first point, the importance of Paris, is very clear. It was

here that Jean de Meung, who used and translated the letters
c. 1280, worked; and at least two, and probably all three, manuscripts of 1290–c. 1330 come from Paris. These manuscripts are:
Troyes 802, which was sold to Robert dei Bardi, chancellor of the
university of Paris, by the cathedral chapter of Paris in 1346;
Paris B.N. lat. 2544, which belonged to James of Ghent, a master
in Paris c. 1330; and Paris B.N. lat. 2923, which belonged to
Petrarch by 1344 and probably came from Paris or its neighbourhood.

The second point, the connection of the early manuscript
tradition with the Paraclete, can be inferred from the contents of
MS. Troyes 802. This manuscript has some pecularities of
punctuation and text which suggest that it is a very careful copy
of an early manuscript. In it, the letters, which occupy ff. 1–88v,
are followed without a break by a collection of texts for the discipline and organisation of a community of nuns (partly printed
*P.L.* 178, 313–326 and analysed by Monfrin, pp. 12–13). Although
there is no formal proof that this collection was made at the
Paraclete or by Heloïse, we know from the charters that have been
preserved that the last years of Heloïse's life were a time of considerable growth and prosperity, for which the rules in the Troyes
collection seem well adapted.

For most of these details the careful account of the manuscripts
by Monfrin, pp. 9–31, should be consulted. Perhaps I should add
that my own examination of the manuscripts nearly twenty years
ago led me to the view of the history of the collection expressed in
the concluding paragraph of my essay. I am glad to find that M.
Monfrin has come to a very similar conclusion, which he expresses
in the following words (p. 60): 'La présence de notre *corpus* au
Paraclete à une date ancienne donnerait à penser qu'il a été mis en
ordre dans cette abbaye; par conséquence par Héloïse ou d'accord
avec elle: ce qui serait de conséquence. Malheureusement toute
certitude manque. Peut-être sera-t-il possible de préciser un jour.'

# 7

## PETER OF BLOIS:
## A TWELFTH CENTURY HUMANIST?

### I

The man I have chosen as the centre-piece for this lecture was once very famous. He was one of the few writers of the twelfth century who wrote a work which was an immediate success without being either a text-book for the schools or a work of edification for a monastic audience. It took the form of a collection of letters, and it was intended to be read as a single work—a solid, learned, unspecialized book for anyone who could understand Latin and was interested in serious problems of conduct and human affairs. It caught on at once. Moreover, and this is still rarer, it kept its popularity. Looking through my notes, I find descriptions of two hundred manuscripts, and another fifty or even a hundred could perhaps be found by relentless diligence. Those I have noted are distributed through the medieval centuries roughly in the following way: seven from the twelfth century, forty-two from the thirteenth, thirty-nine from the fourteenth and a hundred and twelve from the fifteenth. This distribution is interesting, for it shows that though the work was a production of the early age of scholasticism it was not eclipsed by the learning of the Renaissance, and it was growing rapidly in popularity towards the end of the Middle Ages. Moreover, the manuscripts show the same tenacity in every country in Europe, except perhaps Italy, where the conscious superiority of the later humanists was most pronounced. Everywhere else the letters of Peter of Blois continued their triumphal progress to the end of the Middle Ages and beyond. As we should expect from a writer who (despite his name) spent most of his working life in England, the manuscripts of English origin are the most numerous; but those from France are a close second—fifty-three as compared with fifty-seven—and Germany with fifty-one is scarcely behind France. Indeed, it was in Germany in the fifteenth century that the letters of Peter of Blois were most widely read.

They were printed in Brussels before the end of the fifteenth century, and continued, though with diminishing appeal, to be admired and read in the sixteenth and seventeenth centuries.[1] Their second editor, Jean Busée, writing in 1600, described how he had read the letters when he was a student of theology, and had been so impressed by the gravity of their style, the variety of their argument, the acumen of their judgments, the profusion of their quotations from Holy Scripture, the authority of the important people to whom they were written, and their remarkable freedom in castigating vice, that for twenty-five years he had cherished the plan of producing an edition. By the time that he brought the plan to completion, however, Peter of Blois's long run of good fortune was almost at an end. He was ceasing to be read as an author in his own right, and he gradually became merely a source from which scholars hoped (though generally in vain) to extract historical information. The decline from literary and scholarly eminence to historical rag-bag was steep, and it has been aggravated by an exasperating scarcity of solid fact among the gay rags. The historical information has turned out to be meagre, the genuineness of the letters has been doubted, and, worst of all, many of the finest ornaments have turned out to be not so much borrowed as downright stolen. The cries of reprobation have arisen on all sides: his kindest critic, J. Armitage Robinson, is obliged to grant that he is 'a vain, ignorantly learned, hopelessly inaccurate man' only redeemed by being 'very real'.[2] More recently a Belgian scholar has described him as a specialist in plagiarism who shows a certain ability in covering his tracks, which would lead us to admire his handiwork if the plagiarism were less revolting. 'Fi, le vilain!' he concludes with zest.[3]

It is impossible not to sympathise with these adverse judgments, and at one time I felt their force to the full. I had spent a

---

[1] There were three editors in these centuries: Jacobus Merlinus (Paris, 1519), Joannes Busaeus (Mainz, 1600), and Petrus de Gussanvilla (Paris, 1667). The last of these forms the basis of the reprint in *P.L.* 207, with the supplementary letters added by J. A. Giles in his edition of 1846 (4 vols.).

[2] J. A. Robinson, *Somerset Historical Essays*, 1921, p. 140. The essay on Peter of Blois in this volume (pp. 100–140) is still the best general account of his life, though it needs to be corrected at many points in the light of later studies of English episcopal charters in the late twelfth century. Among these studies, see especially C. R. Cheney, *English Bishops' Chanceries, 1100–1250*, 1950, and *Hubert Walter*, 1967.

[3] Ph. Delhaye, 'Un témoignage frauduleux de Pierre de Blois sur la pédagogie du xiie siècle', *R.T.A.M.*, 1947, xiv, 329–31.

long time thinking about Peter of Blois, comparing manuscripts and editions, tracing his sources and testing his assertions, and everywhere behind the attractive exterior there appeared to be a deep emptiness, a lack of thought, of originality, of anything but conventional feelings—and of course, that terrible plagiarism. I can understand the unusual note of vituperation which appears in many modern judgments on Peter of Blois: it springs from a sense of deception, of hopes unfulfilled, of labour lost. There is the stale smell of second-hand clothes. It is not pleasant. Yet it leaves a problem, the problem of Peter's long success. And I am glad to take the opportunity of reviewing in the light of later experience some years of work that at one time seemed rather unprofitable.

## II

It is first of all necessary to know something about our author, and I can think of no better introduction to him than to sketch the position in which Peter of Blois found himself at the moment when he was putting together the collection of his letters. He wrote many other works, but the letters are the work on which his fame has always rested. All his earlier works were a preparation for his great achievement, and his later ones were off-shoots from it. The letters alone gave him a European position.

The decisive moment that set him on his road to lasting fame was the year 1184, and more precisely the period between the death of Archbishop Richard of Canterbury on 16th February, and the appointment of his successor, Baldwin, in December. Peter of Blois was then a man in his early fifties. Although he was a Frenchman by birth and wholly French in sentiment and speech, his life had become irreparably tied up with England. For the past ten years he had been in the household of Archbishop Richard, and for the last year or two he had occupied the respectable position of chancellor to the archbishop. It was not a very brilliant position for a man of his age and abilities, and now that the archbishop was dead the future was very uncertain.

He was a man with no very obvious marketable commodity. From a worldly point of view it must be said that he had not made the best use of his time as a young man. Our very earliest view of him comes from a time about 1150, when he was a law student at

Bologna.[1] The choice does credit either to his own or to his parents' perspicacity. Both Roman and Canon law were in the first vigour of their scholastic revival, and Bologna was the centre of the whole movement: the earliest glossators were at work there on Roman law, and in Canon law the great text-book of Gratian was beginning to carry everything before it. These subjects were the special products of Bologna, and through either of them the opportunities for advancement were very great. But Peter showed no aptitude for either branch of the law. In Roman law indeed he had the double misfortune of combining a lack of aptitude for the essentials of the subject with an enthusiasm for its trappings:

> The secular law (he wrote) wantoning in its glorious panoply of words and in its elegant urbanity of speech, violently attracted me and inebriated my mind.[2]

A strange perversity, we may think, to revel in the verbosity of Justinian and to remain indifferent to the new views of law and society beneath the verbiage, but historically we can understand Peter of Blois's peculiar emphasis. Bologna had been a school of rhetoric before it became a school of law. The two subjects flourished side by side, and the distinction between them was by no means clear in the mid-twelfth century. But no one could have more thoroughly confused the two subjects than Peter of Blois, or more thoroughly committed himself to the view that law was essentially a branch of rhetoric. He came in the course of time to speak with extraordinary bitterness about the study of law. By that time he had seen many men rise to the highest eminence in Church and State as a result of this study, and he had himself been an advocate—an unsuccessful one—in at least one famous case.[3] He lived in a world in which the professional study of law had become increasingly important everywhere; but it was not for

[1] The important information about his studies in Bologna is in *Ep.* 211, where Peter says that he was a companion and pupil of Baldwin, the later archbishop of Canterbury, in the school of Hubert Crevelli, later Pope Urban III. It appears from *Ep.* 143 that Conrad, later archbishop of Mainz, was another pupil. These letters fix the date of Peter's student days in Bologna in the early 1150s.

[2] This account of his love of Roman law comes from the letter to his friend and master Baldwin which Peter wrote from Paris, whither he had gone after leaving Bologna (*Ep.* 26).

[3] In 1187 he was Archbishop Baldwin's advocate at the papal court in his dispute with the monks of Canterbury. Peter found himself no match for the great Roman lawyer Pillius who conducted the case for the monks (Gervase of Canterbury, *Opera Historica*, ed. W. Stubbs, i, 366–9).

him, and his disappointment perhaps sharpened the edge of his vituperation.

But when he left Bologna, he was still a young man and these bitter thoughts lay far in the future. He believed himself in love with the law. Solacing his leisure hours with the study of the Code and Digest, he reluctantly moved to Paris to study theology. We find him there in about 1155.[1] Once more, no rising young man could have made a better choice. Peter Lombard, another migrant from the law school at Bologna, was at the height of his productivity and influence. His *Sentences*, fundamental in the teaching of theology for the rest of the Middle Ages, must already have existed in the form in which we have them; his Commentary on St. Paul was already becoming famous. Peter of Blois could scarcely have arrived at a more propitious moment, and we know that he attended lectures in which the new methods of theological debate were applied to a wide variety of problems. Alas for his academic future, these lectures left no mark on him whatsoever. He was as deaf to the charms of theological debate as he had been to those of legal science. It was only when he was an old man, having nothing else to do, that he developed a strange taste for writing up his lecture notes of fifty years earlier.[2] In the long intervening years they had lain undisturbed. Nothing in his writings suggests that he ever looked at them, and he certainly did not keep abreast of later developments in theological debate.

This was not because Peter was uninterested in the subject-matter of theology; but in his prime he viewed it from quite a different point of view from that of the Parisian masters of the new age. He was interested wholly and exclusively in the elaboration of mystical interpretations of the Holy Scriptures. This was a highly respectable theological interest with a long history behind it in the twelfth century, and an almost equally long history ahead of it; but it was not the predominant interest of the Parisian theologians. They preferred to ask questions and solve problems rather than to accumulate mystical analogies. Peter of Blois

---

[1] He seems to have had two periods of study in Paris: the first as a schoolboy about 1145–7, when he probably studied under John of Salisbury; the second after leaving Bologna, when he studied theology and probably supported himself by teaching grammar. The first period is referred to in *Ep.* 240; the second in *Epp.* 9, 26 and 51.

[2] For some account of these letters, of which Miss E. Revell has prepared an edition, see my note 'Some new letters of Peter of Blois', *E.H.R.*, 1938, liii, 412–24.

never turned against academic theology as he turned against the academic study of law, but he was never a man to solve problems. He liked to think of himself as a theologian, but the truth was that he valued the allegories of Scripture for the same reason that he had valued law, as an embellishment to his prose and an extension of his powers of expression. He used his learning to surprise his reader by the richness of his imagery. He was not the only man of his generation to see literary possibilities in the exploitation of Biblical imagery. Many of the cunning effects of the poets and satirists of his generation came from their Biblical echoes, and like them Peter appropriated the Bible, its imagery, its allegories, its histories and examples for his own purposes. In this art he was outstandingly successful.

We emerge from these brief glimpses of Peter of Blois's early life with a picture of a man who frequented the schools in a period of academic expansion without sympathy for the new scholastic disciplines, fostering that most dangerous of ambitions in a student, the ambition to be a writer. What he did when he left Paris, we do not know for certain. Probably he became a schoolmaster teaching grammar and rhetoric at Tours.[1] His prospects were bleak. It is the universal testimony of the time that students with worldly ambitions abandoned grammar and rhetoric for the study of law and theology with all possible speed; and this was something that Peter, who did not lack worldly ambition, either could not or would not do. No doubt there was still room in the world for grammarians and rhetoricians in positions of importance, but on the whole they were being left behind in the race for promotion.

The only area of development in these studies which held out some hope of practical usefulness was the art of letter-writing. One of the conspicuous features of the late twelfth century was the growing importance of carefully drafted letters in the conduct of business—not the brief and trenchant writs which are the clearest manifestation of the first age of effective government, but the elaborate unfolding of complicated matters which now occupied the chanceries of Europe. The rapidly expanding business of the papal curia in particular called forth a flood of petitions, appeals, complaints, charges and counter-charges from every

---

[1] This period of his career is very obscure, but it seems to be referred to in *Epp*. 12, 43 and 101.

quarter of the western world. They all needed careful drafting by men who had more than a smattering of law together with a taste for polemic and a command of the ornate diction of correct epistolary style. The conduct of international affairs and the business of bishops and monasteries required something more refined than the routine hack-work of low-grade clerks.

The great age of political letters and propaganda still lay in the future, but the chanceries of the late twelfth century were already equipping themselves for this new stage of political consciousness. It was here that the expert letter writer could find a niche, and a large number of treatises on letter-writing were written at this time to help to equip men for this modest niche. These treatises are among the minor scholastic products of the twelfth century, and those that survive are no doubt only a small proportion of those that were written. They did not have a high survival value for they make desperately dull reading, and they are generally accompanied by a selection of model letters only slightly more interesting than the treatises which they exemplify. But they were written because they were needed, and we have good reason for thinking that this was the kind of activity in which Peter of Blois was engaged in the mid-1160s. It was not an employment to satisfy an ambitious spirit. From a practical point of view it was an unlucky moment for the study of rhetoric: too late to lead to scholastic eminence, as it might have done fifty or a hundred years earlier; too soon to catch the full tide of political business which called for men of learned eloquence a hundred years later.

It is not surprising, therefore, that Peter was ready to take part in a political gamble which nearly brought him to greatness and to ruin. In 1166 William of Sicily had died, leaving his young son under the care of his widow, Margaret. She was a member of one of the great families of the Angevin Empire, and she looked to her relatives to support her against the local opposition so often encountered by foreign wives in great positions. Her call for help was answered with alacrity, and the party of Frenchmen who set out to take over the government of the kingdom of Sicily in her service included Peter of Blois and his brother William. The political involvements of those years do not concern us, but after a year or so of precarious power the attempt ended in revolt and bloodshed. Peter was lucky to escape with his life. In 1168 he was back in France. This was the lowest point of his career. He was without friends, and his qualifications for future employment were obscure. He offered his services in all directions—to King Henry II, to the archbishop of Rheims, to the bishop of Chartres. In the end he was glad to find refuge with the archdeacon of Salisbury.[1] It was distinctly a *pis aller*, for a man who had almost become an archbishop in Sicily. But his new position kept him in touch with important people, and this was something he enjoyed.

Slowly he climbed the ladder: from the archdeacon of Salisbury he migrated to the service of the archbishop of Rouen[2]; and from this service he passed in 1174 to that of the newly appointed Archbishop Richard of Canterbury. In 1182, without abandoning the service of the archbishop, he became archdeacon of Bath. He was never to rise higher, and the death of Archbishop Richard at the beginning of 1184 made his future once more uncertain. There was no assurance that the archbishop's successor would require his services. Peter might be obliged to fall back on the rural insignificance of his archdeaconry, a fate from which his duties with the archbishop had hitherto saved him. It was in these circumstances that he set about making his bid for literary fame.

As an author he had already some small successes to his credit. Nearly ten years earlier, when he may still have hoped for something better than a place in the archbishop's household, he had addressed three small treatises to various people. One of these, which he presented to Henry II as a memorial of his victory over his enemies in 1173, has a certain interest for us, for it was here that he first struck the vein which was to make him famous. The work was called a *Compendium in Job*.[3] It was not a work in massive theological scholarship, and it made no attempt to cover the ground already covered by St. Gregory in his great treatise on the Book of Job. We may call it a contemporary adaptation of the theme of Job's sufferings and final prosperity to the person and circumstances of Henry II. It presented a lively criticism of present-day life and manners, a Mirror of Princes encased in the Biblical, legal and rhetorical diction which we are soon to see more fully displayed.

[1] For this phase in his career see J. A. Robinson, *op. cit.*, pp. 103–5.
[2] We catch a brief glimpse of him in this service in 1172 when (in a lowly position among the clerks) he witnessed a charter of the archbishop of Rouen (Archives of Calvados, H 1842).
[3] *P.L.* 207, 795–826.

He followed this up with another work commemorating the greatness of King Henry II. He must have hoped for great things from this, for he took more trouble with it, and tells us more about it, than about any of his works, except his letters.[1] But it cannot have had a large success, for no copy of it has ever been found. Certainly it led to no promotion.

## III

In 1184, therefore, he found himself with only one solid literary asset—the copies of his letters written during the last twenty years.[2] No doubt in the course of his duties he had written many business letters of no general interest; but the letters he wished the world to read were written on grand or delicate occasions, when dignity and weight were required. Most important, he wished the world to see his own personal letters; it was in these that he stood forth as a mentor of the great in his own right. Indeed he has some claim to be considered as the first man of letters in our modern sense of the word in English history, and one of the first journalists in Europe. He was the first to admonish all and sundry about their manners, morals and duties, unbidden and out of turn. Others had written because their pastoral office or position required them to write. Peter of Blois wrote only because he wanted to write, because he wanted to shine, and because the exercise gave him satisfaction.

How many of the letters, of which the drafts lay before him in 1184, had actually been sent, and in what form they had been sent, we shall never know. These are some of the mysteries with which Peter of Blois surrounds himself, and there seems no way of penetrating them. Perhaps he really did send them all, for he seems not to have been troubled by the thought that he had no right to speak. He felt to the full the dignity of a literary man.

[1] In *Ep.* 77 he refers to the work in these terms: 'Ego in libro de praestigiis fortunae, quem vestro committo corrigendum examini, actus domini regis Angliae Henrici secundi pro mea parvitate magnifico.' In addition to this letter, he mentions the composition and correction of the work in *Epp.* 4, 14, 19, and lists it among his works in his *Invectiva in depravatorem*, *P.L.* 207, 115.

[2] In giving the date 1184 for the first collection of the letters I am guided by the following considerations: the latest datable letters in the first recension belong to May 1183 or thereabouts, and the earliest datable letters in the second recension are shortly after May 1185. Between these dates, Peter's long period of unemployment in 1184 provided the best opportunity and incentive for making the collection.

Authorship invested him with a prophetic mantle and he spoke *urbi et orbi*: when he wrote, he looked through his correspondent to the great world beyond.

Certainly he wished his letters to have a wide public. Others no doubt had wished this before him. We have all written letters which we regretted to see lost to the world. But I think we can claim that he was the first of the important medieval letter-writers to arrange for the circulation of his own letters, and to write with this circulation in mind. This is a somewhat surprising fact, for if we take a quite general view of the great and famous medieval letter collections, Peter's comes at the end of a long series. The series begins with Gerbert, and continues through Fulbert, Anselm, Ivo of Chartres, Hildebert, St. Bernard, Peter the Venerable, and John of Salisbury. But none of these collections owed its origin to the desire for literary fame. Most of them were put together by disciples or pupils after the death of their author; others were preserved as an *aide-memoire* for the author or for those who worked with him. No-one before Peter of Blois had faced the difficult task of presenting his own letters to the general public as a record of his personality and opinions. Many have followed him, and they have all found the task embarrassing.

The causes of this embarrassment have never altered, and since Peter of Blois was the first to try to overcome them we may follow him a little further at this point. The main cause of the embarrassment is of course a moral one: to admonish a friend in private is praiseworthy, but to publish the admonition to the world, especially if the friend happens to be a royal minister or a bishop, is very deplorable. We all know the extraordinary prevarications and subterfuges to which Alexander Pope was reduced in order to appear an unwilling publisher of his own letters; and Pope's case is instructive, for he was a man of high moral purpose, whose letters contained, in Swift's opinion, 'the best system that ever was wrote for the conduct of human life.' Peter of Blois's purpose was very similar—to present in an apparently haphazard way a true system for the conduct of human life. He too was faced with the problem of explaining himself, and he found a less discreditable escape from the embarrassment of self-display than Pope: he simply claimed that the king had urged him to make the collection, and that he had unwillingly obeyed the royal command. Whether this somewhat unlikely statement is true or not we cannot tell. It is certain that the project of publishing his own letters caused a good deal of unfavourable comment. To these critics he replied that his letters were published as models for beginners, as contributions to the public welfare, and as an act of charity.[1] The charity we may reasonably question, but there can be no doubt about the first two aims of the collection.

The first aim of providing a collection of models for beginners may seem the less important of the two, but we must remember that this is how Peter himself had begun his career, and it was the meeting of this need that provided a steady public for Peter's letters for several centuries. As a token of the seriousness of his aim he wrote a treatise on the epistolary art at about the same time as he produced the collection of his letters. It exists in only one manuscript, and it has never been printed.[2] While the letters went on to fame and fortune, the treatise to which they formed a body of illustrations was forgotten. Rightly so. Peter's treatise, like all the others of the same kind, deserved to be forgotten. It belongs to the moment of time when the art of rhetoric was being contracted to meet the needs of a business age. Peter's treatise has many marks of the sharp controversy which had been raging for at least fifty years between those who wished to keep rhetoric as the central subject of humane education and their opponents who wished only to satisfy a practical need for proficiency in letter-writing. On this question, as on so many others, Peter's position was ambivalent. He could not forget that he had been a school-master, and that from his earliest days a love of words had been his one unqualified enthusiasm. But he was also a temporarily unemployed civil servant, and it was in the practical world that his future, and the future of those for whom he wrote, lay. So he compromised. His treatise dealt with each of the seven branches of writing, but it was only on letter-writing that he had much to say. He offered a compromise between the 'perplexed prolixity' of the full course of rhetoric and the meagre diet of practical text-books. But he also set out to be fully abreast of modern practice: he seems, for instance, to have been the first to explain publicly the stylistic secrets of the papal chancery.

[1] *Ep.* 92.
[2] The manuscript is Cambridge University Library MS. Dd. ix. 38. The date of the treatise is determined by its mentioning Lucius III (Sept. 1181–Nov. 1185) as pope. In the preface Peter is called archdeacon of Bath, a position which he did not hold till 1182. The work is briefly described by E. Langlois, *Notices et extraits des MSS. de la Bibl. Nat.*, 1895, xxxiv, ii, 23–9.

It seems clear that in Peter's mind there was a close connection between the publication of his letters and his treatise on the art of writing. The collection was successful because it provided models of fine writing in all the recognized modes. Letters of command, deprecation, exhortation, commination, consolation, increpation and premunition: they were all there. Peter was too self-confident a writer to observe all the rules laid down in his treatise, but his liberty was the liberty of the master. Beginners in the art, if they noted his lapses in the use of the *cursus* or the absence of the divisions he had taught them to expect, were also presented with a plentiful supply of thoughts and phrases, quotations and arguments to meet all the situations of life.

Although they were published as models, the letters were quite free from the atmosphere of the school-room. Peter intended his letters to take their place beside the great letter-collections of the past. They were to be at once a monument to his virtuosity in the elaborate art of epistolary rhetoric and the reactions of a man of the world to the problems and policies of the day

But here a fresh difficulty arose. Virtuosity in a highly developed art implies the expenditure of a great deal of midnight oil, much polishing and revision, and an artificially contrived perfection of form. Writers of text-book examples had no need to feel any embarrassment about this; but it will not do for a man of the world. The effect of spontaneity is spoilt by contrivance. Peter of Blois wanted his letters to appear as red-hot reactions to events, and he was anxious that he should himself appear to be sincere and generous, indignant at the wickedness of the world, ill-used by critics, devoted to friends but sometimes betrayed by them, speaking earnestly to evil-doers, giving advice in high places, and so on. If reactions are to seem plausible, if rage or scorn are to win approval, if condolences are to touch the heart, they must appear to come from the heart. They must not look like gestures performed before a mirror.

Peter of Blois was here in a difficulty which had faced none of his predecessors, and he was obliged to tell a lie. The letters, he declared, were put before the public 'in that native rudeness in which they were first conceived'. Nothing had been changed: they came before the world without embroidery; if he had known that they would appear in public and might offend delicate ears, he would have polished them with a more diligent file; he would have collected them with a more careful vigilance. But such as they were, he put them forth to instruct those who came after him.

To one vigilant critic, who derided his letters as a farrago from the works of other men, he made the ingenious reply that he wrote his letters so fast that he would not have had time to plagiarise. He was abnormally sensitive to criticisms of this kind, and quite reckless in devising ways of answering them. For nothing is more certain than that the criticisms were true. The letters certainly drew extensively and often verbatim from other men's work. Equally certainly they had been extensively revised before publication, and they continued to be revised through many editions. However deplorable the lack of veracity, his explanations showed an appreciation of the essential nature of letter-writing which sets him apart from the writers of school-books. He was the first to feel the need for these subterfuges, but by no means the last.

As well as providing examples of epistolary style and a wide range of comment on the world, Peter of Blois also aimed at displaying himself to the world. We are never allowed to forget the man behind the pen. Like Petrarch and like Pope he sought to project a perfect image of himself in his letters, though unlike them he fails to convince us that the image and the reality are closely related. Let me give you some examples of his self-portraiture and you may judge how far it is reliable. In the first example, written in his school-mastering days, he gives an account of his early education:

> I know that it was of great value to me to have been instructed in the art of versifying when I was a boy, and to have been ordered by my master to take my material not from fables but from true histories. It was also very valuable to me to be compelled in adolescence to learn by heart and repeat the urbane and elegant letters of Bishop Hildebert of Le Mans. Besides the other books which are famous in the schools, it was very valuable to me that I frequently looked into Trogus Pompeius, Josephus, Suetonius, Hegesippus, Q. Curtius, Cornelius Tacitus, Titus Livius. All these authors inserted in their histories a great many things useful for edification and for the completing of general knowledge. I also read innumerable other authors, who have nothing to do with history. In all these writers the diligence of modern

writers can pick flowers as in a garden, and gather honey for
themselves from their sweet speech.[1]

This is a valuable piece of twelfth century scholarly autobiography—provided that we recognize it as a curious mixture of
fact and fiction. Moreover the element of fiction easily predomin-
ates, and it is this that Peter wishes to impress on our minds. The
small significant fact is drowned in the noisy rhetoric of make-
believe. The sonorous list of great names is what we are meant to
notice, but it has long been recognized as fictitious. It is only the
character and complexity of the fiction that seems not to have been
fully understood. Peter had certainly not read, or even seen, all
the authors whom he claims frequently to have looked into.
Worse still, he borrowed the whole list from John of Salisbury;[2]
and ironically enough, John of Salisbury, who had read more
classical authors than anyone else in his generation, had certainly
not read all the authors whom he mentions in this ill-fated passage.
In both authors the list is a piece of rhetorical elaboration, and
the only way in which Peter of Blois differs from John of Salisbury
is in his use of the first person singular. John of Salisbury does
not quite say that he has read these works. His list is a trick of
rhetoric; but Peter turns rhetoric into autobiography. Yet
beneath the rhetoric there is a grain of genuine autobiography.
There is no doubt that he was taught in his youth to make verses,
and it is very likely that he learned by heart the letters of Hildebert,
who had died in about the same year that Peter was born. These
facts almost escape notice, but they are significant for the future of
medieval education.

If we turn to the statutes of Oxford University in the fourteenth
century we find the course of elementary instruction is precisely
this: the masters were to give their pupils copies of verses and well-
turned letters, full of easy metaphors, plain rhythms and grave
*sententiae*, to be learnt by heart.[3] In the course of time the letters
of Peter of Blois were used for this purpose, as he had used the
letters of Hildebert. The letters of Hildebert stand at the beginning of the drift from the study of the ancient authors to the study
of the moderns, which gradually transformed the language and

---

[1] *Ep.* 101. Another passage in the letter is discussed by P. Delhaye, op. cit.
[2] *Policraticus*, viii, 18 (ed, C. C. J. Webb, ii, 364).
[3] S. Gibson, *Statuta antiqua universitatis Oxoniensis*, 1931, pp. 21–2.

literature of the Middle Ages. It was a transformation in which Peter of Blois had a place, but in the passage I have just quoted and in several others his aim was to impress us with the extent of his classical learning. There is no need to doubt that he had read a wide range of well-known classical authors, but the vast majority of his quotations from them come straight from John of Salisbury. Peter's worst enemies have, I think, never fully plumbed the depth of his 'plagiarism' or realized the extent to which the imposing edifice of his classical learning was borrowed from his older friend and contemporary. What his letters effectively demonstrate is the exhaustion of classical learning as a source of inspiration, and the rise of a new style and new authors to a position of independent authority. Peter of Blois is a man of this new world pretending to belong to the old. But then, the pretence of antiquity is a mask of many new beginnings.

In anything that Peter of Blois says about himself, and in much that he says about other people, we must expect to find this mixture of *Dichtung und Wahrheit*. But the reasons for the intrusions of fiction vary. In our first example Peter wished to clothe himself in the authority of great names. In the next one, which comes from his middle period—probably from the year 1184 when the collection was being made—an image from the past is used to romanticize the present. Peter is replying to a detractor who had accused him of plagiarism:

> I say confidently, and I appeal to the testimony of many, that I have always been accustomed to dictate my letters as quickly as they can be written. This speed certainly excludes the vice and suspicion of being a compiler. I say it for the sake of truth and not boastfully. The archbishop of Canterbury has sometimes seen me, as you yourself and many others can bear witness, dictating on different subjects to three different scribes and keeping them fully occupied, while I myself both composed and wrote a fourth letter—a feat which only Julius Caesar is said to have equalled.[1]

That Peter of Blois was capable of writing at great speed is very likely, and many passages in his letters suggest that they were written under pressure. It may sometimes have fallen to him as

[1] *Ep.* 92.

chancellor of the archbishop of Canterbury to supervise the work
of three scribes while he composed a letter. But the point of the
passage is in its classical allusion. The legendary image of Julius
Caesar imposed itself on the simple facts of office routine. Once
more the distortion came from an evocation of the classical past;
and once more the source of the image went no further back than
John of Salisbury, from whom Peter borrowed it.[1] But the source
is really unimportant; what matters is the purpose, which is here
the embellishment of events by mixing past and present, symbol
and reality. This principle of embellishment is everywhere at
work in the writings of Peter of Blois.

Finally, here is one last example from his later years, when his
interests had decisively changed and the change had coloured his
view of his own past. Peter is writing to a lascivious poet rebuking
him for introducing (in his colourful Biblical phrase) the habits of
the Gentiles into the sanctuary of the Lord:

> I too (he writes) at one time occupied myself in writing
> frivolities and amorous poems, but by the Grace of Him who
> set me apart from my mother's womb, I put away such things
> when I became a man. The serpent of Moses devoured in
> me the serpent of Pharaoh when the sweet taste of theology
> extinguished the knowledge of vain things. The water of
> Jericho was sweetened by the salt of Elisha when he
> approached the waters and said 'There shall not be any more
> death or sterility in them'. The wisdom which is from above,
> as St. James says, is first pure, then peaceable. Repudiate
> therefore the adulterous embraces of worldly wisdom and
> embrace the study of salvation and present it as a chaste
> virgin to Christ.[2]

Here again there is a substratum of fact. Peter of Blois in his
younger days had been a poet of love. At some point in his career
—though not quite as early as he says—he began to write in a
different style on moral and ecclesiastical subjects. But the
abhorrence with which he speaks of his earlier pursuits was a very
late development; and the flood of Biblical imagery gives a quite
misleading impression of his early conversion. In middle age he

[1] *Policraticus*, vi, 15 (ed. C. C. J. Webb, ii, p. 41).
[2] *Ep.* 76. The date is about 1195.

had written of the change in his habits in quite a different vein:

> Volo resipiscere,
>     linquere,
>     corrigere,
> quod commisi temere.
> Deinceps intendam
>     seriis:
>         pro vitiis
> virtutes rependam.[1]

And later he wrote:

> Olim militaveram
> pompis huius saeculi,
> quibus flores obtuli
>     meae iuventutis.
> Pedem tamen retuli
> Circa vitae vesperam
> nunc daturus operam
>     militiae virtutis.[2]

In these elegantly turned lines of moderate repentance there is nothing of the evangelical fervour which coloured his later recollections of the past. Nor indeed is the evangelical fervour, though it often reappears in his later writings, easily distinguishable from the colours of rhetoric. The Bible had always been part of his rhetorical stock-in-trade, and this stock only became more overwhelmingly abundant with the passage of time. It would be quite unwise to assume from his highly emotional language that he had become a fervent ranter. Equally however it would be unwise to conclude that the change in his rhetoric tells us *nothing* about a change in his outlook. The relation between appearance and reality is always difficult to establish, and in the case of Peter of Blois, using an idiom to which many of the clues are lost, the relationship is even more ambiguous than usual. Peter shared with all his contemporaries an inclination to portray men in a cloud of literary and Biblical allusions, with a strong rhetorical

---

[1] F. J. E. Raby, *Oxford Book of Medieval Latin Verse*, no. 239, from *Carmina Burana*, ed. A. Hilka and O. Schumann.

[2] This is the beginning of a poem which Peter sent to a friend probably in 1185 (*Ep.* 57): it was sent as an example of his more mature style.

light playing upon them: only when he and his contemporary were seen in this light did he think them worthy of a literary memorial.

He was not a hero or a saint, and he knew it. His letters were an escape from the extreme ordinariness of his humdrum existence. In them he spoke like a hero, and stood up on equal terms with those who were far above him in their station in life. But while he denounced ordinariness in others, he knew it to be his own fate. He would have wished, he said, to be martyred for the faith, but the opportunity never seemed to come. He would have wished to inhabit the mountain tops where the athletes of the spirit were to be found, but he had to resign himself to be saved with Lot in the modest cities of the plain. It was only in his letters that he was able to stand in indignation on the mountain top and survey the vices and follies of mankind. To sustain this position, however, it was necessary to paint an idealized picture of himself, his learning, and his superiority to human failings, and to generalize the shortcomings of others.

## IV

As a literary enterprise the collection of letters put out in 1184 succeeded beyond all expectation. Till the end of his life, Peter basked in the fame that they brought him. He defended them against criticism with the ferocity of a tigress defending her young. He could never leave them alone. The briskness of the demand made it possible for him to bring out a succession of new editions. Between 1184 and 1189 he added a few letters, and he dropped some which now seemed unworthy of his literary greatness. Seven years later he added nearly forty new letters and omitted his ineffectual call to the Crusade which had failed. Five years later he added a dozen new letters and padded out the old letters with a new load of classical and Biblical learning. But though the letters brought him an enviable place in the literary world, they brought him no material advancement. The anxieties of the year 1184 had been dispelled when Baldwin, his old fellow-student at Bologna, was finally appointed archbishop of Canterbury in November. Peter was taken into his service, and for the next six years he took a leading part in all the archbishop's affairs—his long dispute with the monks of Canterbury, his propaganda for the

Crusade, his relations with the king. But he rose no higher in the world. He went on the Crusade with the archbishop in 1190, and he buried him in Syria the same year. After this he found it more difficult to get employment. On his way back to England he joined Eleanor the Queen-Mother, and he wrote some letters for her, urging the release of King Richard from captivity. Then he spent a few years with the new archbishop of Canterbury, Hubert Walter, and in 1201-2 we find him briefly in the household of Geoffrey, archbishop of York.[1] By this time he was getting very old, and his career was almost at an end. He managed to make his position more comfortable by exchanging the archdeaconry of Bath for that of London in about 1200, and here he seems to have spent the last twelve years of his life. There was nowhere else for him to go. He had quarrelled with his nephews in France, and no-one wanted him in his native land. So he went on, a foreigner unable to speak the language of the land in which he had lived for over forty years. He complained of age, weakness and criticism, but he continued to write till his death, probably in 1212.[2]

Ever since his return from the Crusade his mind had been turning away from the moral and political issues which had so greatly occupied him during his years in the household of the archbishops of Canterbury, and he began to write a series of works of a more purely religious character—on Confession, of the duties of a bishop, on Christian friendship, and on the reform of the Mass. The last two are the most interesting, for they show the growth of a new effusiveness in his religious aspirations. The treatise on Friendship is now accorded a very low rating among critics, because nearly all the substance was borrowed (without acknowledgement) from Aelred of Rievaulx. But it has a considerable biographical interest. It illustrates Peter's increasing devotion to the ideals of Cistercian piety, especially its interior sweetness and sensibility. It provides also the best examples of his prose style in its last phase, of his growing love of strongly emotive words,

[1] His employments from his return to England in 1191 to his retirement from official business in 1202 are only sparsely documented. Evidence for Peter's movements will be found in *Epp.* 87, 109, 124, 135, 144–6; *Literae Cantuarienses*, ed. J. B. Sheppard, R.S., iii, 379; L. Landon, *Itinerary of Richard I*, Pipe Roll Soc., 1935, p. 139; *Memorials of Fountains Abbey*, Surtees Soc., i, 133n.; *E.H.R.*, 1938, liii, p. 415.

[2] For these last years, see *E.H.R.* 1938, liii, 412–24. The latest survey of the evidence for the date of his transfer from the archdeaconry of Bath to that of London is D. Greenway, 'The succession to Ralph of Diceto, Dean of St. Paul's', *Bull. of the Institute of Historical Research*, 1966, xxxix, 86–95.

and his search for a deeper emotional response to religion in himself.[1]

This was the burden of his plea for the reform of the Mass, about which he wrote three letters to the new Pope Innocent III. He wanted the words of the canon of the Mass to be brought up to date, dropping old colourless phrases and filling the whole central act of Christian worship with 'burning words' expressive of the intense devotion which he had learned from Cistercian literature.[2]

Peter was nothing if not contemporary. In revising his letters, his latest reading was pressed into service, and it often smothered the original contents of the letter with its amplitude. In one of his revisions of his letters he included large extracts from a recent work, the *Verbum Abbreviatum* of the Parisian master, Peter the Chanter, but he had the good sense to drop these intrusions of class-room learning in his latest recensions.[3] Nevertheless his mind began to turn back to his own theological studies as a young man, and several of his last letters, which never found a place in the normal collections, seem to be nothing more than a writing-up of notes he had made long ago in Paris.

His last work shows him in a curiously uncomfortable state of mind. The title he gave it was *De Fide*.[4] In substance it was a collection of authoritative definitions and arguments which had been used to rebut the heresies of the past. But the purpose, which he explains in the preface, was to quieten his own intellectual doubts. They were very late in coming to him, but it somehow adds an unexpected attraction to his personality to think of the archdeacon, ill and lonely, sitting down to calm and fortify his mind by compiling a survey of past errors and replies.

---

[1] *De amicitia Christiana et de caritate Dei et proximi, P.L.* 207, 871–958. There is a modern edition by M. M. Davy, *Un traité de l'amour du XIIᵉ siècle*, 1932, but the editor did not realise that the treatise is largely a rewriting of Aelred's *De Amicitia spirituali* and *Speculum Caritatis (P.L.* 195, 659–702, 505–620). Several analyses of the relation between Aelred and Peter (none of them entirely satisfactory) have been published: see E. Bickel in *Neues Archiv*, 1924, 223–34; E. Vansteenberghe in *Revue des sciences religieuses*, 1932, xii, 572–88. Ph. Delhaye in *R.T.A.M.*, 1948, xv, 304–31. Any future editor would have to take account of the recension of the work with a dedication to William of St. Mère Eglise, Bishop of London, in Bodleian Library MS. Laud misc. 368.

[2] For the three letters on the canon of the Mass (one of them partly but inaccurately printed as *Ep.* 236) see *E.H.R.*, 1938, pp. 421–4.

[3] There are two manuscripts of this recension: Lambeth Palace MS. 421 and Bodleian MS. 570.

[4] Jesus College, Oxford, MS. 39 (unprinted).

## V

What are we to make of so strange and awkward a character, and of an achievement so long admired and now so dead? Was he a learned man or a charlatan? Was he—to put him in the bracket to which he is generally assigned—a humanist? This last is the epithet most often, though rather grudgingly, applied to him. He is said to be the last faded bloom on the delicate plant that had flourished in the first half of the twelfth century and then slowly withered.

In the literary, academic sense in which the word has been traditionally used in universities, I am sure he must score rather low marks as a humanist, and nothing would have annoyed him more than this judgement. He was after all a teacher of Latin before everything else. He was certainly the master of a style greatly admired throughout the Middle Ages, copious, ornate, learned, glowing with burning words. If we can enter into the spirit of it, if we can follow its involved and intricate course through a maze of Scriptural and classical allusions and metaphors, and if we can accept its strange mixture of pious commonplaces and vituperation, we shall have to admit that the language of Peter of Blois is a powerful instrument. But surely it could never be recommended by a post-Renaissance classical scholar as a model.

Nor do I think he would score many marks for appreciation of classical literature. Despite his considerable fund of reading and his furious claims to much more than he possessed, I know no remark of his which shows the slightest genuine feeling for any one classical author. Indeed, he really preferred the letters of his contemporary Hildebert to those of Seneca, the language of Justinian or Aelred of Rievaulx to that of Cicero, the rhetoric of Bologna and Tours to that of classical Rome. He never speaks, as Petrarch does, of the discovery of a classical author as marking a stage in his spiritual development, or bringing a revelation of new truth or opening up a new experience. On the contrary, he used everything as it came to hand to embellish his prose and to illustrate his argument without caring about its source.

In all this he was typical of the twelfth century scholarly revival. The scholars of that age had no strong feeling for their sources. They had no nostalgia for the past, unless it were the nostalgia for the dream-world of King Arthur or Alexander. They had no desire to find a refuge in the past. This nostalgia and desire for refuge were products of the despair and disillusionment of the fourteenth century. The scholars of the twelfth century looked back only for the quite practical purpose of equipping themselves to look forward. The ancient authors were a mine of information on science, philosophy, human nature and human speech to be worked over till they had given up all their secrets. It was in this spirit that John of Salisbury worked, patiently picking over the literary deposit of the past. The names of Lucan, Macrobius, Martianus Capella, Ovid, Cicero, follow each other in his pages with a fine impartiality, each in turn pointing a doctrine or adorning a sentence. Once the nectar had been extracted, John of Salisbury passed on like a bee to another flower, diligently, unemotionally, not stopping to consider whether it was a cowslip or clover, so long as it gave up its treasure. He made it unnecesary for anyone to do that work again, and it would be foolish to blame Peter of Blois, who came after him, for not sucking away a second time at the same material. It is not his plagiarism, but his denial of it that sets him apart from his contemporaries.

The truth is that the growing humanism of the twelfth century was not mainly to be seen in its literary appreciation of the Latin classics, but in its theology, law, philosophy and politics. What ancient Latin literature contributed to the higher reaches of learning was a store of grand and magnanimous actions, and much information about the constitution of the universe. But in the end it was in the works of Aristotle and Justinian that the ancient past provided the chief instruments of twelfth century humanism. The ordered system of thought and practice that emerged from these sources was a great achievement: we may almost say, the fundamental achievement of European thought. Peter of Blois did not contribute much to this achievement but he owed more to it than he suspected. He gave it an airing in his letters. Just as Addison being similarly under-employed in political life aimed at bringing 'philosophy out of closets and libraries, schools and colleges, to dwell in clubs and assemblies, at tea-tables and in coffee-houses', so Peter of Blois brought the learning of his time, if not to coffee houses and assembly rooms, yet to bishops, abbots and clerks, who were busier men than he, and to students and writers who hoped to embellish their prose.

He was no innovator; he was not a powerful thinker; he was not a technically proficient lawyer or theologian. His great merits were his extreme sensitivity to the climate of thought in which he lived, and a power of expressing the changing moods of his time in colourful and ornate prose which appealed to generations of readers. He fell for everything: now all for the Crusade, now for the Inner Life; now all for government, now deploring its corruptions; now all for love, and now for chastity. He expressed every turn of thought with equal vigour. His description of Henry II is the first tolerably realistic portrait of any English king. His account of that Christian firebrand, Reginald of Chatillon, gives us our best view of the passions aroused by the disasters which preceded the Third Crusade. His account of the miseries of court life is certainly more vivid than any other description of this time, and it was sufficiently alive three hundred years later to serve as a model for Aeneas Silvius—a humanist who affected to think little of Peter of Blois—when he attempted a similar work.[1] The list could easily be prolonged, and it establishes Peter of Blois as one of the most effective spokesman for his age.

To be perceptive and articulate, to bring to a wide public the ideas of the schools and the events of public life, and to keep an audience for four hundred tears, constitute a fair claim to fame. But these qualities of rapid assimilation and unfettered utterance also help to explain some of the uncertainties in Peter's own breast. It is in these uncertainties that he is most clearly a humanist.

He was uncertain about himself and about his future. There was little room in society for a man of his unspecialized talents. He could do many things well, but nothing with distinction except with his pen. The pen without influence or position or fortune is a frail support, and if Peter of Blois repels us by his strident assertivism and prevarication, we must remark how insecure and lonely he was. He is never more convincing than when he speaks of the loneliness of his long exile in a foreign land. It is this uncertainty, and the literary ambitions which grew out of his unease, which gave him some of the characteristics of the later humanists of the Renaissance. The intense seriousness with

---

[1] *Der Briefwechsel des Eneas Silvius Piccolomini*, ed. R. Wolkan, i, p. 329: Aeneas flatters Adam of Moleyns by telling him that his letter was far superior to those of Peter of Blois—a form of flattery which shows that Peter was generally considered the best. For Aeneas's own use of Peter, see *op. cit.*, pp. 453–87.

which he asserted his position as an independent man of letters, the vehement protestations of originality, and his desire for fame, were grounded in his fears. He foreshadowed a time when authorship, struggling out of hierarchical and scholastic restraints, would become a profession, and the author a formidable power in society. But that time had not yet come.

Another of his uncertainties concerned the true claim to be made for his literary productions. He might have claimed with justice that they were notable embodiments of the new rhetoric, that they combined the excellencies of the schools of Tours and Bologna, that they were adorned with the learning of Paris and with the imagery of Cîteaux, that his letters were—in the words of the later Oxford statute—*litterae compositae verbis decentibus non ampulosis aut sesquipedalibus, et clausulis succinctis, decoris, metaphoris manifestis, et quantum possint sententia refertis.* All this would have been true, and it represented his real title to fame. It was for these qualities that his letters continued to be read: they gave him his claim to be numbered among the great *dictatores* of the Middle Ages. Why then did he not make these claims, which were true, but others which were false? Because the influences which were guiding medieval literature away from its classical models were not yet clearly recognized, nor wholly respectable. Peter of Blois deplored the decline in the study of the classics; but he did not see how inexorably this decline had been prepared by the great generation of writers at the beginning of the century; nor could he see that he was himself an illustration of the decline and of the triumph of new interests and new standards of taste.

Lastly, he was uncertain about his own faith. He was not one of the numerous cynics of the late twelfth century. Throughout his literary life he maintained a strong preference for the simplicities of the Cistercian or Carthusian Orders in contrast to the elaborate rites of the Benedictines, and this preference grew with the years. In his old age the language of religious fervour came to him more and more easily, and we begin to hear a great deal of the liquifying of the soul in torrents of eternal delight. It is hard to take this language quite seriously except as the expression of an unfulfilled aspiration. But, as we know, it too—like much emotional religion of the late Middle Ages—was grounded in doubts and hesitations about the formulas of faith.

Peter of Blois was a man of many hesitations and uncertainties; hesitating between old and new, between the religious life and the world, between solitude and business, between faith and unbelief. This was one reason for his success: he had something for everyone. But there was one thing which he never doubted, and in this he found a refuge from all his doubts. He believed in his powers as a writer. However wrong he might be about himself in other respects, he was right in this, and he was able to persuade others of its truth. His confidence in this belief was prodigious.

This ill-assorted mixture of confidence and uncertainty made him quarrelsome, resentful of criticism and absurdly sensitive to charges which were true. But he maintained his independence with a tenacity of which he was justifiably proud. He made sacrifices for this independence, and if fame be worth having, the sacrifices were worth making. For an ambitious man, to end as an archdeacon is failure. But an archdeacon who is read for four hundred years and not forgotten after seven hundred and fifty years cannot be called a failure. That is the success he would have desired, and for this success, worldly failure was essential. If he had been busy and rich, a bishop in his native land, he would have been forgotten. Perhaps he realized this when he refused a bishopric. But perhaps the bishopric (it was Rochester) was too poor, and he was too proud, to accept. Perhaps he was never even offered it, and he is telling a lie when he says he refused. We cannot be sure. Much is uncertain. But in all these uncertainties of mind and will and self-revelation we seem to see the shadowy outline of a Petrarch or Erasmus.

## NOTE ON THE MANUSCRIPTS

In 1926 the late Mr. E. S. Cohn published a survey of the manuscripts of Peter of Blois's letters (*E.H.R.* xli, 43–60). It was the first attempt to put the complicated history of the collection on a firm foundation, and it is no discredit to Mr. Cohn, who worked first and worked alone, to say that the jungle—there is none more impenetrable than the tangle of a widely disseminated collection of letters—in the end overwhelmed him. I followed him into the jungle, and if I was not overwhelmed it was largely because I had the benefit of his labours and example. With the large-hearted generosity which his friends will remember and which after so many years it is a pleasure to commemorate, he gave me his transcript of the Oriel College manuscript and his friendship to the end. I write this note in his memory.

The first necessity in a jungle is to keep a sense of direction and avoid side-tracks. In studying the manuscripts of these letters there is a similar need to ignore the misleading or insignificant evidence of ninety-five per cent of the manuscripts and to concentrate on those few that show the true line of development. I cannot claim to have done this as well as I should have wished, but it may be of some value to later users of the letters to give a brief account of the growth of the collection, so far as I have been able to elucidate it. In what follows, the following points should be kept in mind:

1.  It is impossible in the space available to note internal changes in the texts of the letters, although these often provide the essential clues to the development of the collection as a whole.
2.  I have divided the history of the collection into six stages, but it is somewhat misleading to present the matter in this simple form. Into every copy of his letters which Peter made or caused to be made he probably introduced additions, subtractions, and alterations appropriate to the occasion. Some of these changes, but not all, were repeated in all later copies. I have tried to concentrate on major permanent changes, but it is not always easy to distinguish them from minor and transitory ones.
3.  A very high proportion of the existing manuscripts show signs of disorders and conflations which are certainly not the work of the author. I have generally omitted these for the sake of simplicity, but some of them provide valuable evidence of the growth of the collection and they would have to be included in a more complete survey.
4.  In indicating the contents of the various recensions I have followed the numbering of the letters in the printed edition (*P.L.* 207) and I have not attempted to show the order in which the letters appear in the manuscripts.
5.  Several letters, which originally formed part of the letter-collection, are printed as separate treatises in *P.L.* 207. They are included in the following survey with these abbreviated titles:

*Canon Ep.*  :  *Canon Episcopalis, P.L.* 207, 1097–1112
*De Conf.*   :  *De Confessione*, ibid. 1077–1092

*De Pen.* : *De Poenitentia*, ibid. 1091–1098
*De Pereg.* : *De Hierosolymitana Peregrinatione*, ibid. 1057–
1070
*In Dep.* : *Invectiva in depravatorem*, ibid. 1113–1128
*Inst. Fid.* : *Instructio Fidei Catholicae*, ibid. 1069–1078

Bearing in mind these limitations, the main stages in the growth of the collection are:

I (1184): *Epp.* 1–15, 17, 19, 21, 22, 24, 26, 28, 30, 32–56, 58–62, 65–75, 77–86, 88, 90–95, 101, 128, 130, 136, 150, 153–6, 158, 159, 162–4, 173, *Inst. Fid.*
*MSS.*: Arras 200, xiii–xiv C.
Chartres 208, xiii C[1]
Cambridge, Corpus Christi College, 425, xv C. (incomplete)
Cues 80, xv C. (omits 85)
London, B.M. Harl. 3684, xv C.
Paris, B.N. n.a.l. 785, xiii C (omits 72, 86, 90–5, 164, 173, *Inst. Fid.*)

II (c. 1189): *Epp.* 1–13, 15, 17, 19, 21, 22, 24, 26, 28, 30, 32–62, 65–75, 77–86, 88, 90–101, 128, 130, 136, 150, 153–6, 158, 162, 163, 173, *Inst. Fid.*, *De Pereg.*
*MSS.*: Aberdeen 205, xiii C. (omits *De Pereg.*)
London, B.M. Royal 8F xvii, xiii C.
Harl. 325, xiii C.
Gray's Inn 7, xiv C. (omits 101, 136, *De Pereg.*)
Oxford, Exeter Coll. 31, xiv C.
Paris, B.N. lat. 16714, xiii C.
lat. 18587, xiv C.

IIa (c. 1195): I place here a group of MSS. containing the same collection of letters as II with a supplement, which illustrates a period of experiment with the text. The MSS. are closely related in text and contents, but with annotations and additions that did not find a permanent place in the collection.
*MSS.*: London, Lambeth 421, xii–xiii C.
Milan, Ambrosian C 103 sup. xii–xiii C.[2]
Oxford, Bodl. 570, xv C.

[1] This manuscript appears to have been among those destroyed in 1944, but I have photographs.
[2] For an account of some of the marginal additions in this MS. see G. Morin, 'Gloriosus Magister Adam', *Rev. Bénédictine*, 1932, xliv.

III (c. 1196): *Epp.* 1–62, 65–75, 77–86, 88, 90–125, 128–131, 242[1]+134 pt. ii, 136, 150, 153–6, 158, 162, 163, 173, 208, 214, *Inst. Fid., De Conf., De Pen.*

*MSS.*: London, B.M. Cotton Vesp. E xi, xiii C.
Oxford, Oriel Coll. 76, xiii–xiv C. (incomplete)

IV (c. 1198): *Epp.* 1–127, 131–5, 137–9, 143–8, *Inst. Fid., De Pen., De Conf., Canon Ep., In Deprav.*

*MSS.*: Berlin 187 (Phillipps 1697), xiii C. (incomplete)
Cambridge, Corpus Christi Coll. 266, early xiii C. (omits 139, 144–8, *De Pen. De Conf., In deprav.*)
St. John's Coll. 55, xiv C. (adds 128 at end)
University Lib. ff. v. 46, xiv C.
Oxford, Bodl. lat. misc. d. 6, xiii–xiv C. (omissions as in CCCC 266)
Paris, B.N. lat. 14, 764, early xiii C. (incomplete)

V (1202):[2] *Epp.* 1–127, 131–5, 137–152, *Inst. Fid., Canon Ep., In Deprav.*

*MSS.*: Erfurt Ampl. F. 71, early xv C. ff. 21$^v$–138$^v$
Karlsruhe 51, xv C (A.D. 1445) (adds *De Pereg.*)
London, B.M. Harl. 3672, xv C. (adds *De Pereg.*)
Royal 10 Axviii, xv C. (incomplete)
Oxford, New College 127, xv C. (adds 209–12, 227, 229, 230, 235, 239–41, 243, see below)

VI (1202–1212): MSS. with late letters that never became part of the collection. Of these, the following letters have been printed: 209–12, 227, 229, 230, 235–6, 239, 240, 241, 243. But there are many unprinted letters in the Erfurt MS and its copy at Bamberg.[3]

Bamberg B.iv. 38, xv C. (A.D. 1472–3)
Erfurt Amplon. F.71, early xv C. ff. 186–197, 200–224
London, B. M. Arundel 227, xiv–xv C.
Oxford, New Coll. 127, xv C.
Cambridge, Sidney Sussex Coll. 92, xvii C.

---

[1] This is an earlier version of *Ep.* 134 part i.

[2] Although I know no MS. of this recension before the xv C. and most of them are in Germany, I am fairly confident that the recension goes back to Peter's lifetime and, more tentatively, that it was discovered in London, together with the large supplement of letters written between 1202 and 1212 by, or for, the German scholar and collector Amplonius Ratinck. (See *E.H.R.* 1938, liii, 412–24).

[3] See *E.H.R.* 1938, liii, 412–24.

# III

## EUROPE AND THE 'OTHER WORLD'[1]

[1] The idea that the British Isles belonged to a world apart from Europe was a commonplace of ancient geography. Isidore, *Etymologiae*, xiv, 6, 2, calls Britain an 'insula interfuso mari toto orbe divisa', and Pope Urban II spoke of Archbishop Anselm as 'patriarcha alterius orbis'. The citizens of Rome, according to Otto of Freising (*Gesta Frederici*, ii, 29) told Frederick I that their city had extended the Empire to the boundaries of the world, 'quin etiam *insulas extra orbem positas* orbi adiciens.' The map on Pl. III illustrates the position of Britain as it was conceived in the early twelfth century.

# 8

## ENGLAND'S FIRST ENTRY
## INTO EUROPE

### I

In these pages I propose to examine some aspects of the first experiment in the political unity of England and the Continent in the century and a half after 1066, and especially the connection between this experience and the growth of a national consciousness. The two themes are not at first sight obviously connected, but we shall see that political measures, especially if they are unwelcome to a large proportion of the population, have some surprising repercussions on popular sentiments and on the growth of a sense of corporate identity.

The sense of corporate identity which came into existence in England after 1066 was associated with an experience of oppression, and it is quite different from anything we find at an earlier date. It is not at all easy to analyse a sentiment of unity among people in very different situations, but it seems clear that by the time of the Norman Conquest Englishmen had already passed through two phases in the development of a national consciousness. The first phase can be observed as early as the eighth century when there was a widespread sense of unity between English people and Germanic peoples on the Continent. The remembrance of a common ancestry pervaded the earliest English literature, and provided one of the main motives for missionary activity in Germany in the eighth century. This recollection was probably still a force to be reckoned with in the eleventh century, but by the time of the Conquest a more insular sentiment had come into existence. It was associated with the possession of a single language, a unique calendar of saints, an ancient royal house, and a deliverance from the fearful danger which had threatened the total destruction of kingdom and Christianity by the Vikings. The events of 1066 started a third phase by weakening or destroying both these early bonds of unity, and by making England part of a continental political system. The Norman Conquest had some very complicated repercussions on the ways in which Englishmen looked on themselves and their position in the world, and we must begin by looking at the immediate effects somewhat closely.

The first thing that needs to be mentioned is the effect of the imposition of a foreign aristocracy. It is easy for Englishmen, who later became accustomed to being a foreign aristocracy in various parts of the world, to forget how grievous a thing it is for those beneath: not perhaps for everyone, but certainly for those members of the subject-race who are most articulate. It was only in the monasteries that articulate Englishmen survived the Conquest with their society intact. The Anglo-Saxon aristocracy had ceased to exist: only the monks remained to speak for them. In one sense the monasteries had very little to complain about. They had kept their lands; they were the only place where Englishmen in the first two generations after the Conquest could live without any obvious diminution of status. The monks of English origin probably formed a majority in the great monastic communities for a generation after the Conquest, and they were an influential part of the monastic population for two generations. Yet they had their grievances; and in tightly-knit communities grievances are much more potent than the mild satisfaction of well-being. They had seen their families destroyed, and with them had disappeared those secular connections which gave a monk some consequence in the world and some expectation of promotion. Within a few years nearly every abbot and high dignitary in the Church was a foreigner. The English monks saw foreigners infiltrating their communities, speaking an unknown tongue, having the ear of the abbot, holding every position of responsibility. These things were hard to bear. Perhaps monks should not have thought of such things, but certainly they did.

Then, beyond these personal considerations, they had a grievance about the demolition of their past. A conquering race always despises the rites, relics, saints and learning of the conquered, and the Normans were no exception. It is a pure illusion to suppose that a common Christianity and rule of life made these differences seem unimportant. On the contrary it only added to the intensity of the hostility. There is no need to record here the tensions which followed, nor the remarkable efforts which were made by the monastic communities to salvage their past and to assert the respectability of the objects of their devotion. The story of the last flowering of Anglo-Saxon culture after the Conquest—fascinating and important though it is—must be told elsewhere. I shall simply give one illustration of the background of racial tension which lay behind the post-Conquest monastic efforts to revive the Old English past.

The Old English aristocracy left only one martyr to the national cause—Waltheof, earl of Northumberland and lord of Huntingdon, who was executed in 1076. His loyalty to the English cause is in fact highly suspect, but he was undoubtedly executed by the Normans as a traitor and this was enough. His body was removed from the place of execution to his local monastery at Crowland, and sixteen years later it was reported to be still uncorrupt. From this date his tomb became the scene of miracles. His body was cared for by Englishmen; Englishmen flocked to his tomb and were cured by his miraculous intervention. The Normans took no part at all in this; they mocked and doubted, and told their tale of treachery. As late as 1120, when the first passions of the Conquest had died away, the story still divided men along national lines: for the Normans Waltheof was a traitor; for the English a hero and a martyr. Then quite suddenly Norman scorn began to retreat before the accumulating evidence of Waltheof's miraculous powers.[1] In a society dependent on miracles for much that made life tolerable, it was hard to be a sceptic for long. Miracles were the main arguments in establishing truth in the pre-scholastic age, and they triumphed in the end. Normans began to frequent the tomb alongside Englishmen, mocking gave way to acquiescence, and historians like William of Malmesbury (who had long hesitated between two opinions) began to adjust their narratives accordingly. The miracles were a common ground where all men could meet. This is one of the earliest signs that the rancour of the Conquest was beginning to fade away: it is also a sign of its early intensity in religious communities.

---

[1] For the English veneration of Waltheof in the face of Norman hostility, see *Liber de vita, morte, et miracula Waltheofi* by William, monk of Crowland (ed. C. P. Cooper, *Report on Rymer's Foedera*, 1869, ii, 87) and Ordericus Vitalis, *Historia Ecclesiastica*, ed. A. Le Prévost and L. Delisle, ii, 260–7, 285–9. For the change of mind of the Normans, see William of Malmesbury *Gesta Pontificum*, ed. N. E. S. A. Hamilton, *R.S.*, 321–2 and *Gesta Regum*, ed. W. Stubbs, *R.S.* ii, 312.

There were other influences also at work to produce an accept-able level of concord in English society by about the middle of the twelfth century. Intermarriage; the gradual replacement of English by French as the vernacular of cultivated people even of English descent; the romanticizing of Old English history; the mere passage of time—all these things helped to produce a single nation at the top, which spoke French but embraced Old English history and legends as its own. Even the grandson of the English hero Waltheof normally spoke French as he moved among the aristocratic families to which he was related; and the descendants of the conquering race found no difficulty in admiring him as the grandson of the English martyr who had resisted the tyranny of the Conqueror.[1]

In the first fifty or sixty years after the Conquest, English monks fought a battle for the survival of English history and traditions in the face of Norman hostility. The battle was won in the end by Englishmen adopting the French language and manners, and by turning Old English history into a French romance. The old insularity had gone for good. The still older unity of the whole English people with the Germanic people on the Continent was not now even a memory. Henceforth the English belonged to a great Continental system; but, as we shall see, the strains imposed by this system helped to create a new insularity and a new national consciousness. It is with this situation that we shall now be concerned.

## II

The Continental connection dominated English government throughout the twelfth century. Nearly everything that happened in English government either stemmed from or was influenced by this basic fact. From the point of view of her Norman and Angevin kings England had two main functions: it gave them a royal title which made them the equals of the greatest rulers of Europe, and it provided them with a base from which they could operate on the Continent. They were mesmerized by the prospect of Continental glory. This may seem to us a strange miscalculation

---

[1] The French habits and connections of the younger Waltheof are well brought out in Jocelyn of Furness, *Vita sancti Walthevi* (*Acta Sanctorum, Aug.,* i, 249–78).

when we consider how much more might have been won in Ireland, Scotland and Wales at a fraction of the cost of maintaining the Continental connection. But these peripheral countries interested the kings of England only intermittently so long as they had a foothold on the Continent. For that matter England itself scarcely interested them. The great governmental development in England during the century was a token, not of their interest, but of their lack of interest in England. It it very doubtful whether the kings had any policy at all in England; they had only expedients for furthering a policy elsewhere. To preserve and extend the Norman and Angevin family inheritance; to press on into the south of France, even perhaps into Italy; to support allies in Flanders and the Rhineland; these were the great objects of the English kings. For these objects they were prepared to take every kind of risk. The variations in their personal character made very little difference: a prudent king like Henry I deviated from all the normal rules of his far-sighted government to seize and keep Normandy; a wise king like Henry II quarrelled with all his family to avoid any diminution in his Continental lordship; even John was willing to rouse and ruin himself in pursuing an impossible policy of restoring his position in France; and so it went on almost to the end of the Middle Ages.

The expectation that England would for ever be joined to the Continent died hard, and it was not kept alive simply by royal ambitions and designs. In most ways the bonds between England and the Continent were closer at the end of the twelfth century than they had ever been. The children of Henry II were European figures connected by marriage with the ruling houses of France, Germany, Castille and Sicily. Henry's eldest son was the most glamorous figure in the society of the French aristocracy. Henry's daughter, who went to Germany in 1168 as the bride of Henry the Lion, had the *Song of Roland* translated into German as a gift for her husband.[1] Nothing could be more French. The intellectual isolation, which had been so marked a feature of pre-Conquest England, was a thing of the distant past. English scholars moved

[1] The German translator of the poem tells us that a certain Duke Henry brought him the book to translate at the desire of his wife, the daughter of a powerful king. There have been various views about the identity of this duke, but the identification with Henry the Lion is much the most likely. (See *Les textes de la chanson de Roland*, ed. R. Mortier: x. *Le texte de Conrad*, ed. J. Graff, 1944, pp. iii–vi).

freely among the schools of Europe. They occupied positions of the highest distinction in Paris and Bologna, and nearly all the masters of Oxford, Lincoln and Exeter had studied abroad. Yet this freedom of movement was not a symptom of equality. Academically, as well as in the *mores* of aristocratic life, England was a colony of the intellectual empire of France, and its colonial status was emphasized by the fact that, while nearly every English scholar of distinction went to France to study, and often did not return, no distinguished French scholars came to England either to study or to teach.

Economically, the links of England and the Continent were as powerful as those of politics and culture. For the first time in its history, western Europe had emerged in the twelfth century as a single powerful and aggressive economic system. In relation to its Moslem and Byzantine neighbours Europe had become a great manufacturing area engaged in large-scale industrial processes, exporting bulky cargoes across seas controlled by western powers. When all allowances have been made for the primitive conditions of commercial and industrial enterprise, and for the stubborn obstacles imposed by rulers on economic development, it is permissible to see twelfth-century England as part of a common market which came into existence despite governments and by the mere force of commercial enterprise. This 'common market' stretched from Yorkshire, through the industrial towns of Flanders and the fairs of Champagne, to the great towns of Italy and the ports on every shore of the Mediterranean. England's function in this system was that of the greatest primary producer for industry and international trade. It was another mark of England's colonial status that it produced the raw materials: the commercial enterprise which moved the materials, and the manufacturing power which processed them, were concentrated abroad.

This then was the situation in the later years of the twelfth century. Not only in politics, but in aristocratic social life and culture, in its economic system and its ecclesiastical organization, England was joined to the Continent. It was an integral but subordinate part of a western European order. Never before or since has the union of England with the community of Europe been so all-embracing and so thoroughly accepted as part of the nature of things.

## III

It is, however, in the nature of all movements towards unity to set up a contrary current, and to make people more conscious of their own identity as the ties which bind them to their neighbours become stronger. We find this expressed in many harmless ways —in dialogues between wine and beer extolling and ridiculing the rival products of France and England, in dialogues between Frenchmen and Englishmen exploring more or less offensively the characteristics of the two nations, and in a variety of abusive jokes on the same theme. One of these jokes, to the effect that Englishmen had tails which they cunningly concealed, had a very long life. It first appeared about the middle of the twelfth century; it spread like wildfire throughout Europe and aroused sniggers at the expense of the English Crusaders when they arrived in Sicily in 1190; it was still going strong in the seventeenth century and was not quite dead in the nineteenth. It is a melancholy testimony to the paucity of good jokes that this one was thought so funny for so long.[1]

The tendency to ridicule our neighbours is in one sense a symptom of unity. But is is also a sign of tension, and the tensions aroused by the political relationship with the Continent go much deeper than these mild jests might suggest. Some of the symptoms are small and unimportant, others are of far-reaching importance; but they all tell the same story. Among the less important was the speech of the aristocracy. Although the English nobility spoke French, their speech was becoming noticeably an inferior dialect. This was remarked even at the highest level. When King Henry II's son Geoffrey resigned his bishopric of Lincoln in 1182, he announced his resignation in a French which was so unintelligible that the archbishop had to ask what he said: 'He is speaking the French of Marlborough', said Walter Map.[2] This is a small symptom of estrangement, but ten years later there was a more important one. In the years 1190–3 we have the first example of a great political figure in England being hated for being French. No doubt there are other reasons for hating William Longchamp,

---

[1] See G. Neilson, *Anglicus caudatus, a medieval slander*, 1896. The earliest evidence for the 'slander' appears to be in Wace, *Le Roman de Brut*, ed. I. Arnold, 1930, ii, pp. 718–9, ll. 13713–13744, about 1150; but there are traces of the story earlier in William of Malmesbury.

[2] Walter Map, *De Nugis Curialium*, ed. M. R. James, pp. 246–7. Map gives the explanation of this *mot*: at Marlborough there is a spring from which whoever drinks speaks barbarous French.

bishop of Ely, royal chancellor, papal legate, and ruler of England during Richard I's absence on Crusade, but one reason given was that he went about with a French retinue of jongleurs and syco-phants, and that he couldn't speak English.[1] This would have been quite incomprehensible as a ground of criticism fifty years earlier.

William Longchamp was an outsider and foreigner whom everyone in England and Normandy could agree to hate, with the conspicuous exception of that other foreigner Peter of Blois. But between the Frenchmen of Normandy and those of England the differences were becoming marked, preparing the ground for the integration of Normandy with France in the thirteenth century, and for the dissociation of both of them from England. There is a formula used in the royal chancery which bears unconscious testi-mony to the widening gap. From 1066 until the first year of Henry II the English kings had a standard formula for addressing their subjects in England: they were their 'faithful people, *both French and English*'. This phrase was used exclusively to distinguish the two classes of men in England: the aristocracy who were 'French', and the people who were 'English'. Before 1155, the phrase was never used, so far as I know, to distinguish the king's subjects in France from his subjects in England. The distinction was regarded as one of race, not geography. But in this year the royal chancery made a sudden change of usage. Thereafter it used the phrase *only* to distinguish all the king's subjects in England from all those in France. From this time therefore, in the phraseology of the royal chancery, all who lived in England, whether nobility or not, were 'English', and all who lived in France were 'French'.[2] It is very striking that this change should have been made when royal policy was more than ever orientated towards extending the Anglo-French connection, and when French had reached its widest diffusion as the vernacular language of England. Royal chanceries are conservative organizations, and they are not apt to be quick in observing social change; so we may be sure that by the middle of the twelfth century, the distinction between the real Frenchmen

---

[1] *Chronica Rogeri de Hoveden*, R.S., ed. W. Stubbs, iii, 141–7, quoting a contemporary letter of Hugh of Nonant, Bishop of Coventry: there is a reply to this letter by Peter of Blois (*Ep.* 89).

[2] The earlier practice persists in the royal charters of the first two years of Henry II (see L. Delisle and E. Berger, *Recueil des Actes de Henri II*, 1909–27, nos. 5, 6, 8 and 10 of the years 1155–6), but thereafter the use of the phrase 'omnibus ministris et fidelibus suis Francis et Anglis' seems to be used only when the charter applied to the Angevin lands in both France and England.

of France and those who merely spoke French in England was very clear.

Certainly those who knew France best, especially the young, were conscious of the difference when they came to England. For one thing, there were no tournaments and there was no chivalry in England. There were only some pale reflections of the tournament in meetings called 'plaideices', which bore as much relation to tournaments as harriers to foxhunts. We know of this difference between England and the Continent from several sources, but it is nowhere more vividly illustrated than in the poetic Life of William Marshal, the man who became regent of England in his old age. When he was a young man, his guardian, the chamberlain of Normandy told him that he should not stay in England long because it was not a good place for chivalry. For chivalry, he said, he must come to Normandy or Brittany, or anywhere in northern France.[1] William Marshal and many other young men of England, led by the heir to the throne, took this advice. They could find tournaments all over northern France about once a fortnight in the season; to stay in England was deadly dull, as they found when the heir was confined to England for a year after the rebellion of 1173.

It was a serious matter that the English nobility had to go to France for exercise in the art of knightly combat. It gave France a distinct military advantage over England, which lasted till the Hundred Years' War. The French nobility who frequented tournaments included men of the highest political importance—the duke of Burgundy, the count of Flanders, the counts of Blois, Clermont, and Boulogne, and many others. But the English came as playboys or adventurers because they had nothing else to do. They were looked on as easy game by the tougher knights of France until the professionalism of William Marshal gave them a reputation for military competence. But they remained rootless and restless young aristocrats with no responsibilities at home.

The boredom of the young in England emphasized the essential difference between England and France. The land of

---

[1] The only exception I have found to this general judgement on the difference between England and France in the twelfth century is in a poem by a Cluniac visitor to England, Richard la Poitevin, in the later years of King Stephen's reign, printed by W. Wattenbach, *Neues Archiv*, i, 600–4. The poet addresses England as a country 'quae nihil a Gallis, sed Gallia mutuat inde quiquid laetitiae, quicquid amoris habet'. It is interesting that this dissentient view should have been expressed at the moment when royal government in England was at its lowest ebb.

France was acquiring a mysterious power to attract interest and inspire affection. No-one felt like this about England. We know of only one Englishman who had a sentimental attachment to English soil similar to that deep and lasting devotion to the soil of France which found its first expression in the twelfth century. This was Edgar Atheling, the last male descendant of the Old English royal house, the man who should have been king. He had wandered far and wide after 1066—in Scotland, Flanders, Normandy, Apulia and the Holy Land. Both the Greek and German emperors had tried to enlist him in their service, but (we are told) he despised all these foreign offers for love of his native land, and he came back to England to live and die as an obscure country gentleman—a Richard Cromwell of the twelfth century with a genuine title to the Throne. Surely, we might think, here was an example to inspire the enthusiasm of his fellow-countrymen. But William of Malmesbury, who reported the story and who loved English history, did not see it like this. He saw it as a tale of folly. He could not understand a man who so loved his native land that he could find nothing sweet except in breathing his native air. He had nothing but censure for the fatuous longing which had led Edgar to turn his back on greatness and wear out his solitary and silent old age in the English countryside.[1]

At the time when William of Malmesbury was passing these strictures on the English patriot, the land of France was acquiring the character which emotionally it has never lost. The *Song of Roland* is the first expression of a new and lasting enthusiasm for the sweet soil of France. The real hero of the poem is not Charlemagne or even Roland, but France, *la douce, la belle*, the sacred land. France is never mentioned in the poem without one or other of these adjectives, and the first of them, *douce* became inseparably attached to the idea of the country.[2]

Englishmen in the time of Henry II were beginning to realize that England lacked something that France possessed. The young heir to the throne would have said it lacked chivalry; but others described the deficiency in more political and more sinister terms.

[1] *Gesta Regum*, ii, 310.
[2] The occasions on which France is characterised as 'dulce' in the Song of Roland are too numerous to mention. In l. 1695, it is also 'la bele'; in l. 2311, *asolue* (redeemed). In similar vein Peter of Blois wrote to his brother when he got back to France from Sicily in 1168, 'Sumus, frater, in dulci Francia, quae sola, teste Hieronimo, monstra non habet. Bonum est nos hic esse . . . Mihi sufficit si illic vivam et moriar ubi natus sum et nutritus.' (*Ep.* 93)

John of Salisbury was one of them. He went to France in 1164 and described his arrival in these terms:

> After crossing the sea I seemed to feel the breath of a gentler breeze after our storms and tempests, and I admired with joy the wealth and abundance on all sides, and a people quiet and contented.

He went on to Paris and a similar scene met his eyes:

> Here, when I saw the abundance of food, the light-heartedness of the people, the respect paid to the clergy, the majesty and glory of the whole church and the various employments of the seekers after truth, I looked on it as a veritable Jacob's ladder with its summit reaching to the skies and the angels ascending and descending. In the excitement of my happy pilgrimage I was forced to say, 'Truly the Lord is in this place and I knew it not', Then that line of poetry came to my mind—
> Happy is the exile driven to this place.[1]

John of Salisbury had good reason to be glad to be out of England at this time, but his impression of the ease of French life is all the more striking because he relished the sense of English political superiority: 'The French fear our king and hate him equally, but so far as they are concerned he can sleep soundly', he wrote. These were prosperous years for England, but there was not much expression of joy. The country was rich, and we have a fine contemporary description of the wealth of London to set beside John of Salisbury's praise of Paris. Yet the contrast is very striking. There was no romance, no liberality, certainly no Jacob's ladder, in London. Even in the mid-twelfth century the city was described as if it were an over-loaded sideboard groaning under the weight of expensive plate and barons of beef, and the chivalry of France would have smiled at the youth of London 'issuing from the gates equipped with lances and military shields'.[2]

There was no doubt that England was wealthy, but in the eyes of contemporaries it lacked the liberality which made wealth praiseworthy. The wealth tended to be used, so they said, not openhandedly, but craftily and for purposes of policy. About 1160

---

[1] *Ep.* 134 (*P.L.* 199, 111–115).
[2] William Fitz Stephen, *Descriptio nobilissimae civitatis Londoniae*, in *Materials for the History of Thomas Becket*, *R.S.* ed. J. C. Robertson, 1877, iii, 10–11.

a canon of Rheims wrote a fairly elaborate account of the English based on this premise: they won their way by guile and gold and not by honest steel; and for relaxation they gave themselves to the pleasures of the table rather than to warlike exercises—to *gula* rather than *galea*. This same canon was I think the first to develop the theme of perfidious Albion, and like many other ideas of this formative period it stuck.[1]

The differences between the lands and peoples of England and France, which writers at this time were the first to detect, remained part of the common stock of European ideas for several centuries. We even find a first attempt to give a scientific explanation of these differences. This is found in a letter of Peter of Celle to Nicholas of St. Albans in about 1178. The author is writing about the Feast of the Immaculate Conception which Englishmen had been specially active in promoting, and he says:

> Your island is surrounded by water, and not unnaturally its inhabitants are affected by the nature of the element in which they live. Unsubstantial fantasies slide easily into their minds. They think their dreams to be visions, and their visions to be divine. We cannot blame them, for such is the nature of their land. I have often noticed that the English are greater dreamers than the French, and the reason is that their brains being moist are easily affected by wind in the stomach, and they imagine that the impressions which arise from their animal nature are spiritual experiences. It is different in France, which is not so wet or windy, and where the mountains are of stone and the earth is weighed down with iron.[2]

This may seem rather far-fetched, but it was a serious attempt to apply contemporary science to an observed social phenomenon. The English were known to be great dreamers, and Peter of Celle dipped into the medical learning of his day to provide the explanation. Dreams were thought to be caused by vapours ascending the veins from the stomach to the brain. So Peter concluded that those with brains naturally humid from the effects of the atmosphere would be specially prone to dream. Moreover,

---

[1] These phrases appear in a poem in which the advocates of Louis VII and Henry II defend their masters in their dispute over the Vexin. It is printed by Hauréau in *B.E.C.*, 1883, xliv, 7–11; see also M. Manitius, *Gesch. der lat. Literatur des Mittelalters*, iii, 959–61.

[2] *P.L.* 202, 614.

since the dreams were caused by the natural state of the brain and not by disorders of the stomach, the sufferers could not recognize the source of their fantasies and mistook them for truth. By contrast the hard earth and dry air of France were conducive to rational argument and clarity of thought, as well as to joy and martial exercises.

## IV

These differences in attitude towards the land and its people in England and France were closely related to differences in the ways in which the royal families and governments were regarded in the two countries. In France the Crown became the chief symbol of French national sentiment. In England national sentiment developed in opposition to the policies of the Crown. The strong sentimental attachment to the French soil became almost synonymous with attachment to the French king. In England a strong sentimental attachment to the past became one of the chief instruments of opposition to the Crown. These divergent tendencies are first clearly to be seen in the late twelfth century and their effects can be traced at least to the end of the Middle Ages.

So far as France is concerned, Louis VII put the matter in a nutshell in a conversation which he had with Walter Map in Paris in 1179. The king was reflecting on the different kinds of wealth possessed by various rulers and he said:

> Few men can have everything. The kings of the Indies are rich in precious stones and rare beasts; the emperor of Byzantium and the king of Sicily are rich in gold and silk, though their men are useless in war and good only for talk; the German emperor has no gold or silk or other luxuries, but he has warlike men and horses. . . . Your lord, the king of England, has everything—men, horses, gold, silk, gems, wild beasts—everything. We in France have nothing: only bread and wine and joy.[1]

Louis VII was a modest man, and modern historians have generally thought that he had a good deal to be modest about; but

[1] *De Nugis Curialium*, ed. M. R. James, p. 225. Walter Map says that the conversation took place at about the time when he went to the Lateran Council which began in March 1179.

he had one priceless asset—he looked on the world without any sense of strain. This was the prime difference between the royal position in France and England. The French king was at ease with his own. He was the epitome of the French scene: he stood for its history, its legends, its virtues, its well-being. Hence, though Louis VII lost many opportunities, he gained men's hearts and minds—and not only those of Frenchmen. Walter Map, after all, was an official of the English king. He took pleasure in his master's fame, and he had no love of France, a land (in his opinion) filled with pleasure-seekers and the home of all evil, including the Cistercians. Yet he was subdued by the lofty humility and mild self-assurance of Louis. He recorded the king's words because they were 'elegantly and truly spoken'. He did not know that he was witnessing the beginning of a great tradition.

For a hundred and fifty years the French kings alone among the kings of Europe enjoyed the help of a constantly favourable public opinion. They grew rich without becoming unpopular; they succeeded without seeming to try. The letter-collection formed by the French king's chancellor Hugh of Champfleury in the course of his official duties between 1150 and 1172, preserves a contemporary record of the familiar co-operation on which the royal government of France depended.[1] The letters show everywhere a lack of strain—most significantly in the relations of king and pope. Among all the letters those of the pope are the most remarkable for their easy assurance of understanding. Alexander III wrote to Louis as a friend. Probably the most important single cause in creating the favourable climate of opinion towards the French kings was the unwavering support which Louis VII gave Alexander III in the early years of his pontificate. It was a critical time in the growth of both secular and ecclesiastical government, and Louis was the only ruler on whom Alexander III could unreservedly rely. Hence the long stream of letters on subjects at every level of importance in which the pope spoke to the king as his only assured friend in Europe. To find a parallel we must go back to the alliance between the pope and the Carolingians in the middle of the eighth century. At that time the pope signified the new alignment of power by transferring to the Carolingian ruler

[1] Printed by A. Duchesne, *Hist. Francorum Scriptores*, 1641, iv, 557–762, and in chronological order in *Historiens de France*, xvi, 1–171. There is a full analysis in A. Wilmart, *Codices Reginenses Latini*, i, 419–30. Hugh of Champfleury is more fully discussed below, p. 177.

the honorific title *christianissimus*, which had previously been reserved for the Roman Emperor. Now, in the crisis of his reign, Alexander III bestowed this title on Louis VII as a regular title of honour, and it had an instant success. At once it became part of the spiritual armour of the French king.[1]

The special relationship between Paris and Rome established at this time persisted almost without a cloud till the end of the thirteenth century. Even the matrimonial offences of Philip Augustus did not seriously strain the relationship. Although Philip braved ecclesiastical censure longer than either Henry II or John, he remained the favourite son of the Church. His biographers ascribed his marital aberrations to magic and his ecclesiastical exactions to imitation of Richard I. They wrote with frank adulation of his persecution of heretics, his expulsion of the Jews, his zeal for the liberty of the church, the miracles which attended the passage of his armies.[2] The French kings were the sole heirs to the sacred kingship of the early Middle Ages.

How different was the situation in England. The English kings had no community or class committed through thick and thin to speak well of them. This is a matter of some importance in a crisis, when governments must depend on instinctive support. Of course the English kings had their share of adulation, but it was not grounded in any institutional loyalty. Hence it quickly cooled under the cloud of disappointed hopes.

It is one sign of the difference between the positions of the English and French kings, that during a period which produced a long succession of contemporary biographies of the kings of France, in England only King Stephen in the royal succession had a biographer. Stephen deserved a biographer because he inspired affection. He was the only English king who could with any remote plausibility be described in typically chivalric terms as 'both rich and humble, munificent and affable, bold and strong, prudent and patient'; but even Stephen's biographer lost heart in the end.[3] To

---

[1] There was no formal 'conferring' of this title, and it was never the exclusive property of the king of France, but in the letters of Alexander III we first find it used as a recurring epithet in writing to Louis VII.

[2] See Rigord, *Gesta Philippi Augusti*, ed. F. Delaborde, Soc. de l'hist. de Fr., 1882, i, esp. pp. 15–17, 24–7, 29–31, 44–5, 49–51; and for excuses for his ill-doings, pp. 124, 129; Guillaume le Breton, *Gesta Philippi regis*, ibid. i, esp., pp. 273–4.

[3] *Gesta Stephani*, ed. K. R. Potter, 1955, p. 3. Mr. R. H. C. Davis, *E.H.R.*, 1962, lxxvii, 209–32, has pointed out the change in the author's attitude to Stephen after 1148.

retain affection a king must somewhere succeed; and Stephen failed everywhere, partly because his virtues were such as no English king could afford to have. Neither chivalry nor sanctity could succeed on the English throne.

If the English kings had no biographers, they made up for it by having plenty of historians; but the historians only underline their failure to inspire affection. While the French royal historians of St. Denis from the time of Abbot Suger onwards were committed to the support of the French Crown, their English counterparts at St. Albans developed a strain of malice highly destructive of the royal charisma.

Monks are notoriously difficult to discipline, but royal servants may be expected to praise their master. Yet in England in the twelfth and thirteenth centuries they too looked with detachment on the kings whom they served. They cared more for the machine than for its master. This is very evident in the work of Roger of Howden, the best historian of the English Crown in the twelfth century. This dour Yorkshire parson, who knew so much about the affairs of government and recorded what he knew with immense elaboration, who served as a royal judge and accompanied the king on Crusade, emerged from all his experiences without a spark of warmth for either of the masters whom he had served. When Henry II died in circumstances of heart-rending misery Howden was content to pinpoint the date and place without comment:

> He died in the year of the Incarnation of Our Lord Jesus Christ 1189, in the month of July, on the day before the nones of that month, in the octave of the apostles Peter and Paul, on the nineteenth day of the moon, on the fifth day of the week, at Chinon, and was buried at Fontevrault, in the abbey of the nuns serving God there.[1]

Having got this fixed, Howden went on to Richard I in the same unemotional way, without a word of pity or praise. When Richard in his turn was killed in circumstances which called out for pity and regret, Howden merely drew up a careful balance sheet: the king's brain, blood and entrails were buried (he reported) at

---

[1] *Gesta regis Henrici secundi Benedicti abbatis*, R.S., ed. W. Stubbs, ii, 71. This is not, as the title suggests, a work by Abbot Benedict, but (as Lady Stenton, *E.H.R.* 1953, lxviii, 574–82, has shown) simply the longer version of the chronicle of Roger of Howden from 1170 to 1192.

Chinon, his heart at Rouen, and his body at Fontevrault at the feet of his father. He then faithfully recorded the poems written on the king's death, with some unflattering lines on the hatred, avarice, crime, lasciviousness, foulness, pride and covetousness which had marred the late king's character. And there he left it.[1] In these heartless records we see a tradition of governmental service sharply contrasting with the monarchical tradition which had been built up in France in the previous half-century. In England we have a tradition of service without affection; in France a tradition of domesticity without, at this time, much professional service.

## V

These contrasts are in many ways unexpected. In the first place the barons of England owed much more to their kings, whether in basic endowments or in subsequent patronage, than the great barons of France. Then also, the contrasts between the two countries developed most rapidly when the political and cultural union of England and France was closest, and when the initial tensions of the Conquest, which had set native Englishmen against conquering Frenchmen, had disappeared. We might in these circumstances have expected a high degree of cordiality and co-operation between the English kings and their baronage, and a growing sense of unity between the aristocratic societies of France and England. These expectations are not fulfilled, and we must ask why.

The key to the situation is to be found in the political aims of the English kings. They were irrevocably committed to maintaining the Continental connection as a main part of their regality. But the support of baronial families in this policy could be relied on only so long as their territorial interests were fairly evenly distributed on both sides of the Channel. In the reign of Henry I this distribution was still sufficiently common for the policy of union with Normandy to command baronial support. But even in his reign the interests of the new families predominantly lay in England; and the old families with widely based interests on both sides of the Channel became increasingly rare. It is impossible to draw up any exact balance sheet, because the process of disintegration was disturbed by some great marriages and acts of royal

[1] *Chronica Rogeri de Hoveden, R.S.*, ed. W. Stubbs, iv, 82–5.

policy, but the main tendency is obvious. At the baronial level the
process was one of disengagement. For the kings, however, the
growing baronial indifference simply meant that ever more costly
and elaborate measures were necessary for maintaining the
Continental connection. Henry I showed the way: a scientific
system of fortifications in Normandy, a pension to the Count of
Flanders, a firm hand with Norman rebels.[1] In the course of the
century the fortifications, pensions and rebels all became more
numerous and more costly. By the end of the century they were
swallowing the greater part of the royal revenue from England,
and to raise money for their maintenance required the most violent
exertions. It is scarcely surprising that the disaster of 1204, which
effectively deprived the English king of his Continental possessions,
was greeted in England without a murmur of dismay. Certainly
the effect of the disaster on the great families of England was
astonishingly small. It was only the king who felt the need to try
to reverse the judgment of 1204; and this led ultimately to John's
undoing.

The exigencies of this royal policy affected the whole system of
English government. The royal resources in England had to be
ruthlessly exploited to meet the expense of actual war and preparation for war abroad. For this end England came to possess the
most highly developed secular administrative machine in Europe.
But there was never enough. This was the English tragedy. The
French kings grew rich without strain; the English kings strained
every nerve but could never be rich enough.

There is a direct connection between the over-great financial
and military burden of this Continental policy and the failure of
the English kings to create any warmth of sentiment operating in
their favour among the most powerful classes of society. The
grasping efficiency of the English kings, made necessary by their
Continental policy, stamped English society with new strains and
divisions at the very moment when the strains and divisions caused
by the Conquest were beginning to disappear.

Despite all their exertions the English kings were poorer at the
end of the twelfth century than they had been at the beginning.
There seems little doubt that the main reason for this was that

---

[1] For Henry I's measures in Normandy, see below p. 213. The system of
fortification which he introduced, is well described in F. M. Powicke, *The Loss
of Normandy*, 1913 (reprint 1961), pp. 187–196.

they had been obliged to give up the greater part of their demesne to get support which they urgently needed. Like many governments at all times they mortgaged the future for the sake of the present. There is still a great deal of mystery about the stages by which, and the reasons for which, the kings allowed themselves to be driven into this position, and I shall not here discuss the complications of this subject.[1] It is enough to say that, largely because of the loss of demesne revenues, the English kings had lost the financial battle long before they lost the military battles which put an end to their effective power in France. Yet the loss of demesne is not the whole story of the financial contrast between the position of the French and English kings at the end of the twelfth century. There was a broad economic contrast between the two kingdoms which worked to the advantage of the French king and aristocracy.

In France the great unbroken area of corn land which stretches from Flanders to the Loire was approaching its maximum medieval development in the late twelfth century. It was on this that the wealth of France, the abundant resources of men, and the amenities of French aristocratic life, were based. This wealth was easy to lay hold of, and in the upper strata of society a great ease prevailed without too much friction or striving, because at the top there was enough for everyone. Especially at the very top there was enough for the king. The French king had no need to be a tyrant. He went from strength to strength without a struggle, and this gave the impression—not lost upon contemporaries—that God was on the side of men who grew rich while taking so little thought for the morrow. The French kings could dissociate themselves from the sordid details of finance. They left their finances in the hands of the Templars, and dealt with them as the head of a great landed family deals with the head of a great merchant bank. We hear nothing of the bustle and menaces of the English Exchequer sessions; there is only the hush of great wealth effortlessly accumulating. The system was very simple. When men are very rich and are getting richer they have no need for elaborate organization or for novelties of procedure. They

---

[1] The problem is discussed at length by R. S. Hoyt, *The Royal Demesne in English Continental History*, 1066–1272; see also my 'Place of Henry I in English History', *Proceedings of the British Academy*, 1962, xlviii, 157–169.

can sit back in peace and joy; they can wait and choose their time to expand. This is what the French kings did.[1]

## VI

One result of these broad contrasts in the development of society and government was that it was possible to view the present with much more satisfaction in France than in England. The intellectual achievements of France in the twelfth century are those of a buoyant, confident, and united society. In England a different state of affairs prevailed. The English magnates, despite their French speech and origin, began to view the Anglo-Saxon past as a golden age. A strong element of nostalgia entered into their picture of an ideal state.

Nostalgia is a symptom of decline, real or imaginary. It seems to be quite absent from twelfth century France. For the French the past was a foundation for the present; for Englishmen the present was a falling away from the past. There were two distinct phases in the history of these regrets. The first phase followed immediately on the Conquest. This was the phase of English regrets for a past destroyed by the foreign conqueror. The articulate members of the defeated race cherished the thought of past greatness as a defence against the miseries of deprivation and insult in the present. This phase had ended by the middle of the twelfth century. By then the bitterness of defeat had been forgotten, the survivors of the disaster had disappeared, and their successors had either been submerged by, or merged with, the conquering race. But no sooner had this source of nostalgia been removed than the conquerors themselves began to feel a strange deprivation. They began to deplore their lack of French freedom. For a time Stephen seemed to promise better things, but this hope proved illusory. So the conquerors too took refuge in English history, and found in the imagined liberties of a distant past a source of present hope.

The first sign of this is in the *Estorie des Engles* of Geoffrey Gaimar, a French poem written for the entertainment of an aristocratic lay audience shortly after the death of Henry I. Here

[1] For a comparison of the revenues of the French and English kings in 1202–3, and for a glimpse of the simplicity of the French system of accounting, see F. Lot and R. Fawtier, *Le premier budget de la monarchie française*, 1932, and the same authors' *Histoire des institutions françaises au moyen âge*, ii, 102.

the Anglo-Saxon past has been appropriated by the new aristoc-racy. The romantic and chivalrous heroes of the story were Anglo-Saxons, who faced their last crafty and treacherous enemy in William I.[1] The canonization of Edward the Confessor, and the growth of the legends of Hereward and Waltheof, were all part of the same movement. By the beginning of the thirteenth century the Conquest was viewed with distaste by men who were French in speech and habits, and who owed their whole family fortune to William I and his successors. Despite this they had had no enthusiasm for the things that had happened since 1066. It was not easy to say when the decline had begun, but in the thirteenth century Matthew Paris believed that it had begun with the Conquest, and he was not alone in this belief: 'To the golden centuries (before the Conquest) has succeeded an age worse than lead; and from that time to this no king of England has been found worthy of the honour of sanctity.'[2] Certainly the best days were over long before 1215. This was the message of another monk, Matthew of Rievaulx, in the last year of King John:

> England, both land and men, lament thy fate.
> Queen of the world thou wast;
> Now is thy gold rusted, thy flower cut.[3]

A year later in 1217, Gerald of Wales took up the tale of woe. He repeated Walter Map's story of his conversation with Louis VII forty years earlier, and he gave it a contemporary gloss. He drew from the story a contrast between the rapacious tyranny of the English kings and the mild, successful piety of the kings of France; and he compared the joy and liberty of the French people with the abject servitude of the English, still ready to obey the kings who had bled them white.[4]

We seem to be back where we started in 1066: the abject Eng-lish lie at the feet of a tyrant. But there was this difference. After the Conquest it had been the native English who lay under the Norman yoke. Now it was the barons of the kingdom, who—

---

[1] Geoffrey Gaimar, *L'estorie des Engles*, R.S., ed. T. D. Hardy and C. T. Martin: compare the very unfavourable account of the treacherous and crafty William the Conqueror (ll. 5385–5404), with the favourable notice of the English rebel Hereward (ll. 5465–5700).

[2] *Historia Anglorum*, ed. F. Madden, R.S., i, 9.

[3] A. Wilmart, 'Les mélanges de Mathieu préchantre de Rievaulx au début du XIIIe siècle', *Rev. Bénédictine*, 1940, lii, 56.

[4] Giraldus Cambrensis, *Opera*, R.S., viii, 317–322, 326–9.

having failed to destroy King John at the time of the Interdict —were exhorted to place their hopes in a second, and this time a real, French invasion. Gerald of Wales indeed is not a very reliable witness. He was a man with a grievance, but he was no fool, and he knew that no one thought of England as the home of freedom, reason and joy. The whole world knew that these things were French, and he thought they could only return with a new French invasion.

These thoughts and images were of long duration. At the very end of the fourteenth century the Duke of Burgundy told Jean Gerson that he had once had a conversation with John of Gaunt, who had said, 'We in England have men of subtle imagination, but Paris has a solid and secure theology'. Gerson gives the explanation: 'France is not ruled by a tyrant, and therefore it loves sound learning'.[1] That was the distinction which had become clear in the twelfth century. France was the home of freedom, reason and joy; England of oppression, dullness and dreams. The oppression was the direct result of the attempt to maintain the Continental connection; the dreams were a relic of Old England.

It was only when England turned away from the Continent to a wider world across the sea that all this was changed—at least in English eyes. If we go on to the eighteenth century, to the last days of the system of European political order created in the twelfth century, we shall find Cowper still fascinated by the old contrast between the mildness and joy of France and the vapours and drabness of England. But he gives these characteristics a new valuation: the mildness of France is a cause of decay; the joy is a feckless escape from misery; the stern English climate has improved the character of men, and the dullness is the mark of liberty and reason:

> Liberal in all things else, yet nature here
> With stern severity deals out the year.
> Winter invades the spring, and often pours
> A chilling flood on summer's drooping flowers;
> Unwelcome vapours quench autumnal beams,
> Ungenial blasts attending, curl the streams;
> The peasants urge their harvest, ply the fork

[1] The conversation is reported by Gerson in his *Sermo de Pace et Unione Graecorum*, ed. L. E. du Pin, *J. Gersonii Opera Omnia*, ii, 149.

With double toil, and shiver at their work.
Thus with a rigour, for his good design'd,
She rears her favourite man of all mankind.
His form robust and of elastic tone,
Proportion'd well, half muscle and half bone,
Supplies with warm activity and force
A mind well lodged, and masculine of course.
Hence liberty, sweet liberty inspires,
And keeps alive his fierce but noble fires.

Meanwhile in France:

Born in a climate softer far than ours,
Not form'd like us, with such Herculean powers,
The Frenchman, easy, debonair, and brisk,
Give him his lass, his fiddle and his frisk,
Is always happy, reign whoever may,
And laughs the sense of misery far away.
He drinks his simple beverage with a gust,
And feasting on an onion and a crust,
*We* never feel the alacrity and joy
With which he shouts and carols, 'Vive le Roy!'
Fill'd with as much true merriment and glee,
As if he heard his king say—Slave, be free![1]

In these lines written in 1780, Cowper deals out the same cards
as his predecessors had dealt six hundred years earlier, but the end
of the game is quite different. Liberty has crossed the Channel,
and with liberty there has come that other element lacking in
twelfth century England: love of the English countryside.
Cowper's lines may stand as the last words in a debate begun in the
time of Henry II and Louis VII. It cannot be said that the
Hanoverian dynasty succeeded as the Capetians had done in
becoming the symbol of liberty and patriotism. The English
tradition of coolness towards their kings worked against them. But
this too was a story with a twelfth century origin.

[1] W. Cowper, *Table Talk*, 1782, pp. 208–23, 234–45.

# 9

# THE PLACE OF ENGLAND IN THE
# TWELFTH CENTURY RENAISSANCE

## I

Culturally the most obvious thing about England in the twelfth century is its dependence on France. It was a colony of the French intellectual empire, important in its way and quite productive, but still subordinate. Scholars, poets, architects and religious reformers in England did the same things as their contemporaries in France, rather less well, and in a provincial and derivative way. England made no great, distinctive contribution in any of the fields which are the special glory of the twelfth century. Among teachers of the liberal arts there is no name in England to put beside those of William of Conches, Thierry of Chartres, and Petrus Helias; there is no theologian to put beside Abelard, Peter Lombard, Hugh of St. Victor, Peter of Poitiers and Peter the Chanter; no canon lawyer to compare with Gratian, Huguccio, or Bernard of Pavia; no-one in the same class as Chrétien of Troyes in vernacular poetry, or Walter of Châtillon, Hugh Primas and the Archpoet in Latin; among monastic legislators only Gilbert of Sempringham has a place—a very modest one—beside the founding fathers of the Carthusian, Cistercian, and Augustinian Orders. In architecture there is no great seminal building like the church of St. Denis.[1] The Crusade fell on dull ears in England until the least English of her kings infused some life into a long-delayed project.

Naturally this admission of inferiority will arouse some protests. In the liberal arts it may be said that if England has no William of Conches, at least it has John of Salisbury. But this

---

[1] Durham Cathedral with its precocious ribbed vaulting, which is the first step towards Gothic architecture, might appear to be an exception; but for the failure in England to develop this idea which transformed the architecture of the Ile-de-France, see J. Bony, 'French Influences on the Origins of English Gothic Architecture', *Journal of the Warburg and Courtauld Institutes*, 1949, xii, 1–15.

objection is not as conclusive as it sounds. John wrote in England, but everything that he wrote he had learnt in France. Then again, he was not a teacher of the liberal arts in England, but a failed academic driven into administration by lack of scholarly opportunities. His case will deserve some attention later, but it does not modify our first judgement. The same may be said about the line of distinguished theologians—Robert Pullen, Robert of Melun, Stephen Langton—who, if not in the same class as Abelard and Peter Lombard, nevertheless made a considerable contribution to the development of the subject. They were all men who went to France to learn their trade and make their careers as teachers, because they found no sufficient opportunities in England. Similarly, the leading English canon lawyers like Alanus, Gilbertus, Richardus Anglicus and Gerard Pucelle all studied and taught abroad, at Bologne and Paris. The same answer would have to be given to anyone who mentions Stephen Harding among monastic legislators. Certainly the English legislator of Cîteaux was among the greatest religious figures of the century—but not in England. He crossed the sea for inspiration and converted no single house or man in England.

It would be foolish to say that nothing of interest was produced in England in these fields of activity. In theology we can point to the works of the group of pupils of St. Anselm, or to the *Isagoge in Theologiam* of an unknown pupil of Abelard who seems to have written his work after his return to England.[1] In law, there is Vacarius at Oxford, and later there are the decretal collections which seem to have been made in English schools. At this modest level of achievement a quite impressive list of works of theology and law produced in England in the twelfth century could be drawn up; but they would only emphasize the derivative and subordinate character of the English contribution to these subjects. The same is, broadly speaking, true of the newer forms of monastic literature. The English Cistercian achievement is remarkable; the writings of Aelred have a lasting importance, but on a European

[1] For the English authorship of the *Ysagoge*, see D. E. Luscombe, '*The authorship of the Ysagoge in Theologiam*', *A.H.D.L.*, 1968, xxxv, 7–16. I agree with Dr. Luscombe's argument except in one particular: if we accept the genuineness of the Prologue, it follows that the work (*quod Galliae transmittit Anglia*) was sent from England to Gilbert Foliot while he was still in France— hence *before* he became abbot of Gloucester in 1139. If so early a date is to be accepted—and there seems no firm evidence against it—several dates in the early history of scholastic thought will need to be pushed back.

view even he is a figure of mainly local interest. The great Cistercian hymn, *Dulcis Jesu memoria* is probably of English origin, but it is after all only a highly successful and moving expression of sentiments which had their origin in France.[1]

We might thus go on for ever tracing the gradual decline from the central and cosmopolitan influences of France and Italy to the local and provincial echoes of those influences in England. There is a fascination and pathos in echoes, with their lingering exaggerations, but if they were the only noises produced in England in the twelfth century they would certainly make rather an uninteresting story. There are however a few areas of English achievement which give a rather different impression of the place of England in the twelfth century renaissance, and it is to them that we must now turn. We may distinguish these areas as the fields of history, science, wonders and government, and discuss them in this order.

## II

The strongest creative impulse in England in the early twelfth century was historical. The monastic houses in the first half of the century were centres of historical activity of the most varied kind. Although this activity produced no world-masterpieces, yet a historian will recognize some outstanding merits in the productions of this period. They are the products of first-hand research. They were written because men found it necessary to their well-being that the past should be known. Hence they have a purpose which gave cohesion and direction to the efforts of many writers. Every ancient monastery that survived the Conquest was compelled to undertake research into the history of its properties, to assemble its archives, and to compare and copy the title-deeds which lay in its chests or were recorded on the pages of Gospel-books. Local pride and piety also prompted a large-scale effort to discover and transmit an historical record of the saints whose relics formed the main wealth of the religious houses. Earlier generations, relying on the sworn testimony of witnesses or the proofs of sanctity furnished by a tradition of miraculous events, had been singularly indifferent to the historical record. The Conquest changed all

---

[1] For the evidence of English authorship see A. Wilmart, *Le 'Jubilus' dit de S. Bernard*, 1944, 219–22.

this. The new foreign prelates threatened the liturgical observances and piety associated with ill-authenticated relics, and the new aristocracy threatened the estates to which no title could be proved.

In these conditions fundamental historical work was a necessity for corporate survival, and Canterbury, Worcester, Malmesbury, Evesham, Ely, Rochester, Abingdon and Durham all produced historical work which ensured the survival of the Old English past. Sometimes this work was extended backwards to become a general account of English history: William the precentor of Malmesbury was the most successful and original practitioner in this field. Sometimes it extended forward to become a review of contemporary events in the light of the past: Eadmer, companion of St. Anselm and the precentor of Canterbury, was the outstanding writer in this genre. Sometimes the work of arranging and transcribing the records of monastic properties was enlarged to embrace ancient laws and legal formulas: the *Textus Roffensis* of Rochester is the indispensible compilation in this field. Sometimes, as at Ely and Abingdon, the record of properties became a history of the monastery and its saints in the framework of national history. Very often the hagiographical and liturgical motive was uppermost, with the result that the very sparse earlier records of local saints were immensely enlarged in bulk and sometimes—though too seldom—enriched with new and authentic detail. Sometimes, as at Thorney and Worcester, the historical work was inspired by a scientific study of chronology which revived a tradition of scholarship going back to the age of Bede.

Before the Conquest historical work in England had become confined to the one narrow channel of the contemporary annals which make up the Anglo-Saxon Chronicle. These annals continued to preserve the immediate reaction to events of a few monasteries after the Conquest. As a vernacular record of contemporary events they are unique in Western Europe: to find a parallel we must go as far afield as Russia. But though these annals catch the imagination and have the pathos of a dying culture, it is to the new forms of historical research inspired by the Conquest that we must look for evidence of intellectual activity. The Conquest gave the English monasteries a motive which is the inspiration of every great historical movement—the conviction that corporate survival depended on the discovery and

preservation of the past. History was not simply an adornment:
it was a necessity.

The necessity was primarily practical. It arose from a com-
munal concern for properties and relics. But it was something
more than this. The monasteries in 1066 were filled with Englishmen who were connected by family ties with the local aristocracy,
the great families of the land, and the royal family itself. Before
the Conquest these monks had been from a secular point of view
the expendable members of their families. But now that their
families had been destroyed or impoverished, they alone among
Englishmen were left to speak for their people and to see the
catastrophe in its widest setting. To a large extent they accepted
the change with resignation, even with admiration. It was God's
judgement on the perjury of the last Old English king. They saw
that the Conquest had brought a new vitality into the monastic life.
And yet they could not forget the past or the injuries and outrages
suffered by their families. However well-affected towards the new
regime, their own interests and those of the monasteries were
equally involved in the claims and traditions of the past. In this
way the natural and necessary interest in the saints and properties
of the monastic houses became the foundation of a much wider
historical curiosity than had been seen in England, or perhaps
anywhere else in Europe, since the time of Bede.

### III

The historical works undertaken in these conditions were not
the only contribution which the Old English monasteries made to
the intellectual life of post-Conquest England. The monasteries
had been the only centres of intellectual and artistic activity in
pre-Conquest England. This monopoly is a fact of the greatest
importance, both negatively and positively, for the intellectual
history of England after 1066. Negatively it meant that England
started its post-Conquest history without the institutions—the
secular cathedral schools—which were the centres of intellectual
advance in northern France. It was only in these schools that the
conditions prevailed which made possible the rise of scholasticism:
a steady flow of pupils free to go wherever they wished in search of
instruction; a steady supply of masters unattached to any monastic
routine and able to teach wherever the demand was greatest; a

curriculum of studies not too deeply rooted in corporate and liturgical needs, and capable of changing as new resources and new interests made their appearance. In the country between the Loire and the Somme it is possible to name some twenty schools which had a continuous history between the middle of the eleventh and the end of the twelfth century. Although their individual fortunes were subject to many vicissitudes, they all shared a common method of study, which was the method of the future.

There is no trace of this tradition in England before 1066. The wealthiest cathedrals were all monastic, and the secular schools were too small and poor to have any importance. Almost none of the books on which the new scholastic disciplines were built were to be found in pre-Conquest England. Even within the monasteries the learned resources of the country were limited, and outside the monasteries they were negligible.[1]

One of the forms of wealth which the Conquest brought to England was the learning of the Continent in the form of books and masters. All the secular schools of England that are known to us were founded after the Conquest, and all their earliest masters came from France. Despite the paucity of evidence we can build up an impressive picture of the multiplication of schools in England as a result of the Conquest. By 1087 there was a school for grammar and music at Canterbury. In the first decade of the twelfth century we find French masters—Albinus of Angers, Theobald of Etampes, and Geoffrey of Le Mans—at Lincoln, Oxford and Dunstable respectively. Shortly after 1110 the canons of Huntingdon obtained the right to have a school in the town and to put down all rival establishments. Before 1112 there was a school at Gloucester. In 1113 the scholars of Winchester and Bath displayed their poetic talents in verses on the deceased abbess of Caen, the king's sister, and in Bath they were sufficiently emancipated by their study of Ovid to make some very indecent reflections on the royal lady. A little later the school of St. Paul's in London was the subject of an elaborate arrangement which indicates that it had been founded some years earlier. At Warwick the earl gave his canons the right to hold a school 'so that the service of God may be maintained by an abundance of scholars'. These brief records,

---

[1] I have reviewed the evidence for Canterbury in *St. Anselm and his Biographer*, 1963, 242–5; and I believe that a review of other centres would give substantially the same result.

which have to be extracted from the most unlikely sources, are certainly very far from exhausting the list of schools founded between the Conquest and the death of Henry I.[1]

There are many signs of a vigorous demand for schools in England in the early twelfth century: the variety of patrons, and the talk of rivalries and monopolies, are sufficient to show this. But we cannot expect immediate greatness in a field in which England had been inactive for so long. It was only in Oxford that there are any signs of a vigorous scholastic community before 1130. Later, Exeter, Lincoln and London all emerged as something more than local grammar schools; but no English school in the twelfth century ever rivalled the greatest of the French schools. The French schools had too long a lead; they had developed the basic disciplines and teaching methods, hence they attracted the most ambitious and the wealthiest students. The English schools could take only a secondary place. They produced nothing of the first importance in the first century of their existence. A scholastic tradition takes a long time to develop, and it was not until the thirteenth century that Oxford could compete on terms of equality with Paris and Bologna.

That is the negative side of the Anglo-Saxon inheritance: a secular scholastic tradition could not be built up in a day or a decade. But there is another side to the picture. The revival of interest in England's monastic past stimulated renewed activity in those fields of intellectual effort in which the monasteries had once been strong. The pre-Conquest monasteries had not quite forgotten the scientific learning of the age of Bede. Indeed it was one aspect of English intellectual backwardness that learning was confined within the intellectual horizon of Bede. We can see this very clearly in the work of Byrhtferth, the most interesting of English monastic scholars in the two generations before the Conquest. His thought is negligible, and his knowledge is only a

---

[1] I list here the more important pieces of evidence for the statements in the text: for Bath (and Winchester), L. Delisle, *Rouleaux des Morts*, 1866, pp. 189, 192; for Beverley, *Miracles of St. John of Beverley, Hist. of the Church of York*, R.S., i, 281; for Canterbury, *Cartulary of St. Gregory's Canterbury*, ed. A. M. Woodcock, no. 1; for Dunstable, *Gesta Abbatum S. Albani*, R.S., i, 73; *Monasticon Anglicanum*, vi, 240; for Gloucester, *Regesta*, ii, no. 1936; for Huntingdon, *E.H.R.* 1903, xviii, 712; for Lincoln, Henry of Huntingdon, *Historia Anglorum*, R.S., p. 301; for London, *Early Charters of St. Paul's Cathedral*, ed. M. Gibbs, nos. 273–4; for Oxford, H. E. Salter, *Medieval Oxford* (Oxf. Hist. Soc.) 1936, 91–3; for Warwick, *Cartulary of Warwick College*, P.R.O. KR Misc. Bks. 22 (E 164-22), ff 8–12$^v$.

thin deposit of ancient science. But he shows a keen aesthetic appreciation of an intellectual system of which he had only a meagre understanding:

We have stirred with our oars the waves of the deep pool; we have had a glimpse of the mountains around the salt sea strand; and with full sail and prosperous wind we have succeeded in pitching our camp on the coast of the fairest of lands.[1]

These are the words of a man with a deep feeling for scientific knowledge, stretching out to grasp the outline of the universal coherence of man and nature. He drew this diagram:[2]

| Season of the year | SPRING | SUMMER | AUTUMN | WINTER |
|---|---|---|---|---|
| Age of Man | CHILDHOOD | ADOLESCENCE | MANHOOD | OLD AGE |
| Element | AIR | FIRE | EARTH | WATER |
| Effects | MOIST & HOT | HOT & DRY | DRY & COLD | COLD & MOIST |
| Temperament | SANGUINE | CHOLERIC | MELANCHOLIC | PHLEGMATIC |

He could not elaborate this system; he could draw no conclusions from it; but it pleased him and it went on pleasing his monastic successors until the early years of the twelfth century. It was a blue-print of universal nature.

The achievement of these men was a modest one, but they kept an interest in science alive until new resources were available to set scientific enquiries in motion again. They performed this feat not by any intellectual discoveries but by a marriage of science with art. The combination can already be seen in Byhrtferth. It can be seen now fully developed in the beautiful astronomical manuscripts of the English monasteries of the eleventh century. And finally, having survived the Conquest, it can be seen in two manuscripts produced between 1085 and 1125 at Peterborough and Thorney, two strongholds of Anglo-Saxon tradition. These manuscripts are compendia of the learning of the pre-Conquest monasteries, and their illustrations will convey an impression of their beauty, their naivety, and their scientific curiosity.[3] They represent a science in which direct observation, new discoveries, and philosophical

[1] *Byrhtferth's Manual, A.D. 1011*, ed. S. J. Crawford, Early Eng. Text Soc., 1929, i. 15.
[2] Ibid. pp. 10–11: the source is Bede, *De Temporum Ratione*, xxxv, ed. C. W. Jones, *Bedae Opera de Temporibus*, 1943, pp. 246–8. Cf. Plate IV.
[3] See Plates III–VI.

speculation have long ceased to play any part. Yet it was in its way an exacting discipline. There was no idea of new knowledge, but there was a foundation of technical accomplishment.

In this area at least Englishmen were equipped to take advantage of the new opportunities which were opened up by the Norman Conquest. The arts of measurement and calculation, vigorously cultivated in some continental schools in the eleventh century, especially at Liège and Rheims, began to have their effect in England after about 1090, with very far-reaching results. The opening stages of this continental influence are dramatically illustrated in an autobiographical fragment written by Walcher, prior of the Benedictine priory of Malvern, who died in 1125. His tombstone can still be seen in Malvern priory, where he is described as a Lotharingian, a worthy philosopher, a good astrologer, a geometer and abacist.[1] He was a man of foreign extraction and education, but he had long lived in England as the following passage makes clear:

> In the year which Dionysius reckons as 1091 A.D. I happened to be in Italy, one and a half day's journey east of the city of *Romona* on 30 October when I saw an eclipse of the moon. It took place before dawn looking westwards, but I had no instrument that would give me the time of the full moon, nor could I see the moon clearly because of thick clouds. I remember seeing it horned like a V but the clouds made it impossible to tell when the eclipse started and ended.[2] When I got back to England I enquired about the time of the eclipse and a certain brother told me this: he said that he had been very busy during the day before the eclipse and did not get home till late at night. When he had had supper, he sat awhile, and then a servant, who had gone out, came rushing back saying that something horrible was happening to the moon. Going out he noticed that it was not yet midnight, for the moon had still some way to go before it was in the

---

[1] C. H. Haskins, *Studies in the History of Mediaeval Science*, pp.113–7, was the first to study Walcher's work, but in common with others he made a mistake in giving the date of his death as 1135: Walcher's tomb at Malvern gives 1125.

[2] These observations are entirely consistent with the scientific data on the lunar eclipse of 30 October 1091, which (at its greatest obfuscation at 5.27 a.m.) obscured only about one half of the moon's surface, leaving (as Walcher observed) a horned segment still visible (see T. von Oppolzer, *Canon of Eclipses*, transl. O. Gingerich, 1962, p. 360). I am greatly indebted to Dr. J. D. North for his help on these and other details of Walcher's observation.

South. I thus perceived that several hours separated the time of the eclipse in Italy and in England, since I saw it shortly before dawn while he saw it before midnight.[1] But I still had no certainty about the time of the eclipse and I was distressed about this, because I was planning to draw up a lunar table and had no starting point. Then unexpectedly in the following year on 18 October, during the same lunar cycle, the moon— as if to favour my studies and by its darkness bring me light —underwent another eclipse.[2] I at once seized my astrolabe and made a careful note of the time of full eclipse, which was a little more than three-quarters of an hour after the eleventh hour of the night. If this time is converted into equinoctial time, it will be found to be shortly before 12.45. Hence, according to the rule which I have explained earlier, the lunar cycle began on 3 October at 19.30 hrs.[3]

I have quoted this passage at length because it is of very great interest for the history of English science after the Conquest. It is a remarkable example of an early attempt at precise measurement, made not for its own sake, but as a necessary basis for systematic calculations. It illustrates too some of the basic difficulties of the pioneer: the difficulty of telling the time, of converting the hours from 'natural' to 'standard' time, of choosing between alternative chronological systems, and making any observations in the weather conditions of northern Europe. The essential tool was the astrolabe, an instrument which had been imported into the West from the Arabs in the eleventh century. It was probably unknown in England before the Conquest, and its introduction made it possible for astronomy at last to advance

[1] Walcher was right to be puzzled, but he was wrong in his conclusion. An eclipse observed in Italy shortly before dawn could not possibly have been observed in England shortly before midnight. The most likely solution to his problem is very simple. On 5 May 1091 there was an eclipse of the moon at 22.23 hrs, very similar to that on 30 October at 5.27 hrs. It seems clear that the former was the event described to Walcher when he returned to England, and the difference in date went unnoticed.

[2] Walcher's anxiety for precision is an important indication of the existence of a new scientific impulse. He wanted to establish by calculation and observation the exact correlation between the phases of the moon and the solar calendar. As soon as he got a fixed point on 18 October 1092 he calculated backwards to 1036, when the moon's cycle began on 1 January, and constructed his table from that date to 1111 when (according to his calculation) the cycle began again.

[3] The greater part of this passage is printed by Haskins, loc. cit., from Bodleian MS. Auct. F. 1. 9, f. 90: I have added some sentences which Haskins omitted.

beyond the stage which it had reached in the age of Bede. It opened up a new range of scientific enquiry in which Englishmen took a leading part, and the Old English monasteries were among the first to welcome the new science.

This can be seen most clearly at Worcester. Of all the Old English monasteries, Worcester was the most successful in preserving its links with the past. While every other diocese in England had a foreign bishop within a few years of the Conquest, Worcester retained till 1095 a bishop brought up in the insular monastic tradition of the Confessor's reign. Bishop Wulfstan was a dedicated preserver of the past. He was responsible for the careful preservation of the ancient documents of the monastery; it was under his influence that the Worcester chronicle, with its comprehensive amalgam of universal and Old English history, was begun. It was also through Wulfstan that the new scientific impetus reached Worcester.

We can see the effects of this new impetus most clearly displayed in the manuscript written by a monk of Worcester about the year 1130 which preserved the record of Walcher's lunar observations of 1091 and 1092.[1] Like the earlier scientific manuscripts from Thorney and Peterborough which I have mentioned, it is a fine folio volume, copiously illustrated and furnished with abundant tables. But here the similarity ends. The illustrations have no artistic adornment—they are strictly practical and scientific, and they are more complicated than any that had been seen in England before. They incorporated the results of the latest astronomical enquiries in Spain. The manuscript is a visible witness to the union of the old Anglo-Saxon scientific curiosity and the new resources of scientific measurement and discovery.

Their chronicle also shows that the monks of Worcester were stirred by the new discoveries. After 1128 it begins to record unusual celestial phenomena with great regard for exact observation—the sun-spots of 1128, the *aurora borealis* of 1130, the darkness which some observers thought was an eclipse in 1133; and in 1138 the chronicler burst into praise of the work of al-

---

[1] See Plate VII. The first half of the manuscript is largely occupied with works on chronology and arithmetic, the product of the traditional science of the eleventh century: the second half, starting with Walcher's treatise and lunar tables, is a product of the Greco-Arabic science of the twelfth century, introduced into England by Petrus Alfonsi, Adelard, and later travellers to Spain.

Khwarizmi and gave an impressive display of his capacity to handle the new science.[1]

The chance survival of important manuscripts allows us to follow the stages of development at Worcester more fully than elsewhere. But there is evidence that a similar process went on in other ancient monasteries. For instance, a manuscript from St. Augustine's, Canterbury, which can scarcely be later than 1100, contains much of the material on the use of the astrolabe that we find in the great manuscript from Worcester. At a later date, probably before the middle of the twelfth century, this manuscript also had the works of Adelard of Bath and Petrus Alfonsi added to it, and the astronomical tables show many signs of use.[2]

Nevertheless it was inevitable that the monasteries, which had helped to form a receptive audience for the new science, should not have been the main centres for its development. Arab science required advanced skills and new texts which could only be acquired abroad. Fundamentally the new learning had no place in monastic life. The studies of the pre-Conquest monasteries were primitive, but they were closely related to the liturgical and corporate needs of the community. Whatever went beyond those needs soon lost the impulse of necessity. After about 1130, therefore, the monasteries were no longer an intellectual force to be reckoned with in scientific progress. We must look elsewhere.

We must look first of all at a small group of men in the West country in the late eleventh and twelfth century. Here Robert, bishop of Hereford, was a friend of Wulfstan of Worcester. Like Walcher, prior of Malvern, he was a Lotharingian and a keen astronomer. In the year in which Walcher observed the moon's eclipse in Italy he put his astronomy to practical use by foretelling from the stars that the dedication of Lincoln Cathedral to which he had been invited would not take place, and he saved himself the trouble of a journey; a trivial incident, but one which shows why many men were interested in astronomy.[3] It seemed to offer the best hope of understanding, and in some measure controlling, terrestial events. The future of this hope was to be a history of

[1] *The Chronicle of John of Worcester, 1118–1140*, ed. J. R. H. Weaver 1908, pp. 28, 31, 37, 53. See Plate VIII.
[2] Corpus Christi College, Oxford, MS. 283. For some of the contents of this manuscript, of which several items are the same as those in Bodl. MS. Auct. F.I. 9, see C. H. Haskins, op. cit., 22–4, 117–118.
[3] William of Malmesbury, *Gesta Pontificum*, 300–1.

disappointments; but the disappointments still lay far ahead, while new methods of calculating and measuring were stirring the first hopes of unlimited knowledge and power.

Robert's successor at Hereford, Bishop Gerard, was another well-known student of astronomy;[1] and at Malvern, Walcher was in touch with a converted Jew from Spain, a physician of Henry I called Petrus Alfonsi, who had brought the elements of Arabic astronomy to England. Another member of this group was Adelard of Bath. He was a secular clerk, and England (as I have already remarked) had no secular schools of any standing comparable to those of northern France. Therefore, like other Englishmen with intellectual ambitions, Adelard had to go abroad to study. Like many others in the years around 1100 he went to Laon; but there he took a step which is so significant for the history of English thought in the twelfth century that his own words about it are worth quoting:

> You will remember, nephew, that seven years ago when I left you and my other pupils at Laon, it was agreed between us that I should inspect the studies of the Arabs to the extent of my powers, while you would acquire a knowledge of the shifting opinions of the French.[2]

Here we see one of the consequences of travel: it encourages further travel. Englishmen who wanted to learn had to travel because the learned resources at home were so meagre. Nearly all of them went to France in the first place: it was near, they were familiar with the language, and its schools were famous. But, having got to France, some of them were tempted to go further. Perhaps they did not like what they found in the French schools. Adelard evidently though that the 'shifting opinions' of the French were unsatisfactory. Another Englishman found the Parisian concentration on glossing texts brutish and dull.[3] There are always

---

[1] Ibid. 259–60. In passages which he later erased, William of Malmesbury reports that Bishop Gerard was said to practise magic because he read a handbook of astrology by Julius Firmicius, and when he died a *codex curiosarum artium* was found under his pillow. From this we may gather that scientific astrology was not yet such a respectable subject as it was later to become.

[2] *Quaestiones Naturales*, ed. M. Müller (Beiträge zur Gesch. der Phil. im Mittelalter, xxxi, 2), p. 4.

[3] Daniel of Morley, *Liber de naturis inferiorum et superiorum*, ed. K. Sudhoff, in *Archiv f. die Gesch. der Naturwissenschaft u. der Technik*, 1917, viii, i, 1–40.

reasons for being dissatisfied with any course of studies, and Englishmen who had already travelled two or three hundred miles to a foreign country found it easy to go some hundreds of miles further in search of satisfaction. Some of them may have been influenced by the English tradition of scientific study, some by the example of Adelard. Whatever the reasons it is clear that a high proportion of the scholars who went to Spain in the twelfth century in search of Arabic science were Englishmen. They included Robert of Ketton, Robert of Chester, Roger of Hereford, Daniel of Morley and Alfred of Shareshull, who all helped to bring Arabic science to England and the Latin West. If we add Adelard of Bath, their activity covers the whole of the twelfth century. Taken as a whole their work shows how scientific studies, opening out from the astronomical calculations which were the main preoccupation of English scholars in the early part of the century, came to embrace every branch of Greek science by the end of the century. Thus, from the monastic studies of the pre-Conquest period, the way was prepared for the encyclopaedic studies of Grosseteste and his pupils in the thirteenth century.

## IV

The monastic monopoly of intellectual life in England before the Conquest slowly broke down in the two generations after the Conquest, leaving a legacy of historical and scientific work which influenced the direction of later English studies. Another area in which a similar continuation of monastic influence is to be seen is in the literature of marvels. Marvels and the expectation of marvels are one of the starting-points of science. Men begin to observe when their attention has been attracted by the unusual— by comets, eclipses, earthquakes, 'signs in the sun and other stars'. In the beginning science and wonders are simply different aspects of the same thing. They were both deeply embedded in the Old English monasteries. If the study of the movements of sun, moon and stars was essential for the formal organization of the liturgical routine, the study of marvels was no less essential for the interior religious and social life of the monasteries. We must imagine those communities as centres of almost perpetual gossip about wonders seen or believed. These stories were the imaginative food on which the devotion of the monasteries fed. They provided the thrills without which life would have been very drab.

These marvels also had a historical interest. The recording of them had a central place in the historical writings produced in the monasteries after the Conquest. There was a good reason for this. Miracles were the chief adornment of the shrines, but unless they were recorded they were lost. The pre-Conquest church had been very negligent in this respect, perhaps because miracles were too plentiful to need recording. But after the Conquest, important questions of cult and the proofs of the efficacy of saints and relics required a record to be made of past and present miracles. The English monks found themselves with a large task on their hands. Most of their productions had only a strictly limited interest, but there was one form of compilation which had a very wide appeal, and here Englishmen were largely responsible for setting a new fashion. Many of the ancient monasteries were dedicated to St. Mary the Virgin—Malmesbury, Evesham, Worcester among others. They had strong reasons for being interested in the miracles of the Blessed Virgin, especially if they lacked outstanding saints of their own.

One of the first men to put together a collection of Marian miracles from several sources was Dominic, the prior and historian of the monastery of St. Mary and St. Egwin at Evesham.[1] St. Egwin and the other local saints of Evesham were very obscure men, and while Dominic was putting together all that could be recorded of their lives, he also made a collection of the miracles of the chief patron of the monastery, the Blessed Virgin Mary. It was an ambitious collection designed to illustrate the universal sovereignty of the Mother of God and to inculcate the observance of various Feasts and Offices associated with devotion to her cult. Dominic had to search far and wide to get his examples, and at the end he added his single grain from Evesham. It was a miserably small grain, but it was all he could find. He described how a monk of Evesham at the point of death was visited by St. John the Evangelist. St. John said that he had been specially designated by the Mother of the Lord to look after the church of Evesham, and the monk at once recovered and enjoyed good health for a long time. It was a banal story and scarcely deserved

[1] See J. C. Jennings, 'The writings of Prior Dominic of Evesham', *E.H.R.*, 1962, lxxvii, 298–304.

to be written down; but by the strangest of chance, because it was found in one of the earliest collections of Mary stories, it gained a place in European literature.

Dominic was one of the first writers in Europe to make a collection of a type which soon became wildly popular throughout Europe. His contemporary at Canterbury, Anselm the nephew of Archbishop Anselm, appears to have been engaged on a similar collection at the same times, and very soon afterwards William of Malmesbury continued these two collections and made some additions of his own. The movement, still mainly centred in England, then passed from the monasteries to the secular cathedrals, and to the world at large. About the middle of the century a canon of London called Alberic—a man who, like William of Malmesbury, was a considerable scholar and student of classical antiquity—made a conflation of the three monastic collections I have mentioned, and very soon afterwards this collection was translated into French by another Londoner, a clerk called Algar. Sixty or seventy years later a second French translation was made, and in one form or another these English compilations formed the basis of every major collection or miracles of the Virgin throughout the Middle Ages.[1]

The literary and intellectual merits of this activity are not very great, but the rôle of the English monasteries in the creation of a large European literature deserves recognition. The pattern of events is curiously similar to that which we have observed in tracing the English contribution to medieval science. The work done in the Old English monasteries in the early years of the twelfth century was taken up by secular masters and became part of a European movement. Here again the Conquest was responsible for something more than a one-way traffic in ideas from the Continent to England; it provided a European market for the last distinctive products of Anglo-Saxon culture.

The history of these Mary legends is only one example of the great part which England played in the collection and diffusion of legends and marvels of every kind. William of Malmesbury had a passion for the marvellous which he indulged on every possible occasion. This comes out in unexpected ways in his *Gesta Regum Anglorum*, into which he managed to insert the earliest fully

---

[1] See R. W. Southern, 'The English Origins of the Miracles of the Virgin', *M.A.R.S.*, 1958, iv, 176–216.

developed series of stories about the wonders of Rome and the magical powers of Silvester II. John of Salisbury the most sober of English writers, had a more restrained but still keen eye for marvels. He is the first writer in Europe to mention the legends of Virgil's magical powers, which later attained a vast popularity.[1] The Eastern legends which the immigrant Petrus Alfonsi translated into Latin were disseminated throughout Europe. Englishmen were avid collectors as well as seers of visions, and it was a vision of Ailsi Abbot of Ramsey which helped to spread the fame of the Immaculate Conception throughout Europe.[2] As for King Arthur and Merlin, it is doubtful if they would ever have been European figures if their legendary histories had not been gathered together in England. The same love of marvels is also apparent in the manuscripts of bestiaries, herbals, lapidaries and 'Marvels of the East' which come very largely from English sources.[3] William of Malmesbury tells us that Henry I was enchanted by the marvels of other lands, and his famous menagerie was perhaps an expression of this enchantment. As Peter of Celle said, the English were dreamers, and what they dreamed sometimes turned into art, sometimes into literature, sometimes into science, and once into dogma.

## V

The final area in which England made an original contribution to European thought in the twelfth century was in the literature of secular government. Here, as in the other fields that have been discussed, the influence of pre-Conquest institutions is very clear. Although Anglo-Saxon royal government was a very small affair, England was the only country in the West where the pretensions of monarchy did not greatly outrun the means of making these pretensions effective. Consequently the English royal laws of the tenth and eleventh centuries are the only examples at this time of general legislation based on ancient customs and capable of detailed application. This body of law survived the Conquest, and the

---

[1] J. W. Spargo, *Virgil the Necromancer: Studies in Virgilian Legends*, 1934, pp. 9–17.

[2] For the details of transmission see *M.A.R.S.*, 1958, iv, 194–8.

[3] For the English tradition of manuscripts of the 'Marvels of the East' and their association with scientific interests, see M. R. James, *The Marvels of the East*, Roxburgh Club, 1929.

monasteries which gathered up the remnants of Old English science, legend and history, were also responsible for the survival of the laws.

It was at this point, in the reign of Henry I, that an anonymous author appeared who attempted to give this body of law a contemporary relevance in a work variously known as *Leges Henrici Primi* or *Quadripartitus*. His success must be judged to have been meagre, but in the words of F. W. Maitland, he was a man 'engaged upon an utterly new task, new in England, new in Europe: he was writing a legal text-book that was neither Roman nor Canon Law'.[1] These are the words of a great legal historian; but we may put Maitland's judgement in more general terms and say that this anonymous author was the first of a long line of English administrators who have written learnedly about government. He was a man of scholastic learning, capable of quoting the classics, the Fathers, and some parts of canon law: but in his daily work he was an official in the household of the archbishop of York and perhaps of the king, deeply engaged in the business of government. He applied his learning to the work of government, philosophized about law, fitted together the jig-saw of the past, and took a violently partisan stand on the issues of the day.

This kind of man found a place more easily in England than anywhere else in Europe in the twelfth century. From the earliest years of the century the appearance of 'Masters' or (as we should say) graduates in the households of bishops and baron tells a story of the increasing application of learning to the work of government. The household of archbishop Thomas Becket with its famous *eruditi* was the greatest of all associations of learned men of business, and John of Salisbury was the greatest clerk among them. By the third quarter of the twelfth century such men as he were essential for the conduct of business, but they were not yet quite at home in the world. They were exiles from the universities, and they seem to have been regarded by their fellow-administrators with the same sort of suspicion that a graduate used to meet in the business world thirty years ago. They had obscure but potent advantages, and their popularity was not increased by their anxiety to display their learning at every opportunity. John of Salisbury has recorded the uncomfortable position in which such a man found

---

[1] See T. F. T. Plucknett, *Early English Legal Literature*, 1958, 25–30, quoting Pollock and Maitland, *History of English Law*, i, 100–101.

himself in the household of Archbishop Theobald of Canterbury:

> I could ward off in silence the cavilling of my fellow-scholars, and those who call themselves philosophers, but I cannot altogether escape the teeth of my fellow civil servants. To accommodate oneself to everyone and to hurt no-one used to be a sufficient path to favour; but now it is rarely possible to avoid the envy of one's colleagues in this way. If I am silent, I am thought to be ignorant; if I talk, I am accused of being a bore. If I am serious I am said to be an intriguer, if merry a fool. If I had consumed my time with my colleagues in gambling, hunting and the other employments of courtiers, they would have attacked my writings as little as I do theirs. However, it is nothing to me if I am judged by those who fear most the judgement of clowns and fools.[1]

The position of scholars among the philistines became easier as the century went on. Their usefulness became established beyond cavil. They made their way in the royal court, and the highest preferments in the church opened to them. The growing complexity of government made intellectual coherence not only a source of personal satisfaction but an instrument of practical progress. From these twin sources of personal and institutional necessity there came a few books which are our best evidence for the intellectual stimulus provided by the work of government in the time of Henry II: John of Salisbury's *Policraticus* (1159), the *Dialogue of the Exchequer* (1177–9), the *Tractatus de legibus et consuetudinibus regni Angliae qui Glanvilla vocatur* (1187–9), and many of the letters of Peter of Blois from 1174 onwards. These books were not simply manuals or text-books for office use like the contemporary collections of decretals: they aspired in some degree to invest the routine of government with an intellectual generality. They were all written in England, and they provide a glittering testimony to the growing claims of secular government such as we could find nowhere else in Europe.

The histories of the period show the same inspiration. We have seen how the historians of the period up to about 1130 satisfied the need for preserving the Anglo-Saxon past. When this work had been accomplished there was a period in which the

---

[1] *Metalogicon, Prol.*, ed. C. C. J. Webb, p. 1.

historical impulse was extremely weak. Then in 1170 the York-shire parson Roger of Howden began his contemporary history. About ten years later the newly appointed dean of London, Master Ralph de Diceto, started to collect his own records of contemporary events. In 1185 or thereabouts the monk Gervase of Canterbury began his career as a contemporary chronicler. These writers had very different backgrounds but they all showed the same preoccupation with the details of government: they collected administrative and diplomatic documents, and recorded the meetings of the *curia regis*, the visitations of itinerant justices, and the progress of foreign negotiations with unprecedented elaboration. They had no special theme, they glorified no-one. They were of course concerned about events of obvious general significance like the Crusade or an eclipse of the sun; but above all they plodded on from year to year following the intricacies of secular government with a fullness that had never been seen before.

An interest in contemporary secular government was not of course confined to England. But if we look at the evidence for it in France and Germany, we see a notable difference. Abroad we find no work which shows a similar mixture of philosophical interest and practical familiarity. In France government was perhaps too easy, and in Germany too difficult, to encourage any deep interest in its problems.

In France we can find in the career and writings of Hugh of Champfleury a striking illustration of this lack of interest in government. He was chancellor and chief minister of Louis VII from 1150 to 1172. He was a man with an academic training, and he has left a record of his thoughts and aspirations compiled in the course of his official employment. It is a record notable for the absence of any thought about government: all is woe and lamentation for the predicament in which he found himself, remorse for his sins, and fears for his eternal salvation. This would be readily intelligible if he had been writing as a retired civil servant, living —as was ultimately his fate—in disgrace. But it seems that he was writing in the full tide of prosperity:

> I would gladly flee if I could escape from my sad fate; but wherever I go it pursues me, and I—who need counsel and aid—have become the counsellor of others. . . . There are

three things which make me especially anxious: my present
life—is it pleasing or displeasing to God? my death—how
shall I think of God and bear its pains? my eternity—what
judgement shall I receive? shall I be gathered among the
damned? and if I am sent for a time to punishment and exile,
shall I meanwhile be deprived of the vision of God and of the
saints in heaven?[1]

When Hugh of Champfleury finally fell from power, he took
with him into retirement—like many another royal servant—the
documents of his administration, and began to set them in order.
They preserve a vivid picture—but not of the royal government—
only of the demands that flowed in upon government from outside.
Among over five hundred letters, a mere handful are letters
written by the king or his chancellor: all the others are the letters
to the king of popes, cardinals, bishops, abbots, clerks and magnates. They show the cohesive society of France and its relations
with the outside world in great detail; but of the processes of
government it is difficult to find anything more than a shadow.
The contrast between this collection and the collection of letters
that John of Salisbury accumulated at this same time in the service
of the archbishops of Canterbury, or of royal writs that the author
of Glanvill codified and explained, could scarcely be greater.

It would be dangerous to make too much of this single contrast
if it were not borne out by many other indications of the gulf
which separated the French conception of government from the
English. Instead of chroniclers like Roger of Howden, Ralph de
Diceto and Gervase of Canterbury with their strong interest in the
mechanism of royal government, we have a torrent of adulation of
the French king from Rigaud and Guillaume le Breton. There is
nothing remotely like the *Dialogue of the Exchequer* or *Glanvill*.

There can of course be no doubt that Louis VII and Philip
Augustus in France thought deeply about the affairs of their
kingdom. King Philip's thoughts were brilliantly successful, but it
seems unlikely that he spent sleepless nights, as Henry II is
reported to have done, in devising new ways of doing justice or
managing his finances. The thoughts by which he impressed his

---

[1] A. Wilmart, 'Les loisirs ou sentiments intimes d'un Chancelier de France',
*Rev. Bénédictine*, 1939, li, 182–204 (the passage quoted above will be found on
p. 202).

biographers were about ways of freeing Christians from their debts to the Jews—'a divinely inspired intention from which the mind of the most Christian king could not be turned by any attempts to soften his heart with bribes'—or of cleaning the streets of Paris. The passage in which his biographer describes this enterprise conveys a good impression of the intimacy of French government and its lack of elaborate apparatus:

> King Philip was staying at Paris and one day he was walking up and down the royal chamber thinking about the affairs of the realm. He went to the window and looked out on the Seine, it being his habit to refresh his mind in this way. There he noticed the intolerable stench made by carts passing through the city churning up the mud, and he found it insupportable. There and then he resolved on a great and necessary work which none of his predecessors had dared to undertake for its great expense and difficulty. Calling together the burgesses and the bailiffs of the city he gave orders that all the streets of the whole city of Paris should be covered with hard, strong stones.[1]

This is how government worked in a happy state. No doubt the French biographers left out a great deal that ought to have been said, but they showed the French king in the right perspective. Substantially they convey the same impression as Hugh de Champfleury or later, Joinville. The restlessness of the English government in devising expedients was not necessary in France or possible in Germany. The success of familiar collaboration with the right people was the secret of French government; and the failure of this collaboration was the weakness of German government. It was only in England that the complexities of secular government were a matter of anxious thought by men of high ability, and only England produced a literature of detailed elucidation which may broadly be compared with the work of English writers on government between Bentham and Bagehot. Even in Sicily, where the operations of government were studied with something like the same concentration as in England, there was no similar literature.

[1] Rigord, *Gesta Philippi Augusti*, ed. F. Delaborde, pp. 53-4.

## VI

All this does not of course amount to a contribution to European thought and literature comparable to that of northern France. It would be quite wrong to suppose that it did. The French contribution was the contribution of an integrated, buoyant, confident society. The English contribution was the contribution of a divided and hard-driven society. But a society of this kind raises problems, provokes thoughts, and provides opportunities for achievements, which are not found in happier states. The activities stimulated by England's historical position in the twelfth century are tributaries to the main stream of European experience. They were destined to grow in importance; and even in the twelfth century they are sufficient to demonstrate the inadequacy of our initial description of England as a colony of the French intellectual empire.

# IV

THREE TYPES OF PRACTICAL WISDOM

# 10

## RANULF FLAMBARD

### I

The importance of Ranulf Flambard in the reign of William Rufus has always been acknowledged. All the chronicles of the period put him in the forefront of those responsible for the king's unprincipled conduct and lay the blame chiefly on him for the misfortunes they relate. But it was William Stubbs who first gave him a position of long-term importance in English history.

Like all historians of eleventh century society Stubbs was faced with the problem of feudalism. His strong preference for continuity in all things led him to minimise the immediate effect of the Norman Conquest. He sought the origins of Anglo-Norman feudalism in pre-Conquest institutions, but he recognized the difficulty of explaining Norman military institutions as a natural development of Anglo-Saxon arrangements. He therefore looked for a commanding personality to act as an instigator and agent of the 'hardening and sharpening' of feudalism which had become clearly apparent by the early twelfth century. This was the role Stubbs assigned to Flambard: an active, able, unscrupulous innovator, shaping the feudal obligations of lay and ecclesiastical tenants alike in the interests of the king.[1] This account of Flambard's importance was later developed with far less circumspection by Freeman, who pronounced him to be the malignant genius of 'the Feudal System'.[2] Stubbs was too cautious an historian to fall into rhetorical exaggeration of this kind, but he had no doubt that the reign of Rufus and the work of his minister were decisive in the development of military feudalism. Stubbs was no friend to feudalism; so—as a natural corollary—he saw Rufus's reign as a period of stagnation in the growth of royal government, which 'left no traces of administrative power such as mark the rule of his father and brother'.

[1] *Constitutional History of England,* 1874, i, §§ 106–7.
[2] E. A. Freeman, *History of the Norman Conquest,* 1876, v, 377–81.

The story of John Horace Round's attack on Stubbs's account of the development of feudalism in England is one that cannot be retold here, though it has a deep interest as a human and scientific event.[1] The upshot of it was that it left Ranulf Flambard without a historical role. Round claimed that feudalism required no *deus ex machina* in Rufus's reign, because it had already been introduced into England more or less intact at the time of the Norman Conquest. He therefore concluded that Flambard had been assigned a quite unwarrantable share in the development of feudalism in England; and even Round's bitterest enemies (they are almost as bitter now as they were eighty years ago) have not tried to rehabilitate Flambard as the great agent in the 'hardening and sharpening' of feudalism.

All these attacks and counter attacks are now an old story, but they leave us still with Ranulf Flambard on our hands. How are we to account for his contemporary reputation? Did he have any long-term importance? Or was he only a brutal and extortionate character who made a fleeting impact on men's lives? This was how he had appeared before Stubbs and Freeman gave him his unenviable prominence as a force in the historical process, and perhaps he should be sent back to the limbo from which they extracted him. This may well be his true home, but before we dismiss him it may be well to review the evidence once more.

## II

The unanimity of the chronicles is remarkable. They all have something to say about Flambard, and stripped of its rhetoric what they tell us is very consistent. They all agree that he was the chief financial and legal agent of the king. Generally they stress his financial activity, but his work in the law-courts comes a close second, and it is easy to see that contemporaries looked on the two sides of his work as inseparable. This is the universal testimony: 'chief manager of the king's wealth and justice'; 'judge and tax collector of the whole of England'; 'judge of all England after the king'; 'manager of the whole kingdom'; 'chief agent of the king's will'; 'overseer of the business of the whole kingdom'; 'manager and supervisor of the king's courts throughout England'; 'the head

---

[1] J. H. Round 'The Introduction of Knight Service into England', *E.H.R.*, 1891–2, vi and vii; reprinted in *Feudal England*, 1895, see esp. pp. 226–9.

of all royal officials'. These phrases from many different sources describe his position in terms that cannot be paralleled for any earlier or later royal servant.[1]

There is no title which defined his position. Scholars used to think that he was Treasurer, but this is certainly an error.[2] Near-contemporary writers sometimes call him Justiciar, and this is right so far as it goes. He certainly acted at times as one of the king's local or itinerant judges, and sometimes he had some general responsibility, of a kind later associated with the justiciarship. But he was never the Justiciar *tout court*, for this great office did not yet exist, though Flambard's career was an important milestone on the road to its creation.

Royal charters call him simply *capellanus regis*, and this was certainly right; he was one of the king's chaplains. But contemporaries understood that in his case the title was used with a special emphasis; *singulariter nominabatur capellanus regis*, writes one; and another, *Ranulfus vocabatur capellanus regis propter quandam excellentiam familiaritatis*. There is perhaps no better indication that a new power has arisen than the use of a humble title with, so to speak, a knowing wink. Insiders knew that Flambard was not just another royal chaplain; he was the *King's Chaplain*. Geoffrey Gaimar, the colourful historian of the next generation, appreciated what this meant. He describes the king sitting with Flambard at his side when a letter arrived with the news of the revolt of Le Mans. The king took the letter, broke the seal, and handed it to Flambard to read. He was the king's right-hand man, contriving all things to meet the king's needs.[3]

Besides their common testimony to his position, many sources add some individual or local detail of their own. It is a measure of the universality of Flambard's activity that the details have to be gathered from many sides. To understand his impact on individual

---

[1] The evidence of contemporary sources is collected by Freeman, *The Reign of William Rufus*, 1882, ii, 557–67. To the sources he cites there should be added: *Annales monasterii de Wintonia* in *Annales Monastici*, R.S., ed. H. R. Luard, 1865, ii, 36–41 (an important source); Symeon of Durham, *Opera omnia*, R.S., ed. T. Arnold 1882–5, i, 135, ii, 230; Henry of Huntingdon, *Historia Anglorum*, R.S., ed. T. Arnold, pp. 232, 316; *The Life of Christina of Markyate*, ed. C. H. Talbot, 1959, p. 40; *Memorials of St. Edmund's Abbey*, R.S., ed. T. Arnold, i, 86, 156; *Liber Eliensis*, ed. E. O. Blake, 1962, pp. 218–9, 223, 234; *Chronicon monasterii de Abingdon*, R.S., ed. J. Stevenson, 1858, ii, 39; *Historians of the Church of York*, R.S., ed. J. Raine, 1886, ii, 102.

[2] It arose from a confusion with Ranulf, treasurer of the cathedral of York (see *Early Yorkshire Charters*, ed. C. T. Clay, vi, pp. 70, 73–4).

[3] G. Gaimar, *Lestorie des Engles*, R.S., i, l. 5818.

religious houses we must turn to the Abingdon and Ely records and to the miracles of St. Edmund at Bury. For the most lively sketch of his career we must go to Orderic Vitalis writing in Normandy at St. Evroul in the diocese of Lisieux. This might seem an unlikely source of reliable information. But we shall see that Flambard never showed his practical virtuosity more clearly than when he controlled the diocese of Lisieux at the great crisis of his career, and Orderic had reason and opportunity to look closely at this formidable character. Likewise at Durham there was a writer who had seen Flambard at close quarters: his judgement is the best, and his details the most precise, that we have. At Winchester too, the centre of royal government, Flambard was a familiar figure, and the fullest details of his official career are to be found in the annals of Hyde Abbey, which was separated from the royal palace by only a dividing wall. Then, at Huntingdon, Flambard had a wife and family and relatives belonging to the English urban community, and this local association explains his somewhat ignominious appearances in the *Life* of the Huntingdon girl, Christina of Markyate. In York too he was remembered for his testimony in the dispute with Canterbury, and of all unlikely places it was here that the earliest details of his official career were recorded for their bearing on this dispute.

Wherever we look there are men whose paths crossed those of Flambard, and they did not forget it. It would be difficult to find any other person, who was neither a king nor a saint, about whom so many writers of this period had something original to say. Their information was not great in bulk, but it conveys an important impression: Flambard appeared to the men who saw him as something new in their experience. They were not mistaken: he was a new phenomenon in English government. This son of an obscure priest in the diocese of Bayeux was the first man of ignoble birth in English history to climb from the bottom to the top of the social scale by the backstairs of the royal administration. He had many successors, but not many who climbed so far or so fast.

He began his career as a hanger-on of the royal court, perhaps as a servant of Maurice who became the royal chancellor about 1080. He seems at first to have been known as Ranulf Passeflambard, which we may interpret as 'torch-bearer' or 'link-boy'; and Orderic says that Robert the Dispenser was responsible for giving him the name which stuck to him for the rest of his life, 'Flambard', the Torch or Firebrand.[1] The origins are all very obscure, but the name suggests a moment when the fiery young upstart began to blaze a trail of his own.

The earliest steps in his rise belong to the reign of the Conqueror. By 1085 he was keeper of the royal seal under the Chancellor Maurice. Then in 1085, when Maurice became bishop of London, Flambard continued in the royal service. It was at this stage in his career that he was kidnapped by his enemies and carried on a ship down the Thames to be disposed of at sea. The Durham writer gives a dramatic account of the presence of mind and the coolness with which he threw his seal overboard and persuaded his captors to put him back on shore unhurt.[2] These qualities were to save him in future on more than one occasion but he still had a long way to go. By the time of the Conqueror's death in 1087 he was a man of some substance with scattered estates recorded in Domedsay Book. He had small pieces of land in Middlesex, Hampshire, Berkshire, Oxfordshire, Surrey, Wiltshire and Somerset; he had a house in Oxford and two churches at Godalming in Surrey.[3] Most of these lands were held from the king, and they were no doubt his share of the gentle dew of royal favour which has slaked the thirst of royal officials through the centuries. But official service also brought benefits from other sources. His small estate in Middlesex on the lands of Maurice, bishop of London recalls his service with the bishop when he was chancellor. His estates in Somerset and Wiltshire on the lands of the abbeys of Malmesbury and Bath were probably payments for services rendered in the course of business at the royal court. The total value of these estates was not great—about £30 a year—but they were a fair beginning. Flambard was now important enough to have powerful enemies who desired his death; but he also had friends. Best of all, the new king was his friend.

The partnership between Rufus and Flambard can almost be counted among the great partnerships of history between a king and his minister. It was cemented by a like-mindedness which

---

[1] Ordericus Vitalis, *Hist. eccl.*, iii, 310–311.

[2] Symeon of Durham, op. cit. ii, 135–8.

[3] Domesday Book, i, 127 a ii, 49 a ii, 51 a ii, 58 a ii, 157 a i, 30 b ii, 67 a i, 89 b ii, 154 a i, 30 b ii. In addition to these holdings, an *uxor Radulfi capellani* held a very small estate from the king in Herefordshire: it is possible that she was Flambard's wife (D.B. i, 187 b i).

went deeper than self-interest. They were both men of ready wit and audacity, fertile in invention, rapid and irrepressible in action. They were both utterly secular and untouched by the religious ideals of their own, or any other, age. Neither Flambard nor his master can be called respectable. But they suited each other, like Elizabeth and Burghley, or Henry I and Roger of Salisbury. Flambard brought to the work of government an inexhaustible vitality; and Rufus's insatiable need of money provided an incentive for unremitting activity. No other moment in the history of government would have provided such opportunities. It was a time when the agencies of administration were sufficiently developed to repay continuous vigilance, but the machine had not developed beyond the power of one man's control. Flambard initiated the tireless search for money for foreign conquest which is the hall-mark of English government in the Middle Ages. The royal government was always in need of money, and it could never be too nice in its expedients for raising it. If it was more frankly predatory in Rufus's reign than at most times, this was partly because the king and his minister were more than usually contemptuous of ecclesiastical opinion, and partly because they were just beginning to discover the extent to which administration and justice could be a source of profit. First among royal ministers Flambard systematically exploited these sources of revenue. He is the first outstandingly successful administrator in English history.

The most important evidence for these statements comes from the royal administrative and judicial writs of Rufus's reign. It is in them that we find the commentary on the judgements of contemporary writers. By any later standards the writs of William Rufus are not numerous, but they show a fertile inventiveness in developing new forms of royal mandates as instruments of royal administration. Already by the reign of William Rufus royal writs had a long history as a means of making transfers of land and other transactions known to royal officials in the counties. What was new and important was the growing use of the writ as a means of daily communication between the central government and its local officials—ordering them to hear pleas, assess liability, survey property, enforce judgements and secure the king's peace. Writs for such purposes as these are but feebly represented in our archives before the end of the eleventh century, but they are considerably more numerous in the thirteen years of Rufus's reign than in the twenty-one years of his father, and they have become terser and more professional. In these documents we see the emergence of a small body of officials habitually acting together in the king's business. At their head stood Ranulf Flambard, with Urso de Abitot and the stewards Eudo and Haimo as his most regular colleagues.[1]

The growing importance of these officials can be seen in the king's arrangements for the government of the kingdom in his absence. It had been William I's practice when he went abroad —as he did for long periods—to leave the kingdom in the charge of great men like Archbishop Lanfranc and Odo of Bayeux. With Rufus there was a change of emphasis: he left England to the care of a commission of royal officials. Thus from 1097–1099 Walchelin bishop of Winchester, a former royal chaplain, and Flambard were regents. Then in 1099 Ranulf Flambard, now himself a bishop, was left in charge, with Haimo the Steward and Urso de Abitot as his colleagues. There are several writs which preserve the orders sent by the king of Normandy to these ministers in England, requiring action to be taken either by local officials or by a royal officer.[2] These are our earliest illustrations of the elaboration of administrative routine made necessary by the king's absences abroad. With this growth of government by writ we see also the growth of new formulae and sanctions designed to add force to the orders transmitted in this way. The distant origins of the judicial processes of the writs of right and *praecipe* and *novel disseisin* have been traced back to Rufus's writs; and the threat of a £10 fine for disregarding the royal writ becomes a fairly common feature of his reign.[3]

Even without the testimony of the chroniclers the royal writs would be sufficient to show that Flambard stood at the head of the royal administration in the last years of Rufus's reign. What can we discover about the steps by which he reached this position? As we have seen, he was already keeper of the king's seal under the

[1] Flambard appears with Urso and at least one of the two stewards in the following writs of Rufus' reign: *Regesta*, i, nos. 337, 387, 416, 418, 422; ii, no. 377a.

[2] Ibid. i, nos. 416, 422, 424.

[3] For these origins see R. C. van Caenegem, *Royal Writs in England from the Conquest to Glanvill*, 1959, esp. pp. 406–515. The existence of unrecorded developments in William I's reign cannot of course be ruled out but on any assessment the increase in activity under Rufus is very striking. For the £10 fine for neglect of the royal writ under Rufus, see *Regesta*, i, no. 322; ii, nos. 399a, 400a, 485a.

chancellor before 1086, but there is no sign that he had any
independent sphere of action while William I lived. Then quite
early in the next reign we find him in a position of authority in the
Fens. Here the abbot of Ely found himself in difficulties. He was
a very old man, unable to control his tenants. To save himself
from their depredations he called for the help of the royal justices.
Flambard arrived in person and dealt with the affairs of the
monastery with brutal efficiency. He allocated a portion of the
total monastic revenue to the monks at the rate of about £2 a year
a head, and he appropriated the remainder for the abbot. This
lion's share soon came into his own hands when the abbot died and
Flambard assumed control as the king's agent. The monastic
annalist remembered the visitation and the measures that followed
it like a bad dream. Flambard took the view that the monks had
enough when their share of the monastic goods sufficed for the
bare purposes of their monastic life; he himself would look after
the rest.[1]

It is perhaps to this early phase of his career under Rufus that
we should refer a story which Orderic tells of his having persuaded
the king to revise the assessment of the countryside for royal
taxation by measuring it with ropes. Orderic's story cannot be
accepted as it stands for there was certainly no universal reassessment of the kind he describes. But there are signs of various
reassessments in the Fens which may have taken place at this time,
and we know that Orderic visited this area in 1115. The monks of
Thorney for instance evidently suffered from some unrecorded
reassessment, for they visited Rufus in Normandy and obtained a
writ addressed to Flambard and his colleagues ordering them to
reassess the abbey for 'gelds, scots, military service and all dues as
favourably as any honour in England with the same amount of
land', restoring whatever had been taken by the royal officers above
this amount. Ramsey Abbey also suffered from an increase in its
military service at this time, and it too had to obtain an order
from Rufus reducing its service to the old level. Certainly a
reassessment of services, based on surveying and measuring areas
of land, was not beyond the capacity of a government that had
just produced Domesday Book, and there is evidence that rods and
ropes for measuring land were used in Normandy in the eleventh
century and in England in the twelfth. On the whole it seems

[1] *Liber Eliensis*, ed. E. O. Blake, pp. 218–9, 223, 234.

likely that Orderic's story had some foundation, and the Fens, with their growing area of cultivation, were well suited to such an experiment.[1] Whatever the truth about this, Flambard was certainly very active in this area. At Huntingdon, as we have seen, he had a wife and raised a family, and this was probably the first centre from which he operated. A few miles north of Huntingdon lay the abbey of Ramsey. He was there in June 1088 with another royal chaplain witnessing a charter of the abbot Herbert Losinga. In 1090 Herbert bought the see of Thetford for himself, and the abbey of Hyde for his father. It was the most elaborate piece of simony in the reign, and—since Flambard was certainly in charge of Hyde Abbey and probably Thetford also—the transaction could easily have arisen from the local association of the two men. They continued to co-operate throughout the reign, and it is remarkable how many of those writs in which Flambard has a prominent rôle were drawn up in favour of Herbert Losinga.[2]

This association introduces us to the later phase of Flambard's administrative career, and to the activity which made him notorious. From the early years of the reign he was in charge of ecclesiastical sequestrations. According to the well-informed annals of Winchester, he had the custody of the vacant abbey of Hyde as early as 1088, and of the archbishopric of Canterbury in the following year. From this date he seems to have had a general responsibility for all ecclesiastical property falling into the king's hands during a vacancy. He made it a very important part of the royal revenue. The statement of the Winchester annalist that in 1097 he had sixteen vacant bishoprics and abbeys under his care, and that each of them contributed on average 300–400 marks (about £250) a year to the king, cannot be checked in detail but it does not seem extravagant.[3] If so, the king depended on this part of Flambard's activity for about £4,000 a year, or something like one-fifth of his total revenue. In principle there was nothing original in this: that the king should receive the revenues of vacant

---

[1] Ordericus Vitalis, *Hist. Eccl.*, iii, 311–2. For the writs for Thorney and Ramsey, see *Regesta*, nos. 422, 462, and *Cart. monasterii de Rameseia, R.S.*, ed. W. H. Hart and P. A. Lyons, 1884, i, 235. For examples of measurements of land with a rope in eleventh century Norman sources, see F. Lot, *Etudes critiques sur l'abbaye de S. Wandrille*, 1913, p. 40, and Dudo, *De moribus actibusque Normannorum, P.L.*, 141, 652.

[2] *Regesta*, i, 321, 322, 419; ii, 385 a, b and c (LXI b, c and d, p. 411).

[3] *Ann. Winton*, in *Annales Monasticii, R.S.*, ii, 39.

sees was commonplace. The originality of Flambard's activity lay simply in the methodical, businesslike and ruthless fashion with which this source of revenue was exploited. The method of exploitation—pensioning the monastic community and appropriating the remaining revenue—which became associated with Flambard's name at Ely and elsewhere, was already practised in the reign of William I; but Flambard reduced the whole process to a routine. It was also quite normal in the eleventh century that the king should appoint prelates after a vacancy and take a fee from his nominee; it was the stripping away of all pretence, and the naked search for profit, that shocked contemporaries. Business came before everything.

The system was undoubtedly repellent, but the resulting appointments were not obviously worse than those of the preceding or succeeding reigns. Nor did the system hit all monastic communities with equal severity. Those houses which had made a division between the estates of the monastic community and the abbot suffered less than those which had the division thrust upon them by Flambard and his officers. During the vacancy at Durham from 1096 to 1099 it was recorded that the king took £300 a year from the bishopric, but nothing from the monks, who were treated with generosity.[1] Even at Canterbury, where the monks were never slow to sense oppression, there was remarkably little resentment at the treatment of the community during the long vacancy. At Hyde Abbey, which suffered two long vacancies and one simoniacal appointment during the reign, it is somewhat grotesque to find the name of Flambard, the chief agent and instigator of these measures among the benefactors of the church in its confraternity book.[2] At Peterborough, after the disastrous rule of a Norman abbot appointed by the Conqueror, the monks were glad to be able to buy from Rufus—or more likely his agent Flambard—the right of electing an Englishman at last.[3] Like all systems this one also had its bright side; but nothing can hide the fact that the whole system of sequestrations and appointments was designed simply for the more efficient extraction of money.

[1] Symeon of Durham, *R.S.*, i, 135.
[2] *Register and Martyrology of New Minster and Hyde Abbey*, ed. W. de Gray Birch, 1892, p. 67.
[3] The new abbot, Godric, won the praises of the monks, but their freedom did not last long: Godric was deposed by Anselm in 1102, probably for simony. (*Chronicle of Hugh Candidus*, ed. W. T. Mellows, 1949, p. 86)

It was Flambard's success in this business that commended him chiefly to Rufus. The stages of his rise to the top place in the administration can be only sketchily distinguished. A list of the members of the royal household in January 1091 gives him only a humble place—ninth in a list of eleven chaplains. But by September 1093 he had broken through to the top. From this date his name frequently appears in royal writs immediately after the bishops and chancellor, at the head of the clerical and lay members of the royal household. Henceforth he was the effective head of the administration in England in the king's absence. Finance, to which he owed his rise, remained his chief preoccupation, for the king could never have enough. Wherever there was money to be had, there was Flambard. In 1094, when the king had suffered a severe reverse in Normandy and called for the English fyrd, it was Flambard who went down to Hastings and took the soldiers' money for the king instead of their services. In 1096, when every source of money had to be tapped to pay Duke Robert for the lease of Normandy, Flambard's name was at the head of the witnesses of the most famous of Rufus's writs ordering the tenants of the vacant bishopric of Worcester to pay a relief to the king.

Naturally most of the existing evidence refers to his financial dealings with the church, but the promise in Henry I's coronation charter that the heirs of barons shall no longer buy back their lands as in the time of his brother but 'relieve' them with a just and reasonable relief shows the same mind at work in secular affairs. Here again there is no sign of originality in theory. We now know that the principle of hereditary right in feudal tenure had a much harder struggle to prevail than was formerly realized. The king's right to take seisin of the estates of his dead tenants, and to make a new bargain with the heir, took a long time to die. In principle Rufus probably went no further than his father in enforcing this right. But to judge from the wording of Henry's coronation charter Rufus's ministers seem to have dealt with secular fiefs in the same systematic ruthless fashion as ecclesiastical fiefs. We hear of Flambard's operations in secular affairs only in the most casual way as they happened to impinge on ecclesiastical affairs, but the Worcester writ illustrates the method of dealing with the sub-tenants of a great fief.

The writ ordered the tenants of the bishop of Worcester to pay a relief to the king on the death of Bishop Wulfstan, which took place in January 1095.[1] The constitutional issue involved in this demand have often been debated, but the administrative lessons have been overlooked, though I think they are easier to see. In the first place the writ illustrates the extreme alertness of Rufus's government. It acted quickly—probably within a few weeks of Wulfstan's death—and it acted on an assessment of liability that could only have been based on up-to-date local knowledge. Secondly, the writ illustrates the rewards of administrators. Some of the greatest royal officials, like Urso de Abitot, were themselves tenants of the bishopric, but the demands from them are conspicuous by their absence. This was one of the attractions of the royal service: the servants of the king did not have to pay like other men.

So far I have spoken mainly of Flambard's financial activity, but finance easily shaded off into law. Flambard was known not only as the *exactor*, but also as the *placitator*, of the whole of England. This word *placitator* exactly expresses his function: he was the king's advocate, pleading the king's cause and asserting the king's rights in the local courts. Whether he also acted as judge is less clear. Perhaps the functions of judge and advocate were not always clearly distinguished. In any case, it was certainly as an advocate that Flambard won notoriety. No doubt there was much for him to do. Domesday Book shows many cases of disputed possession, and there were many more that it does not show. However imposing the king's position might appear, when it came to local claims the king had to fight for his own like everyone else. In this field Flambard was his chief agent.

The first clear reference to this activity comes from the year 1093. On Sunday, 25 September, on the day of Anselm's enthronement, Flambard appeared at Canterbury to begin a law-suit against the archbishop on some matter affecting the royal rights. Two years later, we find him in Bury St. Edmund's with Bishop Walchelin, the head of the royal government. The two of them intended to spend three days transacting royal business. They were diverted, apparently without any sense of incongruity, from this work to the task of translating the relics of St. Edmund, and

---

[1] *Regesta*, no. 387; Round, *Feudal England*, pp. 308–11; I. Atkins, 'The Church of Worcester from the 8th to the 12th Century', *Antiquaries Journal*, 1940, xx, 209–11.

it was only thus that we come to hear of their visit. It was probably on the same tour that Walchelin and Ranulf, with the sheriff of Norfolk, surveyed the site for a new cathedral at Norwich and allocated the necessary land to Bishop Herbert Losinga. In the following year the same pair were in Devon and Cornwall pressing their claims to land which was alleged to belong to the royal demesne.[1]

Among the miscellaneous writs which illustrate Flambard's judicial activity there is one which throws light on an important feature of royal justice: the power of enforcing or relaxing the king's legal claims, whereby friends could be helped and enemies harassed. We shall never know many details of the see-saw of royal favour and displeasure, nor how much was paid, nor to whom, for acts of clemency, but we can sometimes observe the effects. For instance, the royal writ ordering the sheriff of Norfolk and Suffolk to restore to the bishop of Thetford land which had been adjudged to the king in suits instituted against him by Ranulf the Chaplain, shows how important the good-will of the king and his officials could be. Flambard was here the agent who pressed the royal claims; he was also the sole witness of the writ which freed the bishop of Thetford from the consequences of the royal suit.[2] The two facts were certainly not unconnected. A good deal of the strength of his position probably lay in this double role: he could both urge on the hounds and call them off at will.

The power to intimidate and relieve at will opened up prospects of gain. Flambard, like all royal officers, must have received large rewards from many sources in the course of his duties. The custody of so many abbeys and bishoprics could not fail to bring some personal profit. Of these rewards only a few traces remain. At the beginning of Henry I's reign, Flambard held an estate at Wytham which belonged to Abingdon Abbey—no doubt a result of the vacancy from 1097 to 1100. In Hertfordshire he held the manor of Much Hadham, which belonged to Ely Abbey—a house which had given him many opportunities for profit. In Norfolk he held land of the bishop of Thetford. In Cambridgeshire there are two estates known as Flambard's Manor, in villages where the

[1] Eadmer, *Historia Novorum*, *R.S.*, ed. M. Rule, p. 41; *Regesta*, nos. 385, 399; for Flambard's part in the foundation of Norwich Cathedral, B. Dodwell, *Trans. Royal Hist. Soc.*, 1957, 5th Ser., vii, p. 8.

[2] *Regesta*, ii, 385 c (LXI c, p. 411).

abbot of Ely also held or claimed some land. At both of these sites there are remains of moats which seem to belong to this period, and it is tempting to think that here we have material evidence of Flambard's personal wealth and his passion for building which he shared with every Norman magnate.[1]

In addition, he was a canon of Salisbury and head of two colleges of secular canons at Dover and Christchurch in Hampshire, both in the royal gift. The latter gave him his first chance to show his powers as a builder and organizer on his own account. The college consisted of twenty-four canons, each of whom received a share of the offerings at the altar. Flambard persuaded them to surrender their individual revenues in return for a promise to provide them with food. With the proceeds he began to build the massive church which still stands. As the canons died off he kept their places vacant, intending in the end to make over the whole foundation to a religious order. By 1100 only five of the original twenty-four canons were left, so Flambard's plan was within sight of success. But the death of the king gave him other things to think about.[2]

These operations are an indication that, quite apart from the royal service, Flambard had an insatiable urge for organization and administration. In 1099 his scope for satisfying this urge became even greater. The king gave him the bishopric of Durham. He had reached the peak of his career. For another year he continued as bishop to act as the chief agent of the royal government. Then on 2 August 1100 Rufus was killed and Flambard's career in the royal service was at an end. Worse still, he was a ruined man. On 15 August he was arrested, deprived of his bishopric, and imprisoned in the Tower, the first of all the state prisoners to lie there. A new constellation of power began to appear round Henry I, including most of the officials of Rufus's household. Flambard was to be the scapegoat for the whole regime. But while Henry I was building up his body of supporters, Flambard was himself not without friends. With their help he climbed out of the Tower on 3 February 1101 and escaped to Normandy. He was safe; but the

---

[1] For Wytham, see *Chron. monasterii de Abingdon, R.S.*, ii, 83–4; for Much Hadham, *Regesta*, ii, no. 684; for the land in Cambridgeshire, *V.C.H. Cambs.*, ii, 4, 36, 38.
[2] For Flambard's operations at Christchurch, see Dugdale, *Monasticon Anglicanum*, 1846, vi, 303, and A. H. Thompson, *History of Bolton Priory*, Thoresby Society, 1928, xxx, 20–1. For his canonry at Salisbury, *Regesta*, ii, no. 753; iii, no. 789.

outlook was bleak. He was a runaway bishop with no great family connections; his bishopric was in the hands of royal officers; he himself was liable to be deposed with ignominy at any moment for notorious offences. His position could not have been worse.

## III

If anything were needed to prove that Rufus's confidence in his ability had not been misplaced, Flambard's career in the next few years would provide evidence in abundance. He appeared to be indispensable to government wherever he was. He was no sooner in Normandy than he became the chief adviser of Duke Robert. For once the Duke acted promptly and invaded England, and all contemporaries agreed that Flambard was the mainspring of this invasion. The initial landing on 20 July 1101 took King Henry off his guard, and his position was so shaky that Robert must have succeeded if he had not been a man of exceptional stupidity. In the event he threw away his opportunities. Robert met his brother Henry at Alton in July 1101, and agreed to give up his claim to the Crown in return for a pension of £2,000. Duke Robert good-naturedly but imprudently persuaded Henry to meet Flambard. A writ was issued granting him a safe-conduct to meet the king in London. They met. They came to an agreement. Another writ was immediately issued restoring Flambard to the full possession of his lands and bishopric. On the face of it nothing could be more astonishing than this apparently unnecessary and quite uncharacteristic act of leniency on Henry's part. To a remarkable extent the transaction was kept dark and remained almost unknown till our own days, when Sir Edmund Craster discovered the series of writs which put the matter beyond doubt.[1] The whole thing seemed so unlikely: the king had nothing now to fear; Flambard had nothing to offer. What can be the explanation of this sudden change of fortune?

The explanation almost certainly lies in Henry's determination to conquer Normandy, and in the possibility of using Flambard as an instrument of this over-riding purpose. It was evidently part of the plan that Flambard should return to Normandy and resume his position as adviser to Duke Robert. On this under-

---

[1]'A contemporary record of the pontificate of Ranulf Flambard', *Archeologia Aeliana*, 1930, 33–56.

standing the writs of restitution began to flow from Henry's chancery. The measures taken against him had been so thorough that they took several years to undo, but the greater part of the formality of restitution had been accomplished by the summer of 1102. Archbishop Anselm gave him absolution. The archbishop of York undertook to supervise the work of restoration. Meanwhile Flambard was busy in Normandy and made only occasional visits to England until Henry's final victory over his brother in 1106. During these years he established himself in control of the bishopric of Lisieux, which became vacant in August 1101. First of all he obtained the see for his brother Fulcher; and then on Fulcher's death in 1102 he got it for his own son Thomas, with reversion to another son in the event of his death. The methods he used to impose himself on Duke Robert, and to maintain himself against the rage of ecclesiastical opinion, must remain a mystery, but simony must certainly have played a part. It seems very likely that he escaped to Normandy with a large sum of money, and this may have provided him with resources for his rôle in Normandy, while making Henry I more willing to come to terms with him.[1]

The murky intrigues of these years cannot be followed in detail, but it is certain that, while Henry prepared the destruction of Duke Robert, Flambard was able to maintain a foot in both camps. He passed freely between England and Normandy. When Henry finally invaded Normandy, Flambard was at Lisieux to receive him. Ivo of Chartres seems to have known that he was an agent of the king of England, for he blamed King Henry and not Duke Robert for his tenure of the bishopric of Lisieux:

> What reason, what law (he writes) permits Ranulf Bishop of Durham to cross from one church to another, and by his adulterous presence and the tenure of his sons to invade the church of Lisieux by the violence of the king of England.

He demanded his removal, but nothing happened till the king was ready with a candidate of his own. When the conquest of Normandy was complete and Duke Robert was committed to a life imprisonment, Ranulf quietly left Normandy and returned to his bishopric in Durham. He was safe at last and free to turn his mind to his own affairs.

---

[1] Ordericus Vitalis, *Hist. Eccl.*, iv, 107–10 gives a colourful account of the escape. For Flambard's dealings with the see of Lisieux, see *Hist. Eccl.*, iv, 116–7, and Ivo of Chartres, *Epp.*, 149, 153, 154 (quoted below), 157 (*P.L.* 162).

## IV

He was safe but he had lost ground. Despite the royal writs of restitution in 1101–2 it took years to make good the damage that had been done. His lands had been seized by the royal officers, his cattle had been driven off, his villeins had fled, his neighbours had encroached on his estates, his regal position in the North had crumbled. The results of these misfortunes could not be undone in a day; some results could never be undone. By wonderful agility and exertion he had got back his bishopric when all had seemed lost, but Henry I was too prudent a man ever to make him a member of his inner circle of advisers. He was cut off from the stream of royal favours to which he had been accustomed, and which other men now enjoyed. He had to watch while men of the new generation, like Nigel d'Aubigny, seized estates which belonged to Durham, and he had to wait a long time for redress. It was with the help of men of new families that King Henry secured his own position in Northumberland. He took away areas which had long been more or less part of the diocese of Durham—Hexhamshire, Teviotdale, Cumberland—and gave them to York and his new diocese at Carlisle.[1] Flambard was wise enough to make no protest. He knew how far he could go and how much he still had to lose. He walked very warily where the king was concerned. In 1118 he did not dare sit beside his archbishop, Thurstan, at the Council of Rheims, for fear of stirring up the king's greater displeasure.[2] He was careful to get the king's consent to territorial arrangements in his principality which might be disputed. He took no risks, and he had his reward. In circumstances which invited the extension of royal authority over the whole of the Northern diocese, he managed to preserve his immunity from royal interference and to hammer out the elementary organization of the emergent Palatinate. It was a feat for which he deserved the gratitude of all his successors in the see down to 1832.

The state of the bishopric at his accession is not easy to visualize. In the previous thirty years it had suffered many disasters and the

---

[1] For Nigel d'Aubigny's seizure and belated restitution of lands belonging to Durham see below p. 221; and for the loss of various parts of the diocese, see J. Raine, *The Priory of Hexham*, 1864 (Surtees Soc. xliv), i, 220.

[2] *Historians of the Church of York*, R.S., 1886, ii, 166: the passage is striking because Flambard evidently went as far as he dared in supporting Thurstan in his quarrel with Henry I (ibid. pp. 124, 142).

energies of his immediate predecessor, William of St. Calais, had been more concerned with the establishment of the monastic community at Durham than with the organization of the diocese as a whole. We know virtually nothing about the territorial organization of the bishopric before Flambard. So far as diocesan organization was concerned, William of St. Calais had been content to take his monks into partnership and make the prior of Durham his permanent archdeacon and deputy. There is no evidence at all for the administrative organization of the bishop's regal rights before Flambard.[1]

Into this scene of confusion and frustration Flambard brought the elements of order and clarity. By the time of his death, the pattern of the government of the future was firmly established, with two sheriffs for the secular business and two archdeacons for the ecclesiastical business of the Principality, a well-organized episcopal household, and new families of military tenants. He left things in working order, and little or nothing needed to be undone. Flambard's episcopal household is especially interesting, for he was one of the earliest English bishops to attract scholars to his household. One of these, *Willelmus clericus meus de Curbuil* as he is called in one of Flambard's writs, was soon to be archbishop of Canterbury; another was that still rare thing in government—a man with an academic title.[2] The writs produced in Flambard's name have the stamp of one who was accustomed to exercise royal authority:

> Bishop R. to Papedy sheriff of Norham. Know that I have given Hallowstill to God and St. Mary and St. Cuthbert and his monks. . . . I order you to put them in possession quickly

[1] The fundamental study of the secular organisation of the bishopric is G. T. Lapsley, *The County Palatine of Durham*, 1900. For the ecclesiastical organisation, see H. S. Offler, 'The early archdeacons in the diocese of Durham', *Transactions of the Architectural and Archeological Society of Durham and Northumberland*, 1962, xi, 189–207. For an assessment of Flambard's rôle at Durham, see G. V. Scammell, *Hugh du Puiset, Bishop of Durham*, 1956, pp. 219–220, and most important H. S. Offler, *Durham Episcopal Charters, 1071–1152*, 1968 (Surtees Soc. clxxix), where the fine series of Flambard charters is now collected and critically annotated for the first time.

[2] Offler (pp. 68–72) condemns as violently anachronistic Flambard's charter relating to Godric's hermitage at Finchale in which Master Robert de Chaumont and William of Corbeil appear as witnesses. I am not quite convinced by the argument, but there is in any case other evidence that both these men were members of Flambard's household (*Regesta*, ii, no. 721; Symeon of Durham, *R.S.* i, 258).

and without contradiction; and if you delay, I order my nephew Ranulf to do this without delay, so that I may hear no further complaint in this matter.[1]

It was thus in earlier days that he had spoken in the king's name.

But however strongly he was impelled by an urge to organize, it would be unrealistic to suppose that he had no personal motives in these activities. He had a large family to provide for, and now at the end of his career he had to do for them what he could. His father, who had come to England, died as a monk of St. Augustine's Canterbury, and was commemorated at Durham. One of Flambard's sons, Elias, was endowed with a canonry at Lincoln and an estate in Oxfordshire, and this arrangement was the subject of an elaborate charter which Flambard had the foresight to obtain from the king. Another son (for so he appears to be[2]), William fitz Ranulf, was enfeoffed with two knight's fees on the bishop's estates; for this arrangement too Flambard prudently obtained the king's consent. A third son, Ralph, became parson of Bishop Middleham in County Durham. He served in his father's household, and later he had a very respectable career alongside Thomas Becket in the household of Archbishop Theobald of Canterbury. Of his nephews, one became sheriff of Durham and a landowner in the county; a second became archdeacon of Northumberland; a third, as lord of Ravensworth, founded a family with a long history among the minor aristocracy of the North.[3] In one way and another Flambard planted his family. Flambards are to be found in Yorkshire in the thirteenth century, and many quiet families of

[1] Offler, no. 20.
[2] Offler, p. 74, thinks this unlikely since Flambard never calls him his son and he was 'normally not diffident about acknowledging his children'; he prefers to see him as 'pretty closely related to the bishop'. The relationship must remain uncertain, but I am more impressed by the remarkable terms of the three charters in favour of William fitz Ranulf than by Flambard's silence as to their relationship, for I do not know that he anywhere calls anyone his son. There was certainly no one else whom he took so much trouble to endow; and his emphasis on the king's permission, the consent of the monks, the hereditary right of the beneficiary, and the request for aid are all very striking: 'Quicunque illum manutenuerit et adiuverit et bonum consilium ei dederit benedictionem dei et sancti Cuthberti et nostram et hic et in eternum habeat.' (Offler, nos. 11, 12, 13.)
[3] There are many details about Flambard's family in Offler, *passim*. In addition, for his son Elias see *Regesta*, ii, nos. 1104, 1364; for Ralph, parson of Bishop Middleham, A. Saltman, *Theobald, Archbishop of Canterbury*, 1956, pp. 262, 286, 368, 404, 474, 546; for Ranulf, Archdeacon of Durham, *The Priory of Hexham*, ed. J. Raine, Surtees Soc., 1864, i, 141–2, 167, 220.

Tees and Weardale must to this day have the blood of Flambard in their veins.

These men repaid him with lasting loyalty and service. There are few touching episodes in the Flambard story, but one of them is recorded in two charters of his son Ralph, the parson, and his nephew Osbert, the lord of Bishop Middleham. Nearly twenty years after the bishop's death, in 1146, they came into the church at Durham while Flambard's successor was sitting in full synod. Ralph gave up his church at Bishop Middleham to the monks, 'being moved by the example of that excellent piety with which my father cherished the church and monks of St. Cuthbert while he lived'. Having made this declaration, Ralph and Osbert carried their charters, with their seals and a little knife hanging from them, to the tomb of St. Cuthbert, and then they laid them on the altar between the hands of the bishop.[1] This act of solemn piety and affectionate memory is Flambard's best memorial.

The mention of Flambard's generosity to the monks of Durham seems at first surprising. His reputation in monastic annals has led historians to expect an ogre, and they have found what they expected—a premature member of the Hell Fire Club, robbing the monks in his lifetime, and making an ignominious surrender on his death-bed. This is quite false. Flambard's charters tell a different story. It is true that on his death-bed with many expressions of repentance he restored to the monks lands and revenues which he had unjustly retained. But it does not seem to have been noticed that the total value of the lands he restored was only about £10 a year, and that the offerings which he had wrongfully appropriated had been taken to build the cathedral.[2] These are not evidence of a systematic spoliation, and they were not so regarded by the monks of Durham. Flambard carried through the division of estates between bishop and convent which his predecessor had begun. Perhaps no reasonable division would have satisfied all the aspirations of the monks; perhaps Flambard did not satisfy all reasonable aspirations. But there was no general discontent, nor was there any effort to undo his work. Flambard's final charter shows that the monks had few demands to make. His earlier charters record gifts of tithes and estates with every appear-

[1] Offler, nos. 35, 35a, 35b.
[2] Offler, pp. 104, 109, has made some detailed calculations, which do not differ markedly from the figures I had independently arrived at.

ance of good will. In addition, he enlarged the monastic precincts, finished the building of the church, and enriched it with the elaborate vestments that had become indispensible to the worship of a rich community. On the whole the monks had no reason to complain, and some of them looked back at his pontificate as a golden age.

Whether he was an adequate bishop is another matter. His private life continued to be a source of public scandal and private amusement. Those who knew the story of the saintly recluse Christina of Markyate would learn that her uncle Flambard, the bishop of Durham, had tried to seduce her. Others alleged that in 1125 the papal legate intended to degrade him for incontinence, and went to Durham for this purpose. But the ready wit that had saved Flambard from death at the outset of his career preserved him from degradation at its end. He lured the legate into bed with a less saintly niece than Christina of Markyate, and then burst into the room with companions whom he led in bacchanalian rejoicings.[1] Whatever the truth of these stories, the legate left England in a hurry, and Flambard finished his days in peace.

He seems to have performed the formal duties of a bishop with sufficient diligence. He was a frequent participant at consecrations, translations and other solemnities. He preached at the translation of St. Cuthbert in 1104. When he thought about religion, he thought as other men. There was no incongruity in his final repentance.

His religious benefactions were not large, but they were not purely formal. They expressed something of his own character. In a suburb of Durham he built and endowed the church and hospital of St. Giles for poor persons 'for the salvation of my soul and the redemption of the souls of King William the Conqueror of England and Queen Matilda who raised me up; for the soul of King William who elevated me to the honour of this bishopric; and for the soul of King Henry who confirmed me in that honour'.[2] In this brief sentence he looked back on the history of his rise, and to the moment when he had almost fallen beyond recall. These were the people who had made him what he was. He did not mention

[1] See *The Life of Christina of Markyate*, ed. C. H. Talbot, p. 43; *Ann. de Wintonia* in *Annales Monastici*, ii, 47–8.
[2] Offler, no. 9.

his family in this company. For them he had made provision of another, more material, kind.

It was a strange fate for the boy from Bayeux to be the most princely bishop in England. Only kings could thus have made him almost one of themselves. The hospital was his main personal memorial, but it was not his only benefaction. In the church of St. Giles there acted as doorkeeper for a time one of the most extraordinary men of the North in the twelfth century, the former merchant and future hermit St. Godric. When Godric retired to his hermitage at Finchale in the midst of the bishop's forest, Flambard—at the instigation of his son Ralph—gave him the site. He evidently kept a friendly feeling for the hermit, for men remembered that Godric had left his hermitage only three times, and that on one of these occasions he had come to talk with the bishop at Durham at his request.

There are many signs that Flambard had the warm affections and magnanimity which practical men often find their nearest approach to religion. Undoubtedly the quality which characterized him at Durham, and at all periods of his life, was the power to plan largely and execute boldly. Despite all the restraints put upon him by the absence of royal favour, he made an impression of greatness on those who saw him at Durham: 'impatient of leisure, he went on from labour to labour, thinking nothing done unless new enterprises pressed on the heels of those already accomplished'.[1]

The most talented writer in this golden century of literature in medieval Durham was Lawrence, a monk who had come North in Flambard's lifetime. He looked back in middle age to a time when the greatness of Durham and the genius of its bishop had been well-matched:

> His was a spirit worthy of Durham, worthy of riches, worthy
> of honour, dispensing hospitality with the best. That was our
> golden age, under Ranulf our bishop. His works show his
> wealth, and declare that their author was a truly great-
> hearted man. Durham demands such a man—great in spirit,
> liberal in spending—for Durham is no empty shell for the
> man who holds it.[2]

[1] Symeon of Durham, i, 140.
[2] *Dialogi Laurentii Dunelmensis monachi ac prioris*, ed. J. Raine, Surtees Soc., 1880, p. 22.

Here then he is. Deplorable of course in many ways. But also magnanimous, eloquent without premeditation, bursting with vitality. He brought to the work of government in the king's service and at Durham the ruthless energy of a Viking ancestry. He belonged to the heroic age of government before it became entangled in its own precedents, and before instinct cooled into calculation. By his work he hastened this transition and helped to bring order and routine into the fragile mechanisms of administration. His earthy and tumultuous energies were dedicated to the task of making things work, and though he was guided by no ideals he did less harm than better men who set Europe in arms to create the world of their dreams. The great line of administrators who fashioned and finally destroyed the medieval system of government in England begins with Flambard.

# 11

## KING HENRY I

### I

No English king in a reign of comparable length has left so faint an imprint on the popular imagination or even on the minds of students of history as Henry I. Yet the materials for his reign are neither scarce nor unexciting; they are more varied than for any previous period, and they tell a story of new beginnings in many fields. The earliest documents in the archives of several of the greatest families in our history go back to this reign; the earliest documents of dozens of religious houses belong to the same period. It is the first, and one of the greatest ages of English historical scholarship; if it produced nothing equal to Bede, yet what it produced was the work, not of a single supreme scholar, but of many hands working to meet a widely felt need. At the same time, we have the beginnings of the only purely English religious order; the beginnings of the University of Oxford; the earliest English scholastic writers; the rebirth of English science after a long decline. We have our first Charter of Liberties, which became the immediate inspiration of Magna Carta; the first foreign treaty in our history, embodying a line of thought only extinguished in 1914; the first victory of foot-soldiers over mounted knights, foreshadowing in several particulars the victories of Crecy and Agincourt. We have the first treatise on English law; the first royal financial accounts; the first documents of manorial administration. For the first time it is possible to grasp in some detail the complexity of English government and society.

Why then have the reign and the ruler left so ambiguous an impression? No doubt the main reason is the absence of large personalities, great events, and clearly intelligible policies. Nothing happened of sufficient size to concentrate the attention of historians and to draw together the scattered impressions left by a multitude of unimportant details. Of all the general assessments of the reign, that of Stubbs, written nearly a hundred years ago, still remains the most penetrating. Stubbs misunderstood many of the details, and his generalizations need a radical restatement; but what he tried to say is something which needs to be said. He saw the leading characteristic of the reign in the union of the king and the English people for the repression of feudal violence and the resuscitation of English institutions. Henry I, he says, 'from the first day of his reign, found himself compelled to seek the support of the native English'; 'during the greatest part of his reign he was not only in the closest alliance with the clergy, but the English people, who saw in the clergy their truest friends and champions, uniformly supported him'; and Henry's gratitude, in Stubbs's view, showed itself in the restoration of the local courts of hundred and shire, in the granting of municipal privileges, in strengthening the hands of Anselm and the reforming prelates, and in maintaining good peace by severe and even-handed justice.[1]

These are great claims, but it must be admitted that in detail not one of them will bear inspection. Henry had nothing to fear from the English people; there is not the slightest evidence that any one of his actions was taken to enlist or reward their support. He did not restore the local courts; they did not need restoration. He did all he could to weaken the position of Anselm. He gave municipal privileges as sparingly as possible, and purely for financial gain; and his severe and even-handed justice was more severe than either even-handed or just. Why then is Stubbs's assessment of the reign still worth reading?

In the first place, Stubbs was translating into language intelligible to himself and his readers the universally favourable estimate of Henry contained in all contemporary accounts. Secondly he was giving expression to a feeling which everyone who studies the reign cannot resist: looking to the future, it is here, we feel, that the history of England begins—a history which is neither that of the Norman conquerors, nor that of the Anglo-Saxons, but that of the English Crown and aristocracy. Even if we disbelieve in Henry's goodwill to the English, we cannot help seeing that his reign preserved some of the fundamental features of old English society which the Conquest had threatened to destroy. This is the message of Stubbs, and I believe it has the truth of the matter. But if so, it is clear that his meaning must be expressed in very different terms and illustrated by facts very different from those which he chose as his illustrations.

[1] *Constitutional History*, i, § 110.

## II

We may look first towards the future. If we are right in thinking that the importance of Henry I in English history lies in his
success in establishing certain broad lines of development which
persisted for several centuries, we may expect to find some traces
of this in the work of historians of modern England. Nor are we
disappointed. A medievalist who reads the works on modern
English history which have caused most stir in recent years has a
curious feeling of having been there before. Namier and Tawney,
and the host of supporters and opponents who have followed them,
have succeeded in one unacknowledged aim: they have made
modern history quite surprisingly medieval. They have described
their subject in terms with which any medievalist is familiar from
the time of Henry I onwards. The subjects with which they have
dealt—patronage as an expedient of government and a means of
social climbing, the trade in wardships and marriages, the debts of
great landlords, the rise and fall of landed families, the intricate
web of landlordly rights and interests as determinants of social
change—these things are the very stuff of medieval history,
observable in abundant detail from the early twelfth century but
not earlier.

It is strange that more attention has not been paid to this fact.
If he had borne it in mind Tawney could never have fallen into the
error of supposing that the principles of feudal land-ownership
went down before the practice of economic efficiency only in the
sixteenth and seventeenth centuries; he could never have approved
the hare-brained analysis of Thomas Wilson, who supposed that it
was only in the late sixteenth century that 'gentlemen, who were
wont to addict themselves to the warres, are now for the most part
growen to become good husbandes and knowe as well how to
improve their lands to the uttermost as the farmer or countryman'.[1]
Within the limits of what was possible landowners had been deeply
interested in 'improving' their estates at least from the early
twelfth century onwards. As for the 'rise of the gentry', which
Tawney saw as the main social development of the late sixteenth
and early seventeenth century, this too is a perceptible feature of

---

[1] *The State of England*, A.D. 1600, ed. F. J. Fisher, 1936 (Camden Series,
3rd ser. lii), p. 18, quoted by R. H. Tawney, 'The Rise of the Gentry', *Econ.
Hist. Rev.*, 1941, xi.

the early twelfth century. Whether the gentry were rising or falling in the century before 1640, they had certainly played a far more important part in England since the twelfth century than anywhere else in Europe. And much of the credit for this—if it is a credit—must, as I shall try to show, be given to Henry I.

Henry I is also a significant figure in the history of another aspect of government which has greatly exercised modern historians —I mean the history of patronage as an instrument of government. If the history of patronage ever comes to be written, it will have to begin in the early twelfth century; and the same is true of that aspect of royal patronage on which Professor Trevor-Roper has lately insisted—its importance as a factor in social change.[1] Both these aspects of patronage, the governmental and the social, are of the very greatest importance in the Middle Ages. It would be an exaggeration to say that it was Henry I who made them so; but it was he who first controlled the whole range of government-patronage with which we are later familiar; and it is under him that we can first observe the effects of this patronage at all closely.

It was Namier's greatest service to English history that he described with sympathy and vast knowledge, the system of patronage and its place in the work of government at the moment of its fullest articulation before the rise of parties and principles forever destroyed it. In its details, the system of the eighteenth century is very far from that of the twelfth. But the motives of the men who took part in government 'to make a figure', to better their families and their friends, and to emerge richer than their ancestors, these motives are found perfectly developed—they needed no long period of evolution—in the reign of Henry I. Indeed, for what other reasons could men indulge in so dangerous, laborious and sordid a pursuit? Ideals and principles may only faintly tinge the practice of politics in 1760; they are imperceptible in the secular government of Henry I. No king has been a more devoted Namierite than he. The men who sat at his Exchequer were in a position very similar to the recipients of secret-service money in the eighteenth century. Henry's servants were exempt from Danegeld; George III's pensioners from land-tax. In either case they were better off by about two shillings in the pound. We can find a score of Henry's friends who might have used the language with which Charles Jenkinson in 1770 replied to Townshend's

[1] *The Gentry 1540–1640* (*Econ. Hist. Rev.* Suppl. i).

sneer that his pompous manner did not become a man who owed
his position to his service in the royal government: 'My rise is
from as old a family as his own. I have risen by industry, by
attention to duty, and by every honourable means I could devise'.[1]
Some of them too, like Jenkinson, lived to become earls; but
Henry I would have thought this was going too far, and perhaps
George III thought the same.

In an earlier Raleigh Lecture Sir John Neale described the
system of royal patronage in the government of Queen Elizabeth.
Compared with the well-regulated machine of the eighteenth
century, what he revealed was an immense and chaotic jungle of
offices, bribes and tips supporting the edifice of government. This
is much nearer to the medieval situation. Those who operated in
the jungle of Elizabeth's government did so at great risk and
exposed themselves to much greater unpopularity than the quiet
swallowers of pensions in the government of George III. Elizabeth's beneficiaries had to work, so to speak, in the field, handling
lands, debts, wardships, and monopolies and going personally into
the whole grisly business of making a profit at someone else's
expense. The situation is typical of a much earlier period; it is only
the chaos which has grown. A twelfth-century ruler, having less to
give, could not have afforded to leave so much to the play of
factions as Elizabeth was forced to do; but, in the more restricted
conditions of his time, Henry I operated a machine quite as
powerful as that of Elizabeth. What Neale says about the reign of
Elizabeth can be applied with only minor modifications to that of
Henry I, but only with very great modifications to any earlier
period:

> There were hundreds of offices in her gift, and others which
> could be diverted to her use by the device of recommendary
> letters or verbal orders, sometimes amiable in tone, sometimes
> hectoring, but at all times difficult, if not dangerous, to resist.
> There were also royal lands to be leased or sold, or to be
> granted as reward for services; a source of great wealth and
> most eagerly solicited. Finally there were all those grants by
> letters patent, whether charters, licences, monopolies, or

---

[1] Quoted by L. B. Namier, *The Structure of Politics at the Accession of
George III*, p. 11.

whatever they were, which conferred some benefit on the recipient.[1]

All these elements—even the monopolies—were to be found under Henry I.

How powerful was this machine as an instrument of social change? It has recently been argued by Professor Trevor-Roper that the enjoyment of crown patronage was the most important factor in enabling landed families to better themselves in the century before 1640. Of course this is the sort of proposition that is incapable of proof. Even if we had many more and better statistics than we have, or are ever likely to have, they would always tell us more about the recipients of crown patronage than about quiet families putting a little aside year by year. No doubt, in the end, these quiet processes of economic growth count most in the redistribution of wealth. But, barring a revolution in agrarian techniques, economic growth is a slow business. A family will have to wait a long time to rise significantly by improvements in draining and ditching, manuring and breeding, and the keeping of accounts. For rapid growth some external impulse is needed, and I am quite sure that—whatever may be true of the seventeenth century— royal patronage was the chief external impulse to social climbing in the twelfth century; and it is in Henry I's reign that we can first see this impulse at work, operating in a modern fashion.

It is time to turn to his reign and to draw together at their visible point of origin these factors in the modern history of England: the exercise of patronage as a means of government; the emergence of royal patronage as an instrument of social change and especially as a means of consolidating the position of that class of lesser aristocracy known to historians as the gentry.

## III

Henry I was not a creator of institutions; he contributed nothing to the theory of kingship or to the philosophy of government. He created men. It was his contribution to English government and society to insert into the social fabric men with a direct interest in the success of royal government; men who depended on

---

[1] 'The Elizabethan Political Scene', *Proc. of the British Academy*, 1948, xxxiv, 98–9, reprinted in *Essays in Elizabethan History*, 1958.

royal government for their rise, and on its continuance for their survival. This essential fact about him was noticed by Orderic Vitalis in his famous passage describing the new men whom Henry 'raised, so to speak, from the dust and placed over earls and castellans in power and wealth'.[1] Much has been said about the content of this passage; but there is one thing which is easy to overlook. To raise men was not in itself remarkable: the test came in keeping them loyal. William the Conqueror had raised new men, but their loyalty proved to be of very short duration. Of his eight earldoms only one survived in its original family beyond the early years of the twelfth century. The others disappeared in a succession of unsuccessful rebellions. In the disloyalty of these men the Norman dynasty merely experienced the bitter truth of which the Merovingians and Carolingians had been made aware, that when a dynasty had exhausted its powers of rewarding its friends it could hope for no more loyalty. By the time of Henry I the Norman dynasty was ominously approaching that term of years which had proved fatal to the Carolingian family. New men alone could not save it; without loyalty they could only hasten the decline. It was Henry's greatest achievement that he retained the loyalty of the men he raised up and bound them to his service.

He did not at once discover the secret of success. His earliest measures, though essential for his immediate survival, seemed to be designed to hasten the decline of royal power in England. His coronation charter was no doubt necessary, but on a moderate estimate its concessions can scarcely have cost less than £4,000 or £5,000 a year; the treaty with the Count of Flanders was essential, but it cost another £500 a year; the agreement with Robert of Normandy was a great stroke of policy, but it cost another £2,000 a year. Within a year Henry had parted with perhaps a third of the revenue of Rufus—probably more. Moreover he had been obliged to give his earliest patronage to the families of the Clares, the Giffards and the Beaumonts. These were dangerous friends. Robert of Beaumont, Count of Meulan, used his commanding position to enrich himself without scruple, and, though he remained a loyal and malevolent force in Henry's counsels, he left a son ripe for rebellion. As for the Clares and the Giffards, the boasts of the Ely chronicler about his abbot, Richard of Clare, to whom Henry gave the abbey on his coronation day, show the

[1] Ordericus Vitalis, *Hist. Eccl.*, iv, 164.

dangers to which the king exposed himself by his earliest acts of patronage. The chronicler exults in his abbot's power as he stood in the royal court surrounded by his relatives, the Clares and the Giffards—families (he says) made illustrious by their strength and numbers, capable of overawing assemblies of nobles so that none dared to resist them in their lawsuits or entertain their enemies because of the many murders perpetrated at their hands; even the royal majesty (he adds) was shaken by the frequent terror they inspired.[1] These words take us behind the façade of institutions and legalisms to the brute facts of the situation. It was not by men such as these that Henry was to maintain his position and settle the future of royal government in England.

The great forfeitures of 1102 which followed the destruction of the Montgomery family gave Henry his chance of survival. But they made it by no means certain. His whole situation was complicated by a continental ambition which was often to muddy the stream of English history in the future. He already had England; it was his great aim to have Normandy as well. This was an ambition indefensible in its general purpose, deleterious in its effects, and unjust in the measures by which he was obliged to encompass it. But we must accept it as the aim which in the last resort came before everything else. He spent most of his money and most of his time, and raised up a host of enemies and dangers in order to achieve this end. The defence of Normandy came before every consideration of political prudence. On England this had two effects. On the one hand it involved Henry in his only act of folly in the distribution of his patronage. When he raised Stephen of Blois to a position of the greatest importance in both England and Normandy, it must have been clear even at the time that this was a dangerous step. In the event it was almost disastrous. It was justifiable solely because the defence of Normandy required an understanding with the Count of Blois. This was a calculated risk, but the chief effect of Henry's Norman policy on English affairs was accidental. Since England was mainly valuable as a source of treasure for foreign war, the agents of government who provided this treasure had an importance and freedom which they could scarcely otherwise have obtained. This situation had a profound effect on the development of English society, and the first results are to be seen in Henry's reign.

[1] *Liber Eliensis*, ed. E. O. Blake, pp. 226–7.

## IV

Henry left a large liberty to the men in England who provided him with the sinews of war. He did what he could for them, and they provided him with what he needed. It was rarely that he failed them; but they had to work for what they got. Stephen of Blois could rise to the top with splendid ease, borne upwards by his family connexions and military usefulness. But he was exceptional. Far below him smaller men had to claw their way up the social ladder in the sweat of their brows and under a heavy burden of governmental responsibility. The struggle for power, which in Normandy was crudely military, in England was shifted from the political and military level to the courts; and here the advantage lay not with the very great, but with the men on the spot who worked and manoeuvred and levered their way into the interstices of the feudal structure.

If we wish to see how such men operated, and how the king made it possible for them to operate, we cannot do better than to take a single example, which may in essentials stand for all. The men who 'rise to great places by a winding stair' are necessarily grey figures, and their activities become monotonous by repetition. Yet each successful effort of this kind is in its own way a masterpiece of political manoeuvre. The Pipe Roll of 1130 allows us to trace the fortunes of Henry's servants in some detail, and none more clearly than those of Geoffrey de Clinton, the king's Chamberlain. Clinton's family like that of many of Henry's most trusted servants came ultimately from western Normandy, but it took its name (in all probability) from the village of Glympton in Oxfordshire.[1] Their name is not one which appears in Domesday Book, and there is no sign that the family was of any social consequence before the time of Henry I. But in 1130 Clinton had exemption from Danegeld in fourteen counties—an invariable sign of influence at court. Most of his property lay in a compact group of counties, Warwickshire, Berkshire, Oxfordshire, and Buckinghamshire. If, as seems likely, he was wholly exempt from geld, his total estate in 1130 amounted to 570 hides, which we may roughly estimate as being worth about £500 a year and possibly a good deal more.

The real interest of his position, however, lies not in this large

---

[1] I have to thank Lady Stenton for correcting a false identification of Clinton with Glinton (Northants.) in my original essay.

estate gathered apparently from small beginnings, but in the traces
of the measures by which he was continuing to build it up. The
Pipe Roll shows him engaged in many small transactions which
offered a prospect of permanent gain, and all of them were the
result of his position in the royal government. He had the wardship of the son of William de Dive; he held the land of Roger
Witeng, and half the land of Norman de Martinwest; he had
recently been holding some land of William de Roumara at farm;
he had taken up some debts of the Earl of Leicester and of Nicholas
fitz Godwin; he held the royal manors of Wargrave and Wallop at
farm, as well as the lands of the vacant Abbey of Evesham. How
much of all this he managed to hand on to his son we cannot say;
but when we add that he was Sheriff of Warwickshire where his
main interests lay, the opportunities for tightening his hold on
whatever he held, cannot be overlooked. He had built himself a
castle at Kenilworth, and enclosed his own park (necessarily with
the king's permission); and he had another castle at Brandon on
the upper Avon. A small but significant detail in these castles to
which Sir Frank Stenton has drawn attention is an appropriate
symbol of the manner of his rise: they owed their strength to water
rather than earthworks—to subtlety rather than crude force.[1] The
picture might be that of one of the rising servants of Elizabeth or
James I.

But there is another side to the picture. Clinton was both
working and paying on a massive scale for every step he took. For
the rights, wardships and properties I have enumerated, excluding
the royal manors, he owed the king about £170. For the royal
manor of Wargrave, which was valued at £27 6s. 8d. a year in
Domesday Book, he was paying no less than £80 a year; and for
Wallop, which was noted as being over-valued at about £30 a year
in 1086, he was paying £20 a year. The second of these farms may
have been a bargain, but on the whole he was paying the king
handsomely for what he got. For the Abbey of Evesham he was
paying £40 a year, and for his office at the Treasury which he had
purchased at an unknown figure, he still owed £140 having paid
£66 13s. 4d. in the previous year. In addition to all this, he
accounted to the king for £250 arising from his judicial activities

[1] For these details of Geld exemptions and wardships, etc., see *The Pipe
Roll of 31 Henry I*, ed. J. Hunter, 1833 (repr. 1927); for the fortification of
Clinton's castles, F. M. Stenton, *The First Century of English Feudalism*, 2nd
edit, 1961, p. 202.

in at least seventeen counties, no doubt a mere fraction of the total result of several years' work. But all this did not place him outside the range of minor retribution. He still owed £9 11s. 8d. for some treasure he had lost in Normandy ten years earlier.[1]

Like many others of his class, Clinton was the founder of a house of Augustinian Canons which lay beside his castle and park at Kenilworth. Mr. Dickinson has remarked on the large part which Henry and his servants played in building up this order in England.[2] The sixty-four foundations of his reign, some of them very small, are the proof of the extent to which the Order satisfied the needs and came within the capacity of men like Clinton. It was an Order of compromise—between the world and its rejection, between the splendours of Benedictinism and the trivialities of disorganized colleges of clergy. Its houses could be humble, yet satisfy the founder's desire for independence. Giraldus Cambrensis later put the matter in a nutshell: 'This Order is in the world, yet it avoids the corruptions of the world as far as possible; it is not notorious for drunkenness or excess, and it is afraid and ashamed to become a public scandal for luxury and licentiousness.'[3] These modest and inexpensive virtues appealed to men like Henry I, Roger of Salisbury and Geoffrey de Clinton, and they did not appear unworthy of the support even of St. Anselm and Thurstan of York.

Clinton's benefactions to his new house were liberal. But even in this aspect of his activity it is remarkable how often he was able to be liberal with the lands of other men. The manor of Salford (Oxon.) was not his. It had been held in 1086 by an English nun; she lost it, but recovered it again in the court of King Henry. Nevertheless Clinton was able to give it to his canons. Again, the manor of Woodcote was on the fief of Nicholas of Stafford. It was held by Clinton as his sub-tenant for the service of one knight; but Nicholas was induced for a mere £3 13s. 4d., to relinquish all claim to service and to give the manor absolutely and in perpetuity (he repeats the words with fearful emphasis) to Clinton's foundation. The same procedure, at a cost of £8 3s. 4d. enabled Clinton to

---

[1] *P.R. of 31 Henry I*, p. 37.
[2] J. C. Dickinson, *The Origins of the Austin Canons and their Introduction into England*, pp. 125–30. My calculation of the number of foundations during the reign is based on D. Knowles and R. N. Hadcock, *Medieval Religious Houses in England and Wales*, 1955, pp. 125–60.
[3] Giraldus Cambrensis, *Opera*, R.S., vi, 46–7.

obtain Hugh fitz Richard's manor of Newnham for his canons. The king contributed his manor of Hughenden, but this appropriation of royal rights was only to be had at something like its market price: Clinton paid over £70 for this manor, which had been worth £10 a year in 1086. Such transactions as these enabled Clinton to gather together a sizeable estate for his new abbey, and to make it one of the largest of its Order in England.[1] They were cash transactions. Instead of the spectacle—familiar in an earlier and simpler age—of a great magnate endowing a religious community out of the resources of a well-defined feudal group, we see here a new kind of founder of a new kind of foundation, buying and bargaining to gather a modest estate largely from the resources of his neighbours.

In 1130 Clinton was at the height of his greatness. His nephew had become bishop of Lichfield in the previous year—at a cost, according to Symeon of Durham, of £2,000. He himself probably sat at the Exchequer; certainly his friends sat there. This increased his opportunities and gave him favourable treatment when it came to paying for his chances. Although his farms were paid with scrupulous regularity, he seems to have taken a long time to pay the debts that arose from his speculative dealings. Since the officials of the Exchequer decided how much of any debt should be paid each year, it was clearly an advantage to have friends at the Exchequer. These friends at court could save a man from financial inconvenience. They could do more: they could save him from ruin. At Easter 1130 Clinton came as near to ruin as any servant of Henry I who lived to tell the tale. His enemies accused him of treachery. He was brought before a great session of the royal court presided over by the king's brother-in-law, King David of Scotland—and he was acquitted. But the nearness of disaster is revealed by a Norman charter which mentions that he gave a manor in Normandy to Engelgar de Bohun, another of Henry's new men, for making peace between him and the king.[2] It must have been a narrow escape.

[1] The details of Clinton's transactions are gathered from the Kenilworth Cartulary (B.M. Harleian M.S. 3650, ff. 10ᵛ, 14, 15) with some help from Domesday Book, i, 144 b, 244 a, and *Regesta*, ii, no. 1527. The papal confirmation of 1126 gives some interesting details about the source of some of the endowments (W. Holtzmann, *Papsturkunden in England*, iii, no. 14, *Abh. der Akademie . . . in Göttingen*, 1952, 3rd ser., xxxiii).

[2] The charter which records this gift is quoted in Ordericus Vitalis, *Hist. Eccl.*, iii, 404n.

Engelgar de Bohun belonged to a family which continued to rise. The Clintons remained where their great ancestor had left them.[1] One member of the family in the fourteenth century followed the path of royal service and became Earl of Huntingdon; but he left no heirs. The senior branch of his family remained knights of the shire for another hundred years. They struggled into the Lords, struck a good patch with an earldom in the sixteenth and seventeenth centuries, and a bad one with a succession of cousins and coheiresses in the eighteenth. Tawney lists them among the effete nobility who were victims of the rising gentry in the seventeenth century, but probably the failure of male heirs after a long direct succession did them more harm than anything else. Nevertheless the barony of the Clintons, now in abeyance, survived till the twenty-first baron, a Lord Warden of the Stanneries and Joint Parliamentary Secretary of State in our own day. The family retained a hold on the minor offices of government, but it seldom approached the centre of power after the reign of Henry I.

Despite his acquittal, a doubt must hang over Geoffrey de Clinton's loyalty to Henry I. Yet in his own day the loyalty of Henry's servants was proverbial. William of Malmesbury says that only one of his officials was ever found to be disloyal.[2] Henry's vengeance was terrible and barbaric, but it was a most effective instrument of government. He knew how to play upon the two great motives of human action—fear and hope. And as the fear was a permanent feature of his reign, so was the hope. Henry's servants never had so much that they could not do with more; and Henry always had more to give, because what he gave came principally from the bottomless resources of those who came within reach of his feudal and legal rights.

In almost every county in England Henry raised up men of a middle station among the magnates, in situations similar to that of Clinton, by similar methods and for similar services. Another Midland creation was Richard Basset with his estate of 176 hides in eleven counties centred on Leicestershire. In 1130 he too was

---

[1] Geoffrey's eldest son maintained his father's position by marrying a daughter of the earl of Warwick, but he seems to have played no part in royal administration. See J. H. Round, 'A great marriage settlement', *The Ancestor*, 1904, xi, 153–7; and for his knights' fees, *The Red Book of the Exchequer*, ed. H. Hall, *R.S.*, i, 309, 325.

[2] *Gesta Regum, R.S.*, ii, 488.

paying his way step by step. He owed £133 and six chargers for the right of inheriting an estate in Oxfordshire which his brother had surrendered to the king. He was still paying for the custody of the land of his father-in-law, who had died ten years earlier; and he was paying for other odds and ends of land that had come into the king's hands. He and his colleague Aubrey de Vere, as joint-sheriffs in eleven counties, were responsible for a large additional revenue of £666 from the counties under their control. He was very profitable to the king, and the king repaid his services in kind. Orderic Vitalis describes him returning to his native village in Normandy 'bursting with the wealth of England', building a stone castle and attempting to overawe his humble equals by the magnitude of his operations.[1]

Along the Welsh border there was a succession of families in a similar case; in Worcestershire, the Beauchamps who stepped into the forfeited estates of the Abitot family; in Herefordshire, Pain fitz John; in Gloucestershire and the cantreds of Brecknock, Miles of Gloucester; in the northern counties, William Maltravers, Eustace fitz John and Nigel d'Aubigny; in the eastern counties, William d'Aubigny; in the south and west Humphrey de Bohun and Brian fitz Count. These men were the workers in Henry's administration. They worked and paid for what they got, but they got what they paid for—generally in the form of widows, daughters, heirs, and lands which fell from the grasp of men who could not pay their debts or afford to prosecute their lawsuits. These men were a prey for royal servants who enjoyed a host of opportunities, privileges, and remissions of gelds and fines. Naturally they were not popular. William Maltravers paid for his unpopularity with his life as soon as Henry I was removed from the scene, and others like him must have trembled for their lives.[2] There can be little doubt that if Duke Robert had succeeded in 1100, the opportunities of such men as these would have been greatly restricted by the growth of the great principalities in the kingdom. Perhaps English society would have become more genial and more French. If Stephen of Blois had been successful

---

[1] For these details of Richard Basset's activities, see *P.R. of 31 Henry I*, pp. 63, 81–2 and Ordericus Vitalis, *Hist. Eccl.* v, 68–9. They need to be interpreted in the light of *The Red Book of the Exchequer*, i, 329–30; *Regesta*, ii, 1668; Round, *Feudal England*, 211–13; and Stenton in *V.C.H. Leicestershire*, i, 343.

[2] For William Maltravers, who is an exceptionally interesting example of the type described above, see W. E. Wightman, *The Lacy Family in England and Normandy, 1066–1194*, 1966, 68–73.

after 1135, this might still have happened. At least, among all the confusions of the years after Henry's death, it is fairly clear that the climbers of Henry's reign were at the centre of the opposition to Stephen. It was the men whom Henry had built up and Stephen pulled down who won the battle of Lincoln from which Stephen never recovered. Necessarily, they were loyal to Henry and to his memory, and to each other.

## V

The words of Brian fitz Count are famous as an expression of this lasting loyalty to the memory of the king to whom he owed everything.[1] In 1143 or thereabouts, the bishop of Winchester accused him of being a reactionary, of clinging to the past. Brian gloried in the accusation, and Gilbert Foliot wrote in praise of his loyalty to the memory of the 'good and golden days' of the king who 'brought you up from boyhood, educated you, knighted you, enriched you'. Like most of the others I have discussed, Brian fitz Count owed all his advancement to Henry. The d'Oilly lands and constableship in Oxfordshire, the Crispin honour of Wallingford, a great position on the Welsh border, all came to him as his share of the royal patronage. With his estate of 720 hides exempt from Danegeld, he stood in an intermediate position between the very greatest of Henry's creations, Count Stephen and Earl Robert of Gloucester, and the toilers like the Bassets and the Clintons. But he spoke for them all—all except (by this time) King Stephen.

Long before this testing of their loyalty came to the friends of King Henry, several of them had had to face a greater test. Some time before 1118 Nigel d'Aubigny, the king's chief agent in the north of England, believed himself to be dying. The letter he wrote to Henry has survived. It reads:

> I beg you, my dearest Lord, in whom after God lies my whole trust, to have pity on me in my great need, for the love of God, and for your own sweet nobility. I have been yours while I could, and I have loved you truly and served you most faithfully. In your service and in my own affairs, I have committed

[1] See the correspondence printed by H. W. C. Davis, *E.H.R.* 1910, xxv, 301–3. For his estates and family connections, see J. H. Round, *Studies in Peerage and Family History*, 210–11; F. M. Stenton, *First Century of English Feudalism*, p. 236 n; *P.R. of 31 Henry I.*

many great sins and I have done few if any good deeds; but trusting in your goodness and kindness I have now restored some small pieces of land which I took from various churches. I beg you therefore, dearest Lord, and, since I cannot be present in body, I fall at the feet of your majesty in spirit, with tears and lamentation, begging your pious majesty to concede and confirm those things which I have returned to these churches from my demesne for the redemption of my soul.[1]

D'Aubigny wrote another letter to his brother asking for his help in ensuring that these restitutions were made, and from this it appears that his depredations of church properties were not the only misdeeds he bewailed. Among laymen he had totally or in part disinherited Robert de Cambos, Robert de Witville, William fitz Warin, Ralph de Paveli, Ralph de Buce, the sons of Anseis, Hugh de Rampan, Butin, Gerald, Burnulf, Humphrey Hastings, Russell de Langford, and others.[2]

These letters suggest several reflections. In the first place they bear striking testimony to the deep sense of obligation of Henry's officials to the king who made them. They needed his support to the end. They had risen by influence in courts and in government, and especially by their knowledge of the ways in which central authority could be used to bolster up local power. They feared—and, as many of them discovered, they were right to fear—that if this influence were removed, they were lost. D'Aubigny's list of his misdeeds is very eloquent of the way in which he had used his influence, not by violence but by manipulation, to intrude himself into other men's shoes. We know very few of the details, but we do know that the Durham lands which he appropriated had a long and curious history of complicated descent before they found their way into his hands. These were conditions ideally suited to a man who could bend the law to his will. When the author of the *Gesta Stephani* said that the leading friends and associates of King Henry were afraid to come to Stephen's court because they would have been overwhelmed by the complaints of the poor and the widows whose lands they had turned to their own use, and that they

---

[1] *Feodarium prioratus Dunelmensis*, ed. W. Greenwell, Surtees Soc., 1872, p. 151.
[2] *Historians of the Church of York*, R.S., iii, 54–7.

feared to lose by lawful means what they had unjustly obtained, he probably knew what he was talking about.[1]

That widows and orphans were among the chief sufferers from the legal chicanery and pressure by which the new men grew to greatness, we may readily believe. The fortunes of nearly all these men were founded on marriage, and it was to the king that they owed their opportunity. Richard Basset, as a result of an elaborate agreement made in the royal court, married the daughter of his father's colleague, Geoffrey Ridel, a granddaughter of the Earl of Chester; he obtained the wardship of her brother, and finally (but this was not in the agreement) swallowed the lands he held in wardship. Nigel d'Aubigny married the divorced wife of the forfeited Robert Mowbray, and succeeded to some of his lands and much of his authority in the north. Later he divorced his wife and married again with the king's approval without losing the advantages his first marriage had brought him. Miles of Gloucester owed his great position on the Welsh border to his marriage with Sybil, the daughter of the Welsh princess Nesta and her husband Bernard. This marriage also was made by royal grant and was the subject of an elaborate royal charter. Among the legends of the Welsh border there is a story that a son of Nesta was excluded from his inheritance by this transaction. If this is true, Miles's royal charter was doubly necessary. The invaluable royal servants on the Welsh and Scottish borders, the brothers Pain and Eustace fitz John, both married heiresses who brought them a great increase of local strength. William d'Aubigny did the same in Norfolk. William Maltravers, by a more devious transaction, strengthened his position in Yorkshire by paying the king a great price for the widow and lands of Hugh Laval.[2]

These examples need cause no surprise. If royal patronage was the readiest road to success in the struggle for power, marriage was the easiest road to ready-made wealth, and the king's favour provided the best opportunities for profitable marriage. Never again did the king have so extensive a control over marriage arrangements and the descent of property. The king's control over

---

[1] *Gesta Stephani*, ed. K. R. Potter, pp. 14, 15.

[2] The documents which record these elaborate marriage arrangements are are to be found in F. M. Stenton, *First Century of English Feudalism*, App. no. 4; *Ancient Charters Prior to* A.D. *1200*, 1888 (Pope Roll Soc. x), pp. 8–9, 35–8; *Red Book of the Exchequer*, i, 397–8; *P.R.* 31 *Henry I*, p. 34. The story of the exclusion of Nesta's son is in Giraldus Cambrensis, *Opera*, R.S., vi, 29.

marriages was greatly enhanced at this time by the frequent habit of postponing marriage on the male side till relatively late in life, while the wives were often barely out of childhood. The practice no doubt had its roots in considerations of political and economic advantage. The right opportunity for a man to increase his power by marriage often did not arise till he was at the peak of his career, while the expectations of a woman were as clear at thirteen as they were ever likely to be. Hence arose marriages of wildly unsuitable disparity of age. But one unwelcome result of such unequal unions was seen in the high proportion of magnates who left minors as their heirs and women still young as their widows. Even under the terms of the Coronation Charter the king's control over the fate of wealthy orphans and widows was great; in practice it was much greater.

Henry had a further source of power in the uncertainties which still hung over the right of hereditary succession. His reign is a turning-point in this important matter. At his coronation he had promised to do away with the uncertainty over inheritance which Rufus had found it profitable to exploit, and the charters of Henry's reign are the first to emphasize consistently the hereditary nature of feudal tenures. Impressive phrases expressing the fullness of this hereditary right occur again and again in Henry's charters. At the same time it is remarkable how often the charters in which these expressions occur are themselves an interference with what would later be regarded as the normal course of descent.[1] Professor Thorne has recently pointed out that the king's right of taking seisin of the lands of a dead tenant was no empty formality in the early twelfth century. It gave the king and his officials many opportunities for interfering with the descent of property; and the official on the spot must often, like Nigel d'Aubigny, have been the chief beneficiary of all uncertainties.

Marriages, wardships, the fruits of forfeitures, the opportunities for cutting into the estates of magnates in difficulties of one kind or another—these were the great prizes of royal patronage. And there were other prizes less dramatic in their effects, but sufficiently compelling to induce a strong sense of gratitude in those who enjoyed them, and a grievous sense of dereliction in those from whom the stream of favour had been diverted. No single document provides so clear a lesson in the art of government

[1] *Regesta*, ii, nos. 1719, 1722, 1778.

through minor acts of royal favour as the *Registrum Antiquissimum* of the cathedral church of Lincoln.   The writs of Henry I which are preserved in this Register tell an elaborate story of a king who governed by giving or withholding his countenance in a multitude of small transactions, making life easier for those whom he favoured, and harder for those who stood outside the charmed circle of the king's pleasure.[1]

The bishops of Lincoln were among the lucky ones.  They had earned their right to favour in the royal service, they knew the corridors of power and had the keys to the right doors.  They used their opportunities;  but they used them with a moderation characteristic of Henry's government.  Except at the beginning of the reign they had no outright grant of royal demesne.  The fifty-five writs of Henry I were not the outflowings of a cornucopia, but the injections of a lubricant.  When the bishop built his castle at Newark, the king gave him permission to divert the royal highway, to make his fishpond across the Fossway, to hold a fair, to build a bridge, and to use one-third of his knight service for castle-guard.  He allowed him to exchange land to make a park at Thame.  He gave him a vineyard in Lincoln, and a lodging in the Eastgate of the city.  He allowed him to breach the wall to make a way to his house.  He granted hunting rights in the sokes of Newark and Stowe and throughout the bishop's lands in Lincoln-shire and Nottinghamshire.  He helped the bishop to build up the canonries of his new cathedral by grants of churches; he supported him in his lawsuits; he refrained from pressing royal claims; he forgave his debts; he made his officials available for enforcing legal decisions in his favour; he imposed heavy fines for breaches of episcopal rights.  In all these ways, with little actual expense to himself, the king could make life easier for his friends.

Bishop Robert Bloet of Lincoln, a hard-bitten servant of three kings, enjoyed all these favours for twenty years.  Then suddenly, towards the end of his life, we know not why, he was made to feel the difference between favour and disfavour.  Henry of Hunt-ingdon found him in tears as he surveyed his household dressed not in silks but in woollens.  His lawsuits went awry; pieces of his land were claimed as royal demesne; instead of royal favours, he had fines imposed by men of low birth.  The bishop knew the signs too well; and when his friends recalled the king's kind words

---

[1] *The Registrum Antiquissimum of the Cathedral Church of Lincoln*, ed. C. W. Foster, Lincoln Record Soc., 1931, i 18–48.

about him to cheer him up, he replied out of a long experience, 'The king only praises those whom he wishes utterly to destroy'. There was not much to complain of. No active violence. The king even restored one miserable scrap of land which Ralph Basset had claimed as royal demesne; but Bishop Bloet's days of ease of mind and body were over for all that, until one day at Woodstock he sank down at the king's side and died.[1]

## VI

All the men whom I have so far mentioned were very high in the king's service. They were new men in Henry's day, and for their families the best days lay ahead. There could never at any one time have been more than about twenty such men at the top, pushing the interests of themselves and their families, and succeeding in varying degrees in their struggle for social eminence. But the touch of the royal court could avail much lower down in the king's service. It could even do something to reverse the decision of the Conquest, and help families to regain something of what they had then lost. This aspect of royal patronage turns our attention to the past as well as the future.

It is in this connexion that a discovery made by J. H. Round may be mentioned, for it has never been given the prominence it deserves; nor indeed did he himself notice all its ramifications. In a register of Merton Priory he found a collection of notes on documents which formed the archives of a minor official of Henry I, Bernard the Scribe. What he did not notice was that their information can be supplemented from another unexpected source. Bernard's nephew, Peter of Cornwall, lived to become prior of Holy Trinity, Aldgate, and in the early years of the thirteenth century he made a vast compilation of visions and revelations, culled from the literature and legends of the last hundred years. One section of this compilation deals with the experiences of his own family, starting with his great-grandfather, and including his two uncles, Bernard and Nicholas, both of them scribes in the chancery of Henry I.[2]

[1] For Henry of Huntingdon's story of Bishop Bloet's disgrace see his *Historia Anglorum*, R.S., pp. 299–300; for the king's partial restitution, *Regesta*, ii, no. 1254; and for Bloet's death, *Anglo-Saxon Chronicle*, A.D. 1123.

[2] The charter-notes are printed by J. H. Round, 'Bernard, the King's Scribe' *E.H.R.*, 1899, xiv, 417–30. The family anecdotes are in Lambeth Palace MS. 51, ff. 23–8.

The story which can be put together from these sources is of interest as the rare story of an English, rather than a Norman, family.  Its genealogy may be set out thus:

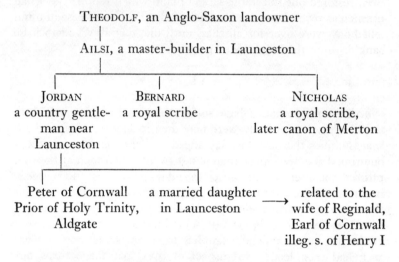

THEODOLF, an Anglo-Saxon landowner

AILSI, a master-builder in Launceston

JORDAN
a country gentle-
man near
Launceston

BERNARD
a royal scribe

NICHOLAS
a royal scribe,
later canon of Merton

Peter of Cornwall
Prior of Holy Trinity,
Aldgate

a married daughter
in Launceston

→ related to the
wife of Reginald,
Earl of Cornwall
illeg. s. of Henry I

Theodulf, the grandfather of Henry I's scribes had been a considerable landowner in Devon and Cornwall before the Norman Conquest. Like most men of his class, however, his sons lost a great part of his estates, and the family survived with a shattered fortune as tenants of the Count of Mortain. One of Theodolf's sons, Ailsi, was the father of our two scribes Bernard and Nicholas. He worked as a master-builder in the service of the canons of Launceston, and held some land outside the town. He had a strong visionary streak in him and a strong attachment to the old church and its patron saint St. Stephen; his miraculous experiences remained a legend in his family, and were a strong influence in forming their later interests. His position—living in Launceston, working as a builder, but retaining some lands which he farmed outside the town—must have been typical of that of many others who had come down in the world as a result of the Conquest.

The documents of Ailsi's son Bernard, prove that something could still be retrieved by a man who moved in the society of the court. They show Bernard engaged in a series of lawsuits in which he steadily improved his territorial position. He pleaded before William of Warelwast, Bishop of Exeter—himself a former royal clerk—and regained a portion of his inheritance in Cornwall. He pleaded before the royal justices in the county court of Devon, and obtained his grandfather's land at Launceston. He pleaded before the barons of the Norman exchequer and recovered a copse and small piece of land in Calvados. He regained from another member of the royal court the churches which had belonged to his grandfather, with their lands and tithes. Besides this work of restoration he was able to step into the shoes of another royal scribe, drowned in the wreck of the White Ship, who had owned house property in Winchester and London. From various magnates of the royal court he obtained churches in Surrey and Northamptonshire; the king gave him a lodging in Launceston; in Winchester the chancellor contributed a tenement, Count Stephen remitted a small rent, and the king was present when he bought a small tenancy-in-chief in Buck Street. The king also gave him a comprehensive royal confirmation of all his lands and churches in Cornwall. In the end Bernard had recreated an estate which might well have supported the dignity of a pre-Conquest thegn. At every step he had been supported by a faithful core of royal officials, and his slightest transactions had the countenance of his immediate superiors in the chancery, Geoffrey the Chancellor and Robert de Sigillo, and other colleagues in the office like William Cumin, William the Almoner, Morel of the Chapel, and so on. He preserved with special care the names of these witnesses to his transactions. Without their backing it is unlikely that this English family would ever have seen better days.

The royal scribes, Bernard and his brother Nicholas, were clerks and left no descendants. They devoted their wealth to enriching their brother's family, their local church at Launceston and the priory of Merton, where Nicholas became a canon. To Launceston they gave among other gifts, the silver-embossed ivory writing-case with silver ink-horn, which they had used in the king's service. The church converted it into a reliquary. As the instrument by which one English family had climbed back into prosperity, it deserved to be held in honour.

Following the practice of celibate clerks in all ages, these two royal scribes looked to their nephews to carry on their work for the family. They left the family inheritance, which they had regained, to their brother Jordan. He moved out of Launceston and set himself up as a small country gentleman among his peasants. He was renowned for his knowledge of the laws and customs of the land, and his help was often sought in law-suits. Most of his life was spent among his peasantry at Trecarrell, four miles from Launceston, but he sometimes made a journey into the town to visit his married daughter. Another of his children was the writer Peter of Cornwall to whom we owe these reminiscences. In the course of time the family became distantly connected with the royal house through the marriage of Henry I's illegitimate son, Reginald, to a local heiress who was a relative of Ailsi's descendants. Reginald became earl of Cornwall, and the whole family held their heads very high, as Peter of Cornwall takes pride in assuring us.

In the nature of things little can be known about families which belonged to this level of society, but it is clear that court connexions could bring benefits for them as well as their betters.

## VII

I do not think anyone will dispute that the men we have been considering rose by using opportunities which came to them from their association with the work of royal government. In the words of Namier speaking of such men in the eighteenth century, they benefited from a situation which 'necessarily distinguishes a man, certainly in his own circle, and opens doors which would otherwise remain shut against him'.[1] The opportunities which were thus provided were essentially the same as those which government was to provide for its servants until the seventeenth century, when a new system had to be devised to take the place of the old patronage of the Crown. These opportunities for advancement continued to be a main motive for participation in government, and they did not greatly alter in character for many centuries after the reign of Henry I. But they can scarcely have existed, or at least can have existed in only a very attenuated form, before his time. For their full development, they required a sophisticated machinery of government, a highly developed system of royal courts and royal justice, a tenurial system at once complicated and yet subjected to a unitary control, at once hereditary and yet full of doubtful points of law. I cannot venture to say that these features

[1] *Structure of Politics at the Accession of George III*, p. 12.

were not present in Anglo-Saxon England; but at least we have no evidence that they were capable of creating an aristocracy as they did in Henry I's reign.

Yet though we think chiefly of the future when we think of these men—of the long history of their families in English affairs, of the rise of others after them along a similar route—nevertheless their rise was made possible by a survival from the Anglo-Saxon period. I am not thinking chiefly as Stubbs would have us do, of the survival of the Anglo-Saxon local courts and central mechanism of government, for these were important only because conditions favourable for their development also survived the Conquest. I am thinking above all of the survival of the tenurial complexities of Anglo-Saxon England. If William the Conqueror had chosen, as he might reasonably have done, to divide England into compact fiefs among his tenants-in-chief, nothing of what I have been describing could have happened. It was tenurial complexity that gave royal officials their opportunities, by making all free tenants more or less equal in the royal courts, and inducing all men, however great, to acquiesce in the growth of royal justice.

This was a state of affairs which foreigners, and Englishmen with continental experience, often viewed with dismay and disfavour. What we see as a basis for freedom, they saw as an opportunity for tyranny. This is how it appeared to a monk of Fécamp, who visited the English lands of his monastery early in the reign of Henry II. He found everything in inextricable confusion, and in explaining the difficulties of the situation he wrote: 'the land has as many lords as it has neighbours, and it is burdened with a multiplicity of dues—hidage, danegeld, 'warscalve' and the aids of sheriffs and royal officials . . . as well as the tyranny of archbishop, archdeacon, dean, etc'.[1] Already England's destiny to be a much governed country was clear, and by some disliked. William of Malmesbury saw another side of the picture in pointing out the great difference between English and Norman society in his day. In Normandy civil strife could go on for years, and the countryside quickly recovered; in England, unless it was stopped at once, the country was ruined.[2] The tenurial structure was too complex to suffer easily the dislocations of civil war.

---

[1] 'Epistolae Fiscannenses: lettres d'amitié, de gouvernement et d'affaires', ed. J. Laporte, Revue Mabillon, 1953, xi, 29–31.
[2] Gesta Regum, ii, 473.

This complexity, which multiplied officials, also gave men of a middle station in society their opportunity. The dispersal and confusion of great baronial interests, whatever this may have meant politically, added immensely to the difficulties of an efficient economic exploitation of their property and virtually condemned whole areas of judicial and military rights to a rapid extinction. The situation described by Tawney as characteristic of the late sixteenth century stems directly from the post-Conquest settlement, and its results are already observable in the reign of Henry I. We already see on the one hand, the difficulties facing men with 'property of a dozen different kinds in a dozen different countries', with majestic but unremunerative franchises, with cumbrous and unreliable methods of estate-management; and on the other hand 'the patient watchers on the shore bringing home fresh flotsam from the wreck of other men's estates'.[1] Already in Henry I's reign the twelfth-century equivalents of the Northumberlands and the Seymours were going down before the prototypes of the Duttons, Winstons, Donningtons, and Chamberlains. They had a long way to go, and the development was not all in one direction. But the tenurial situation which survived from the pre-Conquest period ensured that however the battle ebbed and flowed the midde ranks of the aristocracy would always be thickly populated.

This situation was not created by Henry I, but it could only have been preserved after 1100 by a king of great determination and political insight. Henry was the first king in our history, so far as we know, who treated the business of government strictly as business. Under him the numinous quality of kingship went out almost completely; the splendour of display had no place in his rule; even his passions were subordinated to policy. It is true that Geoffrey Gaimar tells us that he could say much of the feasts and the jokes and gallantry of his court. But he never did so, and it is hard to see what there was to joke about. It was an unlovable reign, and it set an unlovable stamp on much of English history; but it was immensely effective. Both of Henry's brothers had qualities of generosity and magnanimity which he lacked. Rufus had as much determination and ability, but his government was too predatory to last; it clashed with too many interests and stirred up an ever-growing body of opposition, which the devotion of a few friends and officials, and the admiration of the military world,

[1] 'The Rise of the Gentry, 1558–1640', *Econ. Hist. Rev.*, 1941, xi, p. 9.

could do nothing to check. When he died the country was ready for a revolution, which might well have swept away much of the structure of royal government.

Henry I prevented this, and few other men could have done so. He made government predatory yet respectable. The symbol of the change is the replacement of the ready-witted, outrageous, rumbustious Ranulf Flambard, Bishop of Durham, by the sombre, shrewd, financial expert, Roger, Bishop of Salisbury, with his interest in good causes and his wife of whom no one spoke. They were both men of great efficiency in business, but there can be no doubt which of them was better fitted for the period of elaborate compromises which began in the early twelfth century.

The servants were the image of their masters. There have been greater kings than Henry, but none has understood better the art of government. In negotiation he was dilatory and double-faced until the moment for decision arrived, and then he moved rapidly and decisively. In war he never lost a battle because he had first won the struggle for allies and the battle of wits before the fight. Above all, he understood that the first art of government is the art of patronage: to reward his friends without ruining himself; to reward those who mattered, and to ensure that those who were not rewarded continued not to matter. With the exceptions of Count Stephen and Earl Robert of Gloucester, when his hands were forced by the political necessities of the time, he raised no men to great positions at one bound. Some of those who served him rose very high, but they rose the hard way and worked long and hard for what they got. Their greatest incentive was the certainty that lasting gain would follow toil. Hence he never had to cast down again a man he had raised up, and he never lost a friend. By the same token he seldom forgave an enemy. He had a morbid dislike of ridicule, and he punished with a Byzantine ferocity already outmoded in the humaner society of feudal France, not only treachery and rebellion but slights to his dignity and honour. His brother and cousin languished in prison for a quarter of a century, and no one knew whether they had been blinded by the politic king or not. It is certain that neither relationship nor friendship could save them.[1]

[1] There is ample evidence for these traits in Henry's character in Ordericus Vitalis, iv, 167, 337, 459–61; William of Malmesbury, *Gesta Regum*, ii, 487–8; Henry of Huntingdon, pp. 255, 311; *An. Monastici, R.S.*, ii, 50. Orderic (iv, 460) reports that the Count of Flanders was disgusted by the brutality of Henry's punishments for personal affronts.

In all this he had, as Stubbs rightly remarked, the support of the Church. Basically this was because the monastic communities, the chief arbiters of ecclesiastical opinion, preferred his government to any alternative that was available. Ecclesiastical landowners were in the position of lay magnates without the opportunities for playing the dynastic game on equal terms with their neighbours. They could not marry; they could not make family alliances; they could not recruit their wealth, condemned in the course of nature to constant erosion, with the rewards of political service or military command. It was only in the law-courts that they could wage war on equal, and indeed on advantageous, terms. The great churches were extremely tenacious of their rights, and no case was finally lost which could be reopened at a later date. They had no special love for the rights of the king, but their chief hope of withdrawing the issues of property and rights from the field of action, where they were weak, to the courts, where they were strong, lay in supporting the king. All policy in the long run follows the easiest channel towards its goal, and royal government profited from the needs of the Church.

Of course churches too suffered from the depredations of royal officials. We have seen that the church of Durham suffered from the activities of Nigel d'Aubigny; but in the end it recovered what it had lost. The *History* of the monastery of Abingdon is full of accounts of lands lost, only to be recovered again through action in the royal courts. Even land given to royal officials as a bribe for their good offices, even land seized by others with the connivance of royal officials, was not finally lost so long as the possibilities of legal action remained. Thus there arose a natural alliance of interests between the king and the monastic houses which even the reign of Rufus could not shake, and which Henry I was wise enough to foster. He could give them security; they could give him their prayers and their good opinion. He needed both. In his last years he was oppressed by the weight of his sins and the sense of hostility to his exactions. The flow of his monastic benefactions became a flood as the shadows lengthened. He was a man nervous of his health, both physical and spiritual, and he liked to have physicians and men of religion on his side. Both professions served him well. After his death, a monk of Bec saw him in a vision thrust into hell each morning and rescued by the prayers of monks each evening.[1] The community of interests went beyond the grave.

But on this side of the grave, his death left a situation which threatened the destruction of all he had created. We shall not ask whether the reaction was inevitable, but only remark that it was unsuccessful. The strength of Henry I's system—it was more than a system of government, it was an association of families penetrating every county to the Tweed and the Solway, and eating far into the Welsh march—was proved when it survived the dynastic and personal tangles of Stephen's reign. When we remember William of Malmesbury's words about the deep hurt which disorder was capable of inflicting on English society, this survival must be seen as a triumph of Henry's genius for organization. This cold, hard, inscrutable man achieved something more lasting even than the Conqueror. The Conqueror gave England to the Normans. Henry did not restore it to the English, as Stubbs believed, but he ensured the survival of many features of Old English society and government—and even of religious and historical tradition—that might have perished if Robert of Normandy had won the day in 1101.

This is the truth which Stubbs understood, and in a sense it was already understood by the men of the generation after Henry I. They believed that they had found in Henry I the explanation of Edward the Confessor's mysterious death-bed prophecy about the tree returning to its root after three generations. They saw in Henry's marriage with the English princess Matilda, and the succession of their grandson, the fulfilment of the prophecy. On this view, Edward the Confessor was the seer, and Henry I was the instrument of English survival. The details of this interpretation, like those of Stubbs, are pure illusion; but the truth they enforced only becomes clearer when the illusions are swept away, and we see that these years when nothing happened—largely because nothing happened—were decisive in the development of English society. We see also in these years an illustration of the truth which Stubbs believed to be one of the great lessons of constitutional history, that 'the world owes some of its greatest debts to men from whose memory it recoils'.

[1] Cambridge University Library MS Ff. i. 27, p. 217: 'Miraculum terrificum de primo Henrico Anglorum rege filio Willelmi.'

# 12

## POPE ADRIAN IV

### I

The career of Adrian IV is one of the great success stories in English history: he is the Dick Whittington of the twelfth century. We first see him as a poor young man, rejected by his local monastery, wandering from his native land where he had no future; then almost the next thing we know is that he has become a cardinal and shortly, with dramatic speed, pope—the only non-Italian pope in the great period of the papacy from 1099 to 1261, and the only English pope ever.

Nearly all the intermediate stages of his journey are irretrievably lost. His near contemporaries were almost as much in the dark as we are. Yet, when almost everything is unknown, it is strange that we can point to the village, and even with a high degree of probability to the house in the village, where he was born. The house is Brakespeare Farm in the parish of Abbot's Langley in Hertfordshire. It has now nothing medieval about it, but the record of its existence and the association of the Brakespeare family with the house can be traced back to the fifteenth century, and two centuries earlier Matthew Paris records the tradition of his monastery that Adrian IV was born in Abbot's Langley.[1]

Abbot's Langley was a manor of the abbey of St. Albans and this association may explain why Nicholas's father became a monk of the abbey after a career as a minor royal official. Nicholas was probably the younger of two sons, and there are conflicting accounts of his early relations with his father's monastery. The earlier tradition alleges that he received a daily pittance from the monastery until his father drove him away in shame and disgrace; according to the later story, which comes from Matthew Paris, his

[1] There are two independent early accounts of Adrian's origin and youth: William of Newburgh, *Historia rerum Anglicarum* in *Chronicles of Stephen, Henry II and Richard I*, R.S., 1884, i, 109–12; and *Gesta Abbatum monasterii S. Albani*, R.S., 1867, i, 124–5. For Brakespeare Farm, see *V.C.H. Hertfordshire*, ii, 325.

father persuaded the abbot to examine him with a view to his becoming a monk, but he failed the test of literacy. Whatever the truth, he left England without much qualification for future success probably shortly after 1120.

He did not go to any of the places where we should expect to find a rising young man with secular or spiritual ambitions. He went neither to Paris nor Bologna, where intellectual ability could find its reward, nor to one of the Cistercian abbeys, where spiritual zeal at this time was promising a renewal of the monastic life. He went to Provence and became a canon of the community of Augustinian canons of St. Ruf near Avignon. We shall never know what took him there. It was certainly a famous abbey, which had played an important part in the development of the religious life based on the Rule of St. Augustine, but it was not a place likely to attract young men from distant parts. It was the centre of an important association of abbeys in Spain and southern France, but it had no further development ahead of it: like Cluny, but more rapidly, it had risen to the peak of its achievement and faced a slow decline.

The English recruit evidently had some striking business ability, for he rose to be abbot of the monastery: the date is quite obscure, but he must have reached this position by about 1140. It was said that the canons repented of their choice and appealed to the Pope to remove him. Whether or not this is true, he must have had business that took him to Rome and brought him to the notice of the pope in the years between 1145 and 1150, for by 30 January 1150 we find him as cardinal-bishop of Albano. Suddenly we pass from the shifting sands of conjecture and legend, and reach the firm ground of established fact. Probably this promotion should be seen in the context of the papal need to attract able men to the curia wherever they could be found. The business of the curia was rapidly expanding, and the conduct of business required able men. Many of these men came from the great schools of Europe, above all from Paris and Bologne where the legal and theological knowledge necessary for the conduct of papal business was to be found. But, whether they were scholars or not, these men had to be capable of taking firm decisions on a multitude of doubtful, mostly very dull, points of law and organization. They had to be sensible, shrewd, hard-working and reasonably incorruptible men—in a word, administrators.

We may conjecture that Nicholas Brakespeare was conspicuously such a man. The search for the right kind of man had already drawn a few Englishmen into the papal service. As early as 1128 the Pope had tried to enlist the services of an English abbot, Hugh of Reading, but the attempt was foiled by the king who also needed able men about him. Then in 1144 another Englishman, Robert Pullen, a distinguished scholar of Oxford and Paris, became a cardinal and papal chancellor. A little later we find another Englishman at the papal court: he was Boso, a clerk in the chancery and in later years a cardinal and biographer of the popes.[1] It may have been the English connections of these men that brought Nicholas Brakespeare into the papal administration.

Very soon Brakespeare's great chance came. He was sent in 1152 as papal legate to Norway and Sweden. His English origin made him especially suitable for this mission, for England had many ties of trade and speech with Norway. There is evidence of a strong Scandinavian element in the population of Lincoln and Grimsby about this time, and the legate, who came through England on his way to Norway, could easily have found men to help him in his mission. His purpose was to strengthen relations between Rome and Scandinavia and to establish a local ecclesiastical hierarchy. The area was in a state of considerable ecclesiastical disorder; it had lost one source of cohesion without having found another. A century earlier the archbishops of Hamburg-Bremen had extended their patriarchical authority as far as Tronheim and Iceland, but this ecclesiastical empire had long ago collapsed and no effective organization had taken its place. The area was ready for a new impulse and it was this that Nicholas Brakespeare succeeded in providing. In Norway he established an archbishopric at Trondheim with suffragan bishops in places as far afield as Orkney, the Hebrides and Greenland; and in Sweden he laid the foundation for another archbishopric at Upsala. In both countries he introduced an annual tribute on the lines of the Peter's Pence which the English already paid to the pope; and he

---

[1] For the pope's attempt to attract Hugh of Reading to the papal curia, see W. Holtzmann, *Papsturkunden in England*, iii, nos. 15–21 (*Abh. der Akademie Göttingen*, 1952, 3rd ser., xxxiii). For Robert Pullen and Adrian IV's introduction to the papal court, see R. L. Poole, 'The early lives of Robert Pullen and Nicholas Brakespeare', *Studies in Chronology and History*, 1934, 287–97.

reduced to a shadow the last vestiges of Scandinavian dependence on Germany and Denmark.[1]

He seems to have done all this with remarkable tact. The Danish historian Saxo Grammaticus preserved an account of the mission which brings out the combination of firmness and pliability which allowed the legate to get what he wanted without riding roughshod over existing rights. Although Saxo wrote more than half a century later, he preserved a very clear picture of the legate's character, and some of his words are worth quoting here:

> At this time Nicholas, a Roman cardinal, crossed the British sea and gave the dignity of an archbishopric to Norway. He intended to do the same thing for Sweden in virtue of his legatine authority, but the Swedes and Goths could not agree about a city or person worthy of so great an honour, so he refused to introduce this honour with contention among a barbarous people. On his return journey he took the opportunity of returning through Denmark to soften by some new benefits the offence given by his elevation of Norway. He compensated Eskill (bishop of Lund) for the loss of Norway by granting him primacy over Sweden, and promised that this new dignity would outweigh his loss of the old one.[2]

Some of the details in this picture are hard to check, but Saxo's words admirably describe the man we are soon to know as pope: a firm and effective champion of papal rights, and at the same time a pacifier of ruffled tempers and diminished dignities.

## II

Brakespeare was back in Rome by November 1154, and in December Pope Anastasius II died. The prospect was not cheerful. The papacy had been going through a troubled time, and Scandinavia was one of the few bright spots in an otherwise gloomy landscape. The cardinals recognized success when they saw it,

[1] The details of the legation are collected in J. Bachmann, *Die päpstlichen Legaten in Deutschland u. Scandinavien, 1125–59*, 1913 (Hist. Studien, cxv). See also E. Vandvik, *Latinske document til Norske historie fram till år 1204*, 1959, and O. Kolsrud, 'Kard-leg. Nicholas av Albano i Noreg, 1152,' *Norsk Historisk Tidskrift*, 1945, xxxiii, 485–512. W. Holtzmann (*Deutsches Archiv*, 1938, ii, 376–82, and *Studia Gratiana*, 1953, i, 347–8) doubts whether the Norwegian synodal decrees attributed to Nicholas belong to his legation.

[2] *Saxonis Gesta Danorum*, ed. J. Olrick and H. Raeder, 2 vols. 1931–47, p. 389.

and Nicholas was elected pope without opposition on the day after the old pope's death.

He chose an unexpected and significant name, Adrian IV. It was not the name of one of those early popes whose memory had been revived and revered by reformers since 1050. It was a name first used by a pope who was a contemporary of Charlemagne and it had not been used since the ninth century. In the pages of the papal biographies Adrian I was portrayed as a man of action who began his pontificate by putting down disorders in Rome and then continued throughout his reign to fight for papal rights in Italy. He was not, either as a theologian or as a reformer, one of the founders of papal greatness. But he had obtained from Charlemagne the confirmation of all Italy south of the Po as a papal possession; he had fought on all frontiers against the enemies of the papal state; and the list of churches which he restored or enriched occupies many pages. His whole life had been one of resolute action. He was also the pope from whom St. Albans claimed its earliest privileges. We cannot tell which element in the story attracted Brakespeare's attention, but in every way his choice of the name was to prove extraordinarily prescient.

The situation which faced the new pope was full of confusion. The city of Rome was a scene of a violent struggle between commercial and aristocratic groups, which had intermittently denied the pope access to the city during the last ten years. At the time of his election Adrian could not enter the city. His control was confined to the area of the Vatican across the Tiber, and even his palace at the Lateran was beyond his reach. Besides this political and social confusion, the dominant party in Rome was closely attached to a religious leader, Arnold of Brescia, who was one of the first and most important of the popular demagogues thrown up by the Italian cities in the Middle Ages. Arnold had been highly successful in inflaming public opinion against the pope and cardinals, whom he described respectively as 'the man of blood' and 'the den of thieves', and Adrian's predecessors had been quite unable to deal with this firebrand. They had allowed his mastery of the city to grow unchecked, and by 1154 the situation appeared to be quite out of hand.[1] It would be hard to imagine a more unnerving situation for a newly elected pope.

[1] For Arnold of Brescia's position in Rome, see R. L. Poole, *The Historia Pontificalis of John of Salisbury*, 1927, pp. lviii–lxx.

Further afield the situation was scarcely less perplexing. To the south and east the boundaries of the Norman kingdom of Sicily came within fifty miles of Rome. During the last hundred years the popes had been deeply implicated in the rise of this kingdom. They had fostered its early growth, and their alliance with the Normans at a critical period had freed the papacy from dependence on the western Emperor. Yet there had been a price to pay for this. The popes had had to allow the Norman ruler to control the local church in ways that it had been a main aim of the papacy to deny to other secular rulers. When they had given all the privileges in their power, the popes watched their titular vassal with growing alarm. The consolidation of the kingdom under Roger II had been one of the major events in European history, and it had been accomplished in the teeth of papal attempts to extend their own power in the kingdom. Consequently the pro-Norman policy pursued by the popes since Leo IX was now deeply suspect at the papal court.

In their efforts to escape from the clutches of a too mighty vassal, Adrian IV's predecessors had made some efforts to re-establish amicable relations with an acceptable western emperor; also, since the accession of Manuel I at Constantinople in 1143, a rapprochement with the eastern emperor had not seemed beyond the bounds of practical possibility. Here were two possible alternatives to the Norman alliance and when Adrian IV became pope a decision on this question, which might affect the whole future of the papacy, was urgently needed. Roger II of Sicily had died in 1154 and it was essential to decide on a policy towards his successor. Moreover, to add to the complication, there was a new, young and ambitious king of Germany, Frederick Barbarossa, coming down through northern Italy, getting support and enforcing obedience wherever he went. His aim was to reach Rome and to be crowned emperor by the pope. This also presented a problem that required an immediate decision.

Above all there was the problem of Rome. No policy could be conducted while playing cat-and-mouse with insurgents on the papal door-step. For nearly ten years Arnold of Brescia had dominated the Roman scene with complete immunity, but Adrian seems to have understood at once how fragile his power really was. At the beginning of Holy Week 1155 one of the cardinals was attacked by a mob, and the pope replied by demanding the expulsion of Arnold of Brescia. He placed the city under an immediate interdict until this happened. Normally an interdict was a slow and clumsy weapon, but Adrian struck at a sensitive moment when all Rome awaited the Easter festival. Within three days—in time for the reopening of the churches for Easter—Arnold's supporters had capitulated. In a week the new pope had achieved more than his predecessors in ten years, and with this success behind him he set out to meet Frederick Barbarossa between Sutri and Viterbo.

At this meeting he consolidated his success by agreeing to crown Frederick as emperor, in return for his help in seizing Arnold of Brescia and destroying the independent government of Rome. The first of these conditions was duly fulfilled: Frederick's agents seized Arnold of Brescia and he was at once hanged by the pope's chief officer in Rome. The second condition proved more difficult to fulfil. After an inconclusive battle with the Roman citizens, Frederick was obliged to withdraw to the country near Rome. Then the hot weather and danger of disease forced him to retreat altogether. He left Adrian to fend for himself and provided him with a vivid illustration of the limited utility of any alliance with the German emperor.[1]

Meanwhile things had not stood still in the south. Immediately after Adrian's election, William I, the new king of Sicily, tried to come to an agreement with him about their respective rights. The negotiations broke down and William I attacked the border towns of the papal state. In return Adrian excommunicated him and made an alliance with the rebellious vassls of the king, who were supported by Byzantine troops. This alliance of pope, Byzantine emperor and the local enemies of the Norman kingdom was a return to a very old project that had been attempted and then abandoned by Pope Leo IX just a hundred years earlier. After the withdrawal of Frederick Barbarossa it was the only alternative to the Norman alliance. Some members of the curia seem to have been eager to seize the chance of breaking with the Norman king altogether, but it does not appear that Adrian IV was ever deceived by the apparent advantages of this plan. He was right.

[1] The best account of these events is by Otto of Freising, *Gesta Frederici*, ed. G. Waitz (*M.G.H. Scriptores in usum scholarum*), 1912, 132–145. For the suggestion that Frederick's failure in Rome forced Adrian IV to turn to an alliance with the Norman rebels and Greeks in South Italy, see Romuald of Salerno, *M.G.H. Scriptores*, xix, 239.

Although the anti-Norman alliance was at first brilliantly successful, he seems to have sensed its fundamental weakness, and he
wanted to use its initial success to renew the Norman alliance on
the much improved terms that could now be obtained. King
William offered to do homage to the pope for his kingdom, to
allow papal authority to be fully implemented throughout his
territories, and to surrender some border towns, in return for
papal recognition and support. Adrian would have accepted this
offer, but he gave way to his advisers who still had confidence in
their new allies.[1] The soundness of his judgement was vindicated
almost immediately. As soon as the Normans renewed the struggle,
the papal allies collapsed leaving the pope personally in the line
of advance of the victorious Norman army.

In the crisis Adrian showed the calm resolution which marked
his whole career. He was at this time at the papal town of Benevento in the midst of the kingdom of Sicily. He dismissed his
retinue and awaited the Norman king's arrival. The terms of the
agreement which emerged from this meeting were of course not as
good as those which the pope had wished to accept six months
earlier, but they met most of his requirements. He received the
homage of the Norman king and the promise of an annual tribute.
A complicated agreement opened southern Italy, but not Sicily, to
the full influence of papal ecclesiastical jurisdiction. The king
promised to help the pope to regain control of Rome. In its main
lines the treaty provided for the restoration of the alliance between
the pope and the Norman rulers of South Italy, which had been
the mainstay of papal policy in the early years of the century.[2] It
meant that the pope, after considering the possibilities of a German
and then of a Greek alliance, had fallen back on the solution which
Leo IX had first adumbrated a hundred years earlier. It was a
decision which involved the abandoning of grand plans of papal
co-operation with any emperor, whether eastern or western. In
the long run it was a fatal decision. It foreshadowed the end of
Christendom as a united political system, and it meant an acceptance of the schism between East and West as a permanent feature

[1] Boso, *Vita Adriani IV* (*Liber Pontificalis*, ed. L. Duchesne, ii, 394) gives
the terms proposed by King William, and tells us that Adrian would have
accepted them, but 'maior pars fratrum alta nimis et omnino incerta sentiens
consentire nullatenus voluit'.
[2] For the details of the negotiations see Romuald of Salerno, *op. cit.*, pp.
240–1; and for the terms of the treaty of 18 June 1156, *M.G.H. Leges*, iv, i, 588.

of the landscape. Worse still, it committed the papacy to a long, destructive, and ultimately hopeless struggle to preserve southern Italy as a firm basis for papal temporal authority. But it was probably the only practical solution in the circumstances of 1156. Neither the German emperor, nor the Greek emperor, nor the dissident vassals of South Italy, could provide a reliable support for papal policy. Whatever is possible is always in the long run fatal, and Adrian was not a man to seek the impossible. Firmly and decisively he did what the situation required and left the future to others.

## III

While the papal position in southern Italy lay in the balance —that is to say from October 1155, when the success of the anti-Norman alliance was at its height, to June 1156, when Adrian made his final agreement with William I—the pope remained at Benevento, near the centre of the trouble. During these months he had plenty of time to think about other aspects of ecclesiastical policy, and especially about the problem of ensuring the free flow of papal authority throughout the western Church. Adrian was not likely to undervalue this major aim of all papal policy, and during three of his eight months at Benevento he had a friend with whom he could talk about the problems of church government. This friend was John of Salisbury who had come to the papal court on behalf of Henry II of England to solicit the pope's support for a projected invasion of Ireland. The circumstances of this visit and its results are sufficiently important to require some explanation.

At Michaelmas 1155 Henry II had held a council at Winchester at which he proposed an immediate attack on Ireland. Objections however were raised, notably by the king's mother, the formidable Empress Matilda, and the project was postponed.[1] Henry II had no legal case for an attack on Ireland, and it seems likely that he was persuaded to delay his expedition until the pope's support had been obtained. Matilda herself had had long and bitter experience of the consequences of failing to get papal support for her claim to the English crown, and this may well have been a decisive factor in her opposition to the Irish project. At all events the king decided to send a deputation to the papal court.

[1] Robert of Torigny in *Chronicles of Stephen, Henry II and Richard I*, R.S., iv, 186.

The man in England most familiar with the papal court was John of Salisbury, who was at this time a clerk in the household of the archbishop of Canterbury, and he was sent to the pope with a letter setting out the advantages of an English conquest of Ireland.[1] The pope was always a ready listener to the petitions of his fellow-countrymen, and he gave his support to the plan. The papal bull however, which sanctioned Henry's expedition and conferred on him the lordship of Ireland, contained expressions which the king can scarcely have heard with equanimity:

> There can be no doubt (it read)—and you certainly must know this—that Ireland and all islands on which Christ the sun of justice shines belong to the dominion of St. Peter and the holy Roman Church. . . . You have signified to us that you wish to go to Ireland to subdue its people to the rule of law and to extirpate the roots of vice; you say that you are willing to pay an annual tribute of a penny from each household to St. Peter, maintaining intact and undisturbed the rights of the churches of the land. We therefore accept and approve your pious and laudable desire. . . .[2]

In making these statements Adrian IV revived an old papal claim to temporal lordship over the islands of western Christendom derived from the Donation of Constantine; and he implicitly reminded Henry of the terms on which Alexander II had supported William the Conqueror's invasion of England nearly a hundred years earlier. The kings of England had steadily ignored the political implications of these terms, and when Adrian repeated them in a new form Henry hesitated and found other outlets for his energy. It was not until 1172, when he was anxious to demonstrate his loyalty to the Roman See, that he revived his project for the conquest of Ireland. In its main business therefore John of Salisbury's mission to the pope led to no immediate result; but in its side-effects, the mission had results of the highest importance, which (if I read the signs aright) left a permanent mark on English history.

[1] John of Salisbury refers to his mission in *Metalogicon*, iv, 42 (ed. C. C. J. Webb, p. 217). The existence of a royal petition can be inferred from the words of the papal bull describing the king's intentions in invading Ireland.
[2] For the text of Adrian's bull 'Laudabiliter' see Ralph of Diceto, *Opera Historica*, R.S., i, 300, and Giraldus Cambrensis, *Opera*, R.S., v, 317–8.

To understand how this came about we must examine the relations between the pope and John of Salisbury rather carefully, and we shall not be able to avoid a certain amount of conjecture. Since John of Salisbury went to the papal court to get support for the king's Irish project, it is reasonable to suppose that he set out not long after the project had been discussed and postponed at the royal court at Michaelmas 1155. The journey would take about two months, so he could have arrived at the papal court at Benevento about the end of the year. Then, on January 23, 1156, Adrian IV wrote a letter to the archbishop of Canterbury which shows that he was closely informed about the situation in England. What he had heard gave him ground for dissatisfaction, and he wrote to the archbishop as follows:

> You alone in the whole kingdom of England have the right of correcting errors on our behalf, not merely as one who shares our responsibility, but as one to whom we have in some measure given the plenitude of our power. We are therefore very surprised to hear that you have so far forgotten our favours and the dignity conferred on you by the Roman church, that you have presumed to lessen its power in every possible way. We have heard that you and the king between you have put a stop to appeals, so that no one dares to appeal to the apostolic see in your presence or in his. . . . Besides this, you are dilatory and remiss in doing justice to those who suffer injustice, and we have had many complaints that you are so afraid of the king and so eager for his favour that no-one on whose behalf we have written to you can get justice done to him. If we hear any more complaints on these matters we shall make a very strict enquiry into them.[1]

Since John of Salisbury was at this time a clerk in the household of the archbishop of Canterbury, these charges touched him closely. Probably he was himself highly dissatisfied with the conduct of the archbishop. At least his own views, as they are revealed to us in the two books which he completed in 1159, were strongly on the side of papal power and the subordination of the secular to the ecclesiastical ruler. What he thought in January

[1] For the text of this letter, see *Historia monasterii S. Augustini Cantuariensis*, 1858, *R.S.*, pp. 411–13.

1156 is less clear to us, but during the next few months he and the pope had time for talk. The two men became close friends, and when Adrian died in 1159 John of Salisbury looked back to the days he had spent with the pope at Benevento as the greatest days of his life. This is what he wrote:

> Although his mother and brother were still alive, he loved me more than either of them. He used to say privately and publicly that he loved me more than any other human being, and he had formed such an opinion of me that he poured out his inner thoughts in my presence whenever he had a chance. Even though he was pope he welcomed me as a guest at his table, and he made me drink from the same cup and eat from the same plate as he did. It was at my request that he gave Ireland in hereditary possession to the illustrious King Henry II of England.[1]

To our taste it seems something of a breach of friendship to write in these terms, but there is no reason to doubt their truth. The two men talked about the state of the church and John expressed (so he tells us) some common criticisms of the Roman curia:

> Like the Scribes and Pharisees they place on men's shoulders grievous burdens which they will not touch with their own finger. They destroy the churches, raise up law-suits, set at variance clergy and laity, have no pity for the labours and miseries of the afflicted, rejoice in the spoliation of the church, and confuse piety with profit.[2]

The pope took this tirade (which cannot have been new to him) in good part, recalled the story of the revolt of the parts of the body against the stomach, and told John to report without delay any unfavourable comments that he heard. At a more serious level he gave John some kind of commission to see that the pope's interests were represented at the court of the archbishop of Canterbury.

As soon as John returned to England in the summer of 1156 he began to give effect to the pope's commission. He was soon notorious as the upholder of papal privileges and as the man

---

[1] *Metalogicon*, iv, 42, ed. C. C. J. Webb, p. 217.
[2] *Policraticus*, vi, 24, ed. C. C. J. Webb, pp. 67–73.

responsible for archiepiscopal policy. He began to preserve the texts of the letters which he wrote in the archbishop's service.[1] There are a hundred and thirty-five of them and nearly half were written to Adrian IV. Except for a few strays, they all belong to the period between his return to England and the archbishop's death in 1161, and they preserve an incomparable record of the growth of papal jurisdiction under Adrian IV. During the three years from the summer of 1156 to Adrian's death on 1 September 1159 John of Salisbury preserved fifty-eight letters to the pope which illustrate every possible type and stage of judicial business as it flowed from archdeacons' and bishops' courts to Canterbury and thence to Rome and back to England. Sometimes the flow touched the royal courts on its way; sometimes it passed through the archbishop's court; sometimes the archbishop was a mere spectator intervening to promote the interests of a friend or to criticize what had been done at Rome; sometimes he was a papal judge-delegate receiving his instructions from Rome; sometimes he was baffled by litigants in his attempt to carry the pope's instructions; sometimes he sought instructions, and sometimes favours. For litigants new opportunities were opened up, and anyone with money and determination, who saw his case going badly, enjoyed the flattering prospect of a removal to the papal court.

Several of the cases which were thus removed lay in the debatable land between secular and ecclesiastical jurisdiction. Most conspicuous among these were cases about advowsons on which the royal courts would soon tighten their grip. There was even a case against the king himself brought by the younger son of King Stephen: the plaintiff was said to have promised the pope seven hundred marks (£466) for the privilege of bringing it into the papal court. We can see very clearly in these letters how the new opportunities for appeals brought opportunities for many kinds of chicanery—delays, subterfuges, well-timed objections—and how the men on the spot felt frustrated by the inability of the papal court to distinguish between the genuine and the fraudulent. We can see too the appearance of a new kind of expert who could advise litigants on the best mode of appeal and keep simultaneous

[1] *The early letters of John of Salisbury*, 1153–61, ed. W. J. Millor and H. E. Butler, 1955. I have given an interpretation of the origin of the collection in *E.H.R.*, 1957, lxxii, 494–7.

appeals to the king and the pope in the air at the same time. But above all we can see that England's immunity from the operation of papal justice, of which Adrian complained in 1156, had abruptly ceased since John of Salisbury's return from the papal court.

While Adrian IV was pope, John of Salisbury—a mere clerk of the archbishop, without title or position—was one of the most important men in England. Since his return to England in 1156 he had been in a position to give practical expression to the papal view of government. Although the king was quick to scent the danger of this new personality in politics, he could do nothing. About six months after his return to England, John of Salisbury wrote to a friend:

> If anyone in England invokes the name of Rome I am held responsible; if the English church dares to claim even so much as a shadow of liberty in election or in deciding ecclesiastical cases, I am blamed for it—as if I alone told the archbishop and the bishops what they must do.[1]

All this, it would seem, was the direct result of the months he had spent in close contact with Adrian IV. He could speak to the pope with the freedom of a friend. On one occasion he wrote in the name of the archbishop a loud remonstrance against a papal decision:

> Who would think of hanging a boxer to make him fight better? You ordered the bishop to fight and now you tie his hands. We beg your Majesty on bended knees to loose him and to turn your censure against the enemies of the bishop and ourselves and what's more the enemies of the apostolic decrees.[2]

To this remonstrance John of Salisbury added his personal note on behalf of the bishop 'bringing the evidence of his devotion to your Majesty's notice' and bidding the pope remember 'what everyone knows, but very few dare to mention' that he could not live for ever.[3]

The freedom of these remarks expresses very clearly the close

[1] Ibid. p. 32 (*Ep.* no. 19).
[2] Ibid. pp. 74–5 (*Ep.* no. 40).
[3] Ibid. p. 76 (*Ep.* no. 41).

bond between the Englishman in Rome and his friends at Canterbury. Yet this freedom was accompanied by a striking reiteration
of a phrase that was still fairly unusual among the papal titles of
honour: 'your Majesty'. It was not new, but in the rich vocabulary
of epistolary respect 'your Holiness', 'your Paternity', 'your
Eminence' and a multitude of similar phrases formed the ordinary
stock-in-trade of the accomplished letter-writer addressing the
pope. 'Your Majesty' expressed the sovereignty of supreme
lordship. It was the title used by advocates addressing the
pope when he sat in his court as a supreme judge. Never before
had the rôle been so confidently claimed for the pope by a group of
local ecclesiastical administrators. The English friends of Adrian
IV wrote with the confidence of men in control of events. They
could scarcely have known that they were firing the first shots in
a great dispute; but even if they had known it is unlikely that
Adrian IV would have been deterred.

## IV

While his friend and agent in England pressed the papal
claims, Adrian himself continued to show the other side of the
ruler's face. It was an essential part of the strategy of government
that claims to loyalty and obedience should be accompanied by
benefits which sweetened the relationship between the governor
and the governed. It would be wrong to see too Machiavellian a
calculation in this combination, which came quite naturally to
anyone who combined an instinct for politics with a generous
nature. Yet it would be equally wrong to forget the political
inspiration of a ruler's generosity: its naturalness was the secret of
its success.

We have already seen that this onslaught of papal jurisdiction
began with a request from the king for a grant of lordship over
Ireland, and that this was given with a ready though not a careless
hand. The bestowal of benefits and the assertion of rights could
not be separated. They followed one another as naturally as the
night the day. When Henry II wrote to congratulate Adrian on
his election he expressed a pride that was not wholly devoid of a
hope of gain that he shared with other Englishmen. England had
given a gift to the church:

Our western church has—like a new Orient—been found
worthy to give a new light to the world. By the Grace of God
it has restored to Christendom the sun that lately (in the
failure of the Crusade) set in the East.

It was reasonable to expect that Englishmen would receive
some warmth from the sun while it lasted. It was equally reasonable that there should be a price to pay.

None had higher expectations than the monks of St. Albans.
They were perhaps conscious of the need for circumspection, for
they planned their visit to the papal court with great care. It took
them nearly a year to collect the money and gifts that were needed,
and after elaborate preparations the abbot set out. He must have
arrived at the papal court shortly after John of Salisbury, and he
too brought back important messages for the king. If he had had
any doubts about his reception they were soon dissipated: he got
everything that he could think of asking for. On 5 February 1156
the pope took the monastery and monks under his immediate
protection and jurisdiction, and in the course of the same month a
flood of benefits—the contents of thirteen papal bulls—was
poured out on the ancient monastery. Nothing was omitted from
these bulls that could confirm the possessions or enlarge the rights
and dignity of St. Albans and its dependant monasteries. The
pope ordered the Feast of St. Alban to be celebrated in all
parishes and bishoprics in the provinces of Canterbury and York;
the bishop of Lincoln was forbidden to summon any clergy or
laity to meetings or synods on the days when they should go in
solemn procession to St. Albans. Even a slight affront which the
abbot had suffered on his way to the papal court, when the abbot
of St. Benoît-sur-Loire had refused him hospitality, was the
subject of a papal mandate: the offending abbot was to pay the
expenses incurred by his visitor and to bring to the pope in person
the proof of his atonement.[1]

The monks of St. Albans had a special claim on Pope Adrian
but there were other Englishmen who were eager to draw from the
same fountain. One of the pope's early visitors was Walchelin,
archdeacon of Suffolk, and he was sufficiently pleased with his

[1] The abbot's preparations for his journey are described in *Gesta Abbatum*,
i, 125–6; the papal privileges which resulted are in W. Holtzmann, *Papsturkunden in England*, iii, nos. 100–113, 117–119.

reception (as John of Salisbury told the pope) to give the name Adrian to an illegitimate son born during his absence; and then —finding a second visit necessary—to leave instructions that his next child should be named either Adriana or Benevento in memory of his journey.[1]

Another early visitor was Roger, archbishop of York, and the pope gave him even greater cause for satisfaction. Roger had been consecrated only a few weeks before Adrian's election as pope, and he must have been one of the earliest Englishmen to visit the new pope. He returned to England with privileges which confirmed his metropolitan rights and his freedom from the authority of Canterbury. He received papal authority to tighten the discipline of the churches of secular canons in his diocese. Above all he obtained a significant extension of his authority over the Scottish church. Previous popes had supported the claims of York in general terms, but in practice they had allowed, and even encouraged, the expedients by which the Scottish bishops evaded the consequences of their dependance on York. Adrian's privilege promised an end to all subterfuges: it specifically named the Scottish bishops who owed obedience to York, and it promised that the pope would confirm any canonical judgement which the archbishop pronounced against them for failing to show him due obedience.[2]. All this was partly an expression of Adrian's open-handed generosity in dispensing papal favours to petitioners, but it seems also to have been a mark of personal favour, for the papal privilege is remarkable for the friendly familiarity with which the pope recalled the archbishop's prolonged visit to the papal court.

It is not often that papal privileges reveal the personality or inclinations of the pope in whose name they are written. When a man becomes pope his personal characteristics are submerged in his office, and nearly everything that passes under his name is the result of procedures and habits formed long before his time. Moreover, he has probably been elected as the representative of the views of a party within the body of electors, and these men will naturally exercise a strong influence on everything he does or

---

[1] *Early Letters of John of Salisbury*, p. 25 (*Ep.* no. 15).

[2] For Adrian's privileges for York, see W. Holtzmann, *Papsturkunden in England*, ii, nos. 86 and 87, and A. W. Haddon and W. Stubbs, *Councils and Eccl. Documents relating to Great Britain and Ireland*, 1873, ii, Part 1, 231–2. For the change in papal policy represented by these privileges, W. C. Dickinson, *Scotland from the earliest times to 1603*, 1961, pp. 135–6.

writes; they will even write and do in his name many things of which he knows nothing. All this is true, and yet even in the course of dry official business the personality of the pope occasionally expresses itself in unexpected ways. Very few people have left so deep and ubiquitous an imprint of their personality on their official correspondence as Gregory VII. Adrian IV is certainly not in this class. Nor (to mention a quite different kind of pope) is he in the same class as his chancellor and successor Alexander III. Even through all the clouds of common form and rounded eloquence Alexander's letters show everywhere the marks of a powerful professional mind tending and perfecting a beautiful machine. It is impossible to read them without experiencing something of his pleasure in knotty points of law, as he settles down to shake out the perplexities of some matrimonial case, in which kind of business (as he said) the most difficult legal questions are apt to arise.[1] Adrian IV had not a professional mind of this calibre, but in his own way he leaves a remarkably consistent impression in all that he wrote or did.

He appears to have been a man of a singularly amiable and unvindictive temperament; evidently effective and capable of pursuing uncompromising policies in dangerous times, yet without the tense and highly-strung passion of an innovator. At the greatest crisis of his career he chatted to John of Salisbury—a man of no importance in the world—with the relaxed ease of an after-dinner Common Room. He listened to his criticisms with a benevolent smile, and he seems to have borne no grudge against those advisers who, against his better judgement, had landed him in the difficulties which faced him as he talked. His genial disposition is seen in the benefactions. He lavished the riches of papal power on those places and people with whom he had been associated in early life without regard to the good or ill treatment he had received at their hands. The monks of St. Albans were the recipients of his most extravagant bounty, and the canons of St. Ruf also experienced his generosity. For the Norwegians he retained a warm regard, and (we are told by Saxo Grammaticus) he always paid them special honour when they came to the papal court. He seems to have had a strong inclination to support ancient rights and claims,

[1] Alexander III to the Archbishop of Trondheim: 'Vestrae discretionis providentiam non credimus ignorare quod difficiliores quaestiones quae in causis ecclesiasticis contingere solent circa matrimonium emergere consueverunt'. (E. Vandvik, *Latinske Dokument til Norsk historie*, no. 12)

and in this he departed somewhat from the general trend of papal policy. He was less afraid of archiepiscopal rights than his immediate predecessors or successors, and archbishops as widely separated as those of York, Toledo and Grado experienced an enlargement of their powers under his direction.

Adrian IV was a man of business, firm where firmness was essential, easy-going in many details where the expert or the zealot would have been rigorous. In his conduct of Italian affairs he made, without any fuss, decisions of permanent importance for the future of the papacy. And in an apparently casual fashion he gave an impetus to papal claims in England without which the story of Archbishop Thomas Becket might have been very different. His biographer and fellow-countryman, Boso, described him as 'Kindly, mild and patient; eloquent and polished in speech, an outstanding singer, and an excellent preacher; slow to anger and swift to forgive; a cheerful giver, lavish in his alms, unblemished in character.'[1] To this we may add that he was business-like rather than completely professional, courageous and firm rather than audacious, dedicated without losing an easy humanity. He was the best kind of man of the world, a wise and unspeculative opportunist, without malice or envy. Evidently not the stuff of which saints are made, he gave the Roman Church a period of peace and administrative security which laid the foundation for the greatest century of papal government.

[1] *Liber Pontificalis*, ed. L. Duchesne, ii, 389.

CHARTS AND PLATES

# CHART I

## TREE OF KNOWLEDGE (SCHOOL OF HUGH OF ST. VICTOR)

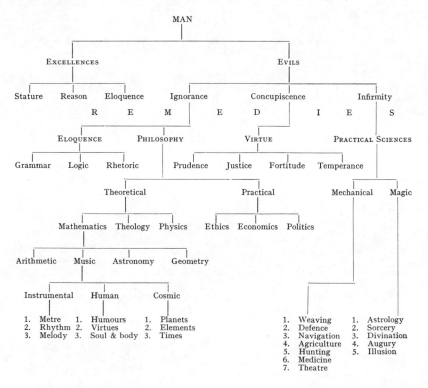

MAN

EXCELLENCES      EVILS

Stature   Reason   Eloquence    Ignorance    Concupiscence     Infirmity

R    E    M    E    D    I    E    S

ELOQUENCE    PHILOSOPHY     VIRTUE     PRACTICAL SCIENCES

Grammar   Logic   Rhetoric     Prudence   Justice   Fortitude   Temperance

Theoretical     Practical     Mechanical   Magic

Mathematics   Theology   Physics     Ethics   Economics   Politics

Arithmetic   Music   Astronomy   Geometry

Instrumental    Human    Cosmic

| Instrumental | Human | Cosmic |
|---|---|---|
| 1. Metre | 1. Humours | 1. Planets |
| 2. Rhythm | 2. Virtues | 2. Elements |
| 3. Melody | 3. Soul & body | 3. Times |

| Mechanical | Magic |
|---|---|
| 1. Weaving | 1. Astrology |
| 2. Defence | 2. Sorcery |
| 3. Navigation | 3. Divination |
| 4. Agriculture | 4. Augury |
| 5. Hunting | 5. Illusion |
| 6. Medicine | |
| 7. Theatre | |

# CHART II

## TREE OF KNOWLEDGE (SCHOOL OF ABELARD)

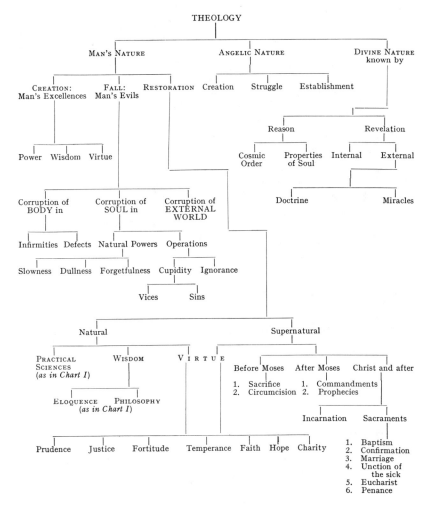

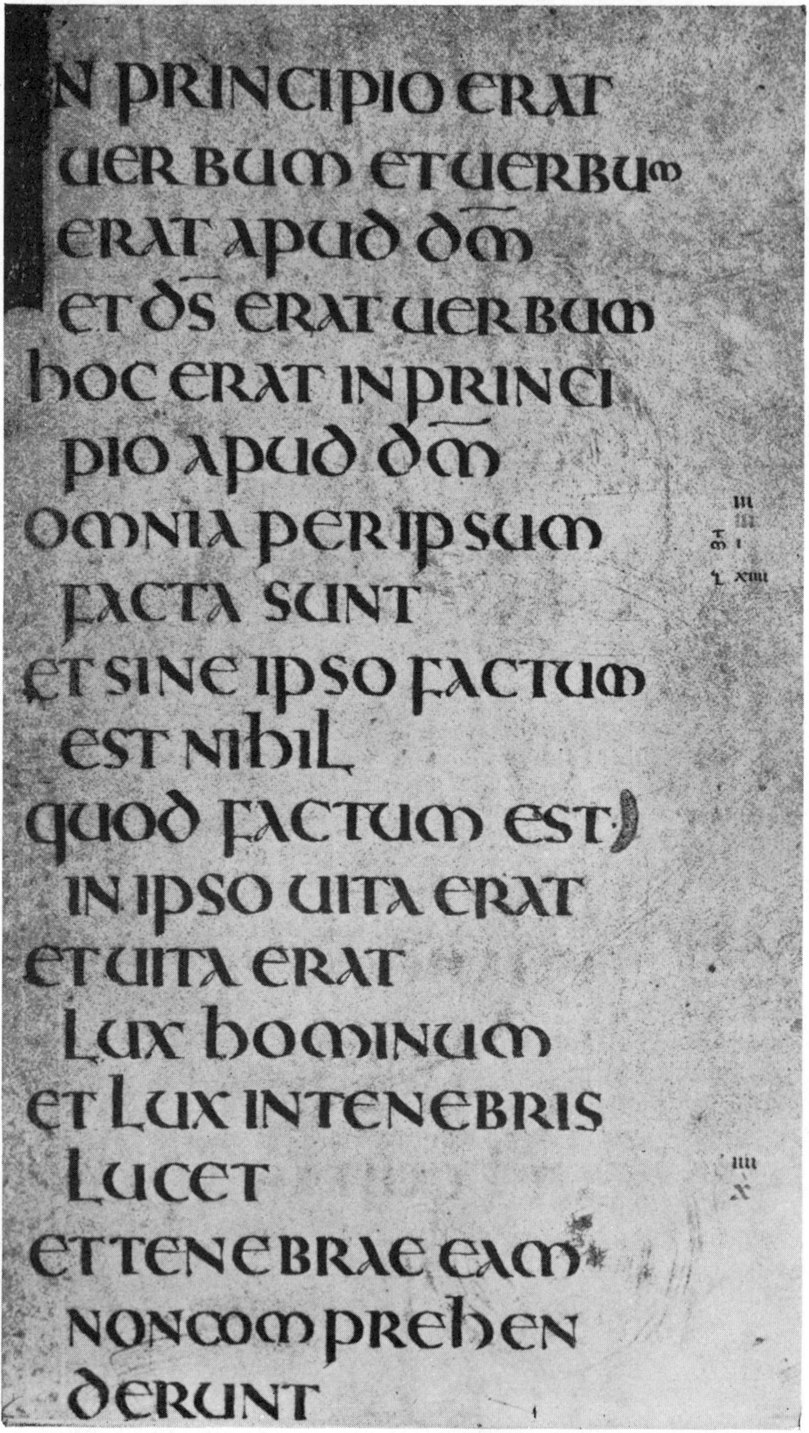

IN PRINCIPIO ERAT
UERBUM ET UERBUM
ERAT APUD DM̄
ET DS̄ ERAT UERBUM
HOC ERAT IN PRINCI
PIO APUD DM̄
OMNIA PER IPSUM
FACTA SUNT
ET SINE IPSO FACTUM
EST NIHIL
QUOD FACTUM EST)
IN IPSO UITA ERAT
ET UITA ERAT
LUX HOMINUM
ET LUX IN TENEBRIS
LUCET
ET TENEBRAE EAM
NON COMPREHEN
DERUNT

The beginning of St. John's Gospel in a Jarrow-Wearmouth Gospel Book.

*Plate I*

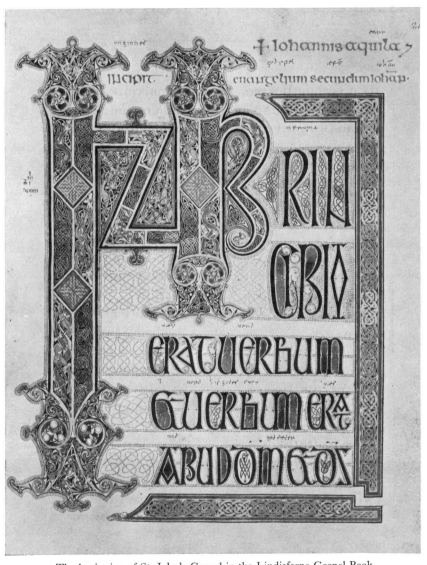

The beginning of St. John's Gospel in the Lindisfarne Gospel Book.

Plate II

Mappa Mundi, 1110–1119. (St John's College, Oxford, MS. 17, f. 6, from Thorney Abbey.)

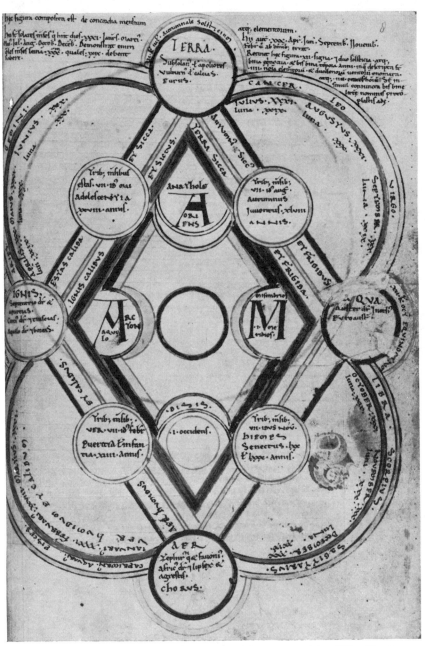

The organisation of Nature, c. 1100. (British Museum, Harleian MS. 3667, from Peterborough Abbey).

Plate IV

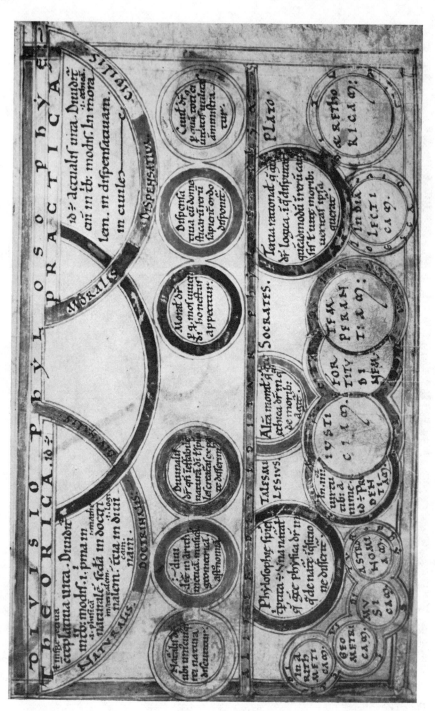

The Divisions of Philosophy, 1109–1110. (St. John's College MS. 17, f. 7.)

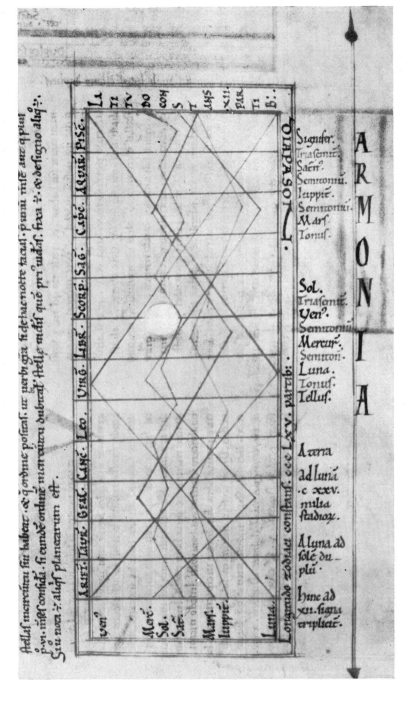

*Plate VI*

The music and movements of the planets, 1109–1110. (St. John's College, MS. 17, f. 38).

Sunspots observed at Worcester, Saturday, 8 December 1128 (Corpus Christi College, Oxford MS 157, p. 380)

Componere hanc figuram recte non leuiter poteris nisi regulas de compositione Astrolabii perfecte noueris Sicut enim ibi componuntur iii circuli pproxtionaliter ita et hic Quem admodum ibi iuxta cuiuslibet puncti latitudine primum imponitur Almuncantarat ita et hic rubens linea confinium venient dier et noctis.

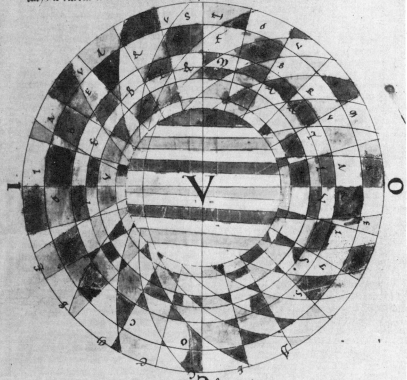

postea sic differentia talis In astrolabio D p primi Almuncantara y secuntur cetera hic autem quantum in qualibet sui parte omnium circulos rubens habet linea tantum in xii diuidio punctis impmunf p quos oblique ducuntur horarii linee Ibi autem et hic sinistra pars huf diuisionif prorsuf eadem est altera u ibi non est.

De compositione

Via plurimi astrolabico scientie compositionis expres sunt uidem nobis in hoc opusculo figure huf describenda compositio Compone in pmus hiemale circulum uxta pagine capacitate seu quante uolueris magnitudinis et diuide illu p iiii equalimat partes impmenf iiii punctof unu supra aliu infra vtvi ad sinistra tua qraf ad dexteram Qui iiii uocaliu positione denotene ita ut supiore denote A ii ye florem E sinistrum I dextrum O et y littera respiciatur in centro. Trahantur autem ii linee in modu crucis una ab A p y ad E altera

A scientific drawing from Worcester, c. 1130. (Bodleian MS. Auct. F.1.9, f. 88).
Plate VIII

# INDEX

Abbot's Langley, 234
Abelard, 41, 45 n., 69, 86–104, 159; hears lectures by Thierry of Chartres (at Paris), 81–2; seduction of Heloise, 89, 91; monk of St. Denis, 89; attitude to sex, 91, 94–5; parallel with St. Jerome, 91–2; abbot of St. Gildas, 88, 101; *Historia calamitatum*, 88 n., 89–93; first letter to Heloise, 97; second, 100–101; third and fourth, 101, 102; hymns, sermons and solutions to problems, 101
Abingdon Abbey, 195, 232
Abitot family, 219. *See also* Urso de Abitot
Adam of Moleyns, 127 n.
Adam de Petit Port, 73
Addison, Joseph, 126
Adelard of Bath, 170–1
Adrian I, Pope, 238
Adrian IV, Pope, 234–52; his origins, 234–5; abbot of St. Ruf, 235; cardinal, 235–7; in Norway, 236–7; elected pope, 237–8; his choice of name, 238; his action against Roman rebels, 238–40; his search for allies, 239–41; agreement with William I of Sicily, 241; at Benevento with John of Salisbury, 242–5; grant of Ireland to Henry II, 243, 245; dissatisfied with Theobald, archbishop of Canterbury, 244; friendship with John of Salisbury, 245; his good nature, 241, 245, 251; resolute character, 240–1; business ability, 235, 252; generosity, 243, 248–51; privileges for St. Albans, 249; and for York, 250; and for St. Ruf, 251; Walchelin, archdeacon, of Suffolk, names his children after, 250

Aeneas Silvius, 127
Aelred of Rievaulx, 35, 124 n., 125, 159
Ailsi, abbot of Ramsey, legend of, 174
Alanus (canon lawyer), 159
Alberic, canon of London, 173
Albinus of Angers, 163
Albion, 'perfidious,' 146
Alexander III, Pope, 251
Alfred of Shareshull, 171
Algar, translator of Marian legends, 173
al-Khwarizmi, 169
*alter orbis*, phrase applied to Britain, ix, 133 n.
Amplonius Ratinck, 132 n.
Anastasius II, Pope, 237
*Anglicus caudatus*, 141 and n.
*Anglo-Saxon Chronicle*, 161
Anselm, St., 9–18; intellectual qualities, 9–10; rationalism, 13–14; 16–17; compared with Pascal and Hobbes, 14–16; love and friendship, 12–13; theological proofs, 13–17, 33; relations with Ranulf Flambard, 198; place in medieval thought, 17–18
Anselm, nephew of St. Anselm, 173
Anselm of Laon, master, 74; teaches Gilbert de la Porrée, 71; and Abelard, 90. *See also* Laon
Aosta, 9–10
Aquinas, St. Thomas, 18, 49–50, 54, 57; *De regimine principum*, 55 n.; *Summa Theologica*, 46–7, 49–50, 54 n., 55 n.
Arabic science, its introduction to England, 170–1
Aristotle, 45–7, 55–7, 61, 80; *Ethics*, 46, 54; *Meteorology*, 46; *Metaphysics*, 46; *Politics*, 54, 55 n.
Arnold of Brescia, 238–40
Astrolabe, x, 167